The Work of Dance

The Work of Dance

Labor,
Movement,
and
Identity
in the
1930s

MARK FRANKO

Wesleyan University Press, Middletown, Connecticut

Published by Wesleyan University Press, Middletown, CT 06459

ISBN 0-8195-6552-0 cloth
ISBN 0-8195-6553-9 paper
Printed in the United States of America
Design and composition by Chris Crochetière, B. Williams & Associates

5   4   3   2   1

Library of Congress Cataloging-in-Publication Data
Franko, Mark.
　　The work of dance : labor, movement, and identity in the 1930s / Mark Franko.
　　　　p. cm.
　　Includes bibliographical references and index.
　　ISBN 0-8195-6552-0 (cloth : alk. paper)—ISBN 0-8195-6553-9 (paper : alk. paper)
　　　1. Dance—Social aspects—United States—History—20th century.
　　　2. Dance—United States—History—20th century. I. Title.
　　GV1588.6 .F73 2002
　　792.8′0973—dc21   2002020843

For Lil', Mafchir, Edie, Buggy, Jack——and the pals
with the great stories, Irwin and Buck, and for Anna
Sokolow and Jane Dudley, in memoriam

Contents

Illustrations

Acknowledgments

The impetus to write this book can be traced to two memories. A child sitting on the floor of a New York dance studio watched his mother take a modern dance class. A teenager in a dance studio in Manhattan's garment district noticed workers spilling onto Sixth Avenue at five o'clock.

It began in 1994 with a graduate seminar called "The Performance of Radicalism," which I taught at the Department of Performance Studies, New York University. Although it was exploratory, that collective work had a decisive impact on this project. I wish to acknowledge the contributions of AnneMarie Bean, Pamela Brown, Leah Garland, Sian Harwood, Sikivu Hutchinson, André Lepecki, Virginia Liberatore, Carol Martin, John McGrath, Lisa Miller, Sumitra Mukerji, Joan Saab, and Lesley C. Wright. I am also grateful to students with whom I continued this work in the Theater Arts Department, University of California, Santa Cruz, in the Department of Cultural Studies, Catholic University of Leuven, and in the Dance Department, Université de Paris 8.

The Getty Research Institute for the History of Art and the Humanities provided time and resources during 1995, and the American Philosophical Society as well as the Committee on Research, University of California, Santa Cruz, generously supported necessary research travel. I was able to complete the book thanks to a senior research fellowship from the American Council of Learned Societies.

Many colleagues have helped my thinking evolve. Discussions with Evan Alderson at various stages of the work are visible to me everywhere in the text. Also important have been exchanges with AnneMarie Bean, Jane Desmond, Donya Feuer, Susanna Franco, Isabelle Ginot, Isabelle Launay, Randy Martin, Felicia McCarren, Joseph R. Roach, Catherine M. Soussloff, Helen Tartar, and Myriam Van Imschoot. Earlier versions of some chapters appeared in journals. John Rouse edited chapter 3 for *Theatre Journal,* Marie-Rose Logan edited chapter 7 for *Annals of Scholarship,* and Ric Alsopp and David Williams edited chapter 5 for *Performance Research.* I thank these journals for permission to reprint.

I am honored to have been able to interview Nadia Chilkovsky, Jane Dudley, Sophie Maslow, and Anna Sokolow. The powerful presence and energy of these artists is enduring testimony to the continuing fascination of their work. I am grateful to the staffs of many research libraries, but especially appreciative of the advice of Peter Filardo, Deborah Bernhardt, Martha Foley, and Erika Gottfried at the Tamiment Institute Library, New York University, and that of Brooks Mc-Namara and Maryann Chach at the Shubert Archive, New York City.

Introduction Dance/Work/Labor

This book explores how work in the 1930s was configured by dance, and how dancers performed cultural work. The performance of work constituted a new direction in American theatrical culture between 1929 and 1941.[1] Work's actual doing became a subject worthy of attention and artistic treatment, and hence the representation of work and workers by dancers and actors could itself be legitimately valued as labor. The coincidence of dance and work, often a question of the collective rather than the singular body, was in turn influenced by Fordist and unionist organizational formations, the administrative structures of the Federal Dance and Theatre Projects, and the Communist Party. During the 1930s, each of these labor organizational formations sustained either direct or symbolic involvement with danced culture. This is not surprising if one considers that the movement of groups through space and in time was of major concern for all parties involved with labor. In the context of production, whether industrial or theatrical, choreography constituted an analytic of organization. The understanding of labor in the Marxian tradition as the expenditure of raw human effort in production engendered new interest in the needs and costs of human movement as well as new questions about the limits and potentials of organized energy.[2] The logic of organization was choreographic when engaged with the physical potentials and limitations of the human body's movement. The logic of choreography was social, even political, when depicting the human prospects and consequences of organization.

This conjuncture of dance and work offers new tools for the dance scholar to study the relation of politics to aesthetics. The 1930s are a unique terrain for such investigation because the politically and ideologically contested status of work was represented as well as masked, claimed as well as rejected, but also reconfigured as either revolutionary or rationalized practices of movement. What is certain is that dance conveyed the physical experience of work in aesthetic and critical terms, bringing laboring bodies into visibility as historical agents.

Work is conventionally thought of as a productive activity, whereas labor is the force that accomplishes it.[3] Let us recall Hannah Arendt's useful distinction between labor and work: "The word 'labor,' understood as a noun, never designates the finished product, the result of laboring, but remains a verbal noun to be classed with the gerund, whereas the product itself is invariably derived from the word for work."[4] Labor, in Arendt's terms, is more like dance than work: it is an action, a process. Because of the ancient intellectual tradition linking dance with play, the movements of dance were the least likely set of movements to become definable as wage earning, and the dance itself was the artwork least suggestive of itself as a stable object or product. The circumstances immediately joining dance to the labor force in the 1930s constitute, therefore, a historically unique moment in which dance contributed to political struggle. The ostensibly ludic qualities of dance were there and then transformed into social energy. My larger thesis is that dance produced ideology but that this "product" was not a commodity inasmuch as it constituted sensuous experience, which is precisely what made it ideologically effective.

This occurred in a decade of economic and social hardship. Cataclysmic news of strikes, racial prejudice, and the rise of fascism abroad reinforced outrage at home. "Exciting events crowded in, one upon the other," wrote black labor activist Angelo Herndon. "Nothing was uninteresting, nothing humdrum."[5] Emotionally extreme social and personal hardship could lead to the excitement of action, rather than to passive depression. The economic and social deprivation caused by the stock market crash of 1929 and the ensuing mass unemployment produced a new sensibility to the body as a crucible of experience and an expressive instrument. Action occupied the forefront of human concerns, and purposeful movement became the occupational drama of life itself in life's most physical and, some might argue, most essential dimension.

Within this lived potential for action against all odds, emotional expression became the social consequence of embodiment. The impediments to action, the difficulty of action within the confines of managed behavior, brought the emotional impulse to the fore as action's essential quality. The political body of the 1930s was an emotional body. Just as the redefinition of dance as work was impossible without a new awareness of the specificity of the dancing body, so the phenomenon of American political radicalism itself could not have emerged without emotionally inflected movement practices. Although the Left may have invented the idea of the emotionally charged proletarian body in motion, attempts were also made to appropriate working-class bodies to rationalized processes of production. Scientific management behind Fordist modes of production—assembly lines—rationalized measurement of workers' physical effort and emotional disposition. This measurement took account of emotional state by seeking to contain it. In this way, both radical and conservative labor organizations actively sought to appropriate or expropriate emotional embodiment.

It is thus not surprising that dance became a central cultural practice of the radical decade. A variety of dance forms with ideological positions on labor crystallized in thirties culture. I contend that these dance forms were in dialogue with each other as well as with their audiences. They set ideologies into motion. As Terry Eagleton reminds us, "Ideology is a realm of contestation and negotiation, in which there is a constant busy traffic: meanings and values are stolen, transformed, appropriated across the frontiers of different classes and groups, surrendered, repossessed, reinflected."[6] Dance culture of the 1930s reveals the instrumentality and value of emotional embodiment itself in the process of being contested and negotiated, appropriated and transformed. This movement occurred at a visceral, visual, and experiential level.

At the radical end of the spectrum, the primary physical practice of "movement culture," a euphemism for the culture of the Communist Party (CP-USA), was indubitably "modern" dance. "In those days," according to Sam H. Friedman, "the trend was toward modern dancing. And the modern dance was taken over by the communist movement. After Martha Graham and, what, Isadora Duncan, the ones after that all belonged to the communists, just as most artists were communist, and most . . . a great many writers."[7] Modern dance of the early thirties had a significant amateur infrastructure. This relatively new form of modern movement was practiced in open dance classes for working-class people, and improvisation study was based on "mass dance" for both men and women. Pageants using amateur dancers, such as Edith Segal's *The Belt Goes Red,* which was performed at the Lenin Memorial Meeting in 1930, satirized labor efficiency by showing assembly line work develop into a workers' insurrection.[8] Modern dancer and political activist Fanya Geltman remembers: "We felt that the workers had to dance, they had to. . . . We went to all the factories, the garment industry, which was a big thing, the ILGWU [International Ladies Garment Workers Union]. We went there, we handed out, and the first night, I

Figure 1: Clenched fists stylize the energy of militant stances, fortitude, suffering, and hope: the look of radical unprofessionalism. Rebel Arts Dancers in Expressions of an Epoch. *(Lincoln Kirstein Collection, Dance Collection, New York Public Library for the Performing Arts, Lincoln Center, Astor, Tilden, and Lenox Foundations.)*

shall never forget. They came in hoards [*sic*], 10 cents we charged, 10 cents a dance. And they came and they came, and they left their machines at night, you know, and they came to dance."[9] Geltman's depiction of this historic moment when dance and labor recognized, as it were, the potential in their relationship, has social and political resonance as well as the aura of psychological necessity. At this early stage, modern dance also served the needs of general theatrical representation by furnishing the backdrop to labor pageants, and providing a movement lexicon for radical theater. Moreover, working-class audiences were coming to see dance in union halls as often as in theaters. Modern dance opened the function Yiddish theater had served for immigrant audiences in New York to a broader working-class audience.[10] The dancing body had didactic, stylistic, and recreational import that artists sympathetic to labor were keen to exploit. The kinesthetic and psychological correlation of labor to danced movement contributed to the definition of modernism as aesthetic ferment with social ramifications.

The contexts for continuity between dance, labor, and culture are thus not

far to seek. The courage to demonstrate or strike did not differ greatly from the "guts" required to dance in front of an audience.[11] A radical individual's strength and confidence to move before the collective gaze could be bolstered in part by community or group support. But the courage to move required a further source of personal strength: emotional conviction derived from the authenticity of a felt politics. This conviction had particular historical specificity. It was rooted in personal experience associated with childhood and consciously realized in situations of impoverishment. As a young girl, Mazie, the main character in Tillie Olsen's novel *Yonnondio: From the Thirties,* is advised by her neighbor Elias Caldwell: "Live, don't exist. Learn from your mother who has had everything to grind out life and yet has kept life. *Alive, felt what's real, known what's real.*"[12] Against the modernist version of "the real thing" with its formalist material sensibility, the radical or socialist (perhaps actually humanist) version proposed feelings as aesthetic materials.[13] Feelings were not required to be romantic or impressionistic inasmuch as they were anchored, as

Figure 2: Not officially communist, the choreographic radical salute betokens left-wing solidarity and aspiration. On the Barricades in the first New Dance Group concert, Sunday, March 26, 1933, Hecksher Theater, New York City. This dance ended the program and led into a march of New Dance Group membership. (Courtesy of the New Dance Group Studio's Archive, New York).

Figure 3: Modern dance provides a choreographic lexicon for popular front musical theater: "Men Awake," the finale of Act 1 of Pins and Needles *(1937), choreographed by Benjamin Zemach. Other choreographers associated with this long-running show were Gluck Sandor, Geordie Graham (Martha Graham's sister), and Katherine Dunham. (Billy Rose Theatre Collection, New York Public Library for the Performing Arts at Lincoln Center, Astor, Tilden, and Lenox Foundations.)*

the word *feeling* suggests, in bodies and bodily sensations. Neither were they based on pop-psychological notions of depth, which the Left characterized as "bourgeois emotionalism."[14] Radical sentiment recognized the materiality of perception as both affective and phenomenal. In this way, emotion was a key to self-projection in the world. Feelings could become aesthetic *and* social material because they materialized in moving bodies.[15] They were e/motional.[16]

In the new century, the urgency and political agency of the emotional body has waned. Performances of emotional conviction, both onstage and off, meet with disparagement as being freakish, or at best, idiosyncratic. Personality has gone out of style. "Personality," wrote Horkheimer and Adorno prophetically in 1944, "scarcely signifies anything more than shining white teeth and freedom from body odor and emotions."[17] But was it by chance or by fashion that the emotional physicality of modern dance spoke for radical causes in the thirties? Might not postmodern cool be another form of theatrical ideology? What does it speak for? What links the waning of our ability or desire to see emotional bodies and the erasure of labor- and class-related issues at century's close?

With political emotion as its backdrop, this book argues that: (1) dance and labor were not just circumstantially contemporaneous but profoundly interrelated during the 1930s; (2) dance was not on the periphery, but at the center of politics; and (3) the bodies of chorus girls, modern dancers, and ballet dancers were protagonists of class struggle. This book is not only about modern dance; ballet and chorus dancing also come in for analysis. The ideologies of these dance forms emerge more clearly through genre comparisons. Viewed across ballet, modern dance, and chorus dance, class encompasses the social class of dancers, the classing of danced genres, and the intervention of dance in class struggle itself.

The ballet/chorus girl and the modern dancer were widely recognized figures disseminated and frequently caricatured in the popular press. Caricature indicates that the broad outlines of divergent choreographic forms were public knowledge. Caricature could play a role in realigning one kind of dance to an adversarial ideological stance. A Covarrubias cartoon labeling stretching and reaching dancers "unhappy moderns" implied that aesthetic innovation in dance was a political dead end.[18] It attempted to short-circuit radical energy and turn public attention away from modernism. Parodies of modern dance in commercial venues such as the Ziegfeld Follies functioned in much the same way. I am interested in satiric discourse for its role in ideological processes. Appropriative caricature always has political stakes, but at the same time it assures what Louis Althusser has called "that minimum of non-existent generality without which it would be impossible to perceive and understand what does exist."[19] Its preponderance is offset by the fact that commentary by Muriel Rukeyser, Dane Rudhyar, Alain Locke, and Michael Gold appeared alongside that of dance critics and satirists.

The generality of caricature can render its object "non-existent" by lumping aspects of modernism that demand differentiation. For example, a comedic Los Angeles version of the Federal Theatre Project's Living Newspapers, *Revue of Revues* (1937), parodied American magazines in dance numbers. One such number, "America Talks Up the Dance," portrayed *Dance Magazine* as a hotbed of radicalism. "Satirizing the ballets of Mary Wigman and Kurt Jooss," wrote one reviewer, "in broad strokes with a ridiculously formalized dance of the workers, it received enthusiastic applause."[20] *Revue of Revues* indicates that by the mid-thirties modern dance was associated with political radicalism in the public mind despite the facts that Mary Wigman was considered fascist by the left-wing press and that *Dance Magazine* was a safely conservative publication. Such inaccuracies testify to the visibility of movement aesthetics in the public sphere, albeit at the level of "non-existent generality."

I shall focus on the thirties as a formative period for the ethos of historical modern dance, as well as for "ethnic" dance, ballet, and chorus dance. A hierarchy of genres began to emerge in the thirties, providing this book's other subject: the genealogy of genre boundaries in twentieth-century American dance. Although social and political criteria were used to evaluate performance during the radical decade, a will to segregate theatrical dance from social issues also materialized at this time. By the 1960s, with the ascendancy of Merce Cunningham and George Balanchine as preeminent choreographers in modern dance and ballet, the critical precedent for formalism was established. Following on the repressive atmosphere of fifties America, this formalist perspective encouraged forgetfulness of the relation between dance and labor.[21]

Precedents for this relation, however, predate the thirties. In the 1920s, Russian theater director Vsevolod Meyerhold elucidated the aims of biomechanical actor training when he noted that "a skilled worker at work invariably reminds one of a dancer; thus work borders on art."[22] The cultural politics of dance in the thirties raise many questions about physical stylization. Why was emotion necessary to political performance in the America of the Great Depression?[23] What was emotion's relation to class consciousness? How did emotional movement aesthetics articulate the ethnicities and genders that actually composed working-class identity? Finally, what role did modern dance play in the articulation of ethnicity and gender as enlisted in the performance of class?

Addressing these questions entails a salvage operation. Radical culture developed a modern and politically engaged performance on the margins of popular culture and aesthetic modernism, but its cultural history was submerged. The aesthetic commitments of cultural radicalism were discounted for their presumed lack of formal integrity. Yet they have never entirely disappeared. Aspects of the radical aesthetic in dance were absorbed, as Ellen Graff points out, into subsequent, less politically engaged performances. Where Graff intentionally blurs the differences between "bourgeois" and "revolutionary" dance as these existed in the thirties, I worry their distinctions. I conceptualize radical dance as based not only on the participation of wage earners in the early thirties and fellow travelers in the late thirties, but also through the kinds of emotions it embodied and called forth in its audience.[24] This analytical direction expands on the notion I developed elsewhere of a politics of expression in dance and develops in particular the following observation about radicalism: "Without emotion, no revolution."[25]

To this purpose, Part I, "Emotion and Form," elaborates a distinction between affect and emotion in order to rethink the form-versus-content cliché that haunts political art. This distinction constitutes an ideological split within modern dance (and indeed within modernism) related to the individualist versus the collectivist ethos of the period. Despite the unavoidable tendency to confuse the meanings of *emotion* and *affect* in ordinary usage, I assign a distinctive meaning to each term: affect occurs when dance has transmitted the essence of a feeling; emotion occurs when dance has transmitted a specific and temporally contingent feeling. There is some precedent for distinguishing between the terms. *Affect,* like its synonym *passion,* evokes a classical philosophical tradition, whereas *emotion* tends to be associated with nineteenth-century romantic sensibility.[26] Following this distinction, *emotion* can be linked with superficial and agitated rather than profoundly motivated movement, while *affect* suggests faculties, state, and inborn propensities. "The affect," writes Deleuze, "is impersonal and is distinct from every individuated state of things."[27] In this way, affect derives from a taxonomy of feelings, whereas emotion is more fluid and circumstantial but also less significant and lasting. This distinction, however prejudicial to emotion, contrasts the personal and the impersonal in a way that I shall find useful.

I use the term *affect* here to denote essential affect—feeling defined by attributes essential to its identification—whereas e/motion shall be understood to puncture "the sanctity of the insularity of the 'subject' to convey historically differentiated experience."[28] If affect emerges from "deep" within the individual, e/motion circulates between subjects in shared social space.[29] I do not align emotion with content and affect with form, despite the parallelism these sets of terms evoke. Form and content are always present in performance: the preeminence of one does not necessarily eliminate the other. What requires demystification is neither form nor content as such, but the form/content binary, which implies form is superior to content in modernist art practices. I do not propose affect/emotion as a binary that would supersede form/content. Rather, I see affect and emotion as merely two among a series of other embodied feelings whose very proliferation disqualifies the mentality of binarism. For example, I suggest possession in chapter 3 as a third figure of embodied feeling in the work of Asadata Dafora.

Martha Graham's choreography will be pivotal in this discussion because her performance of modern individuality was at odds at once with a personal body and a social body. Graham was affective but unemotional because emotion had radical political overtones in the thirties.[30] This realization yields an important insight: emotion was aligned not only with radical social awareness but with personality as well. That is, social awareness in no way precluded a concept of the personal, but actually presupposed it. This is a counterintuitive point. If personality was truly the resource of the left-wing performer, and impersonality the resource of the modernist liberal performer, then dance history overturns the received notion that personality militated against class interests and class representations.

To understand how this was so, I propose that we think of class in the thirties as a pluralistic concept engaged with, if nonetheless conceptually distinct from, race and ethnicity. The majority of working-class persons were African Americans or immigrants of Eastern or Southern European provenance. Ethnicity can be thought of as an identity fashioned by people for themselves on the basis of their cultural heritage. Race can be thought of as an identity assigned to people on the basis of their ethnicity. As workers, people of diverse ethnic backgrounds were characterized by physical traits or behavioral styles endowed with a psychological dimension. From here to racial stereotype is not far to go. For the Left, perceiving ethnicities in the performance of physical and psychological particularity could reinforce the personal values without which radical social awareness was powerless to grow and spread. This was not a performance of stereotype, but a reference to individuated experience as expressive embodiment for general consumption. Ethnicity became a figure of the personal, and for conservative sensibility, of the inessential or contingent. For the Left, however, ethnicity introduced the category of the authentic. The coherence of authenticity expressed differently by different genders and ethnic groups was consolidated in the notion of class. Class itself, however, remained an incomplete project.

Choreographic attempts were made to forge class out of a composite of physical and psychological traits. For dancer and choreographer Jane Dudley, "The problem with ethnicity was to translate a political idea into a do-able dance idiom. So that it didn't stay a mental idea; so it could be conveyed through gesture, and feeling tone, and dynamics, and so forth. Some use of ethnic music is the search for a certain identity that's interesting, and vivid, and rhythmic, and offbeat."[31] The particularity of ethnic music in its "search for a certain identity" guided left-oriented choreographers in their search for movement innovation with social commitment. One dance critic described the amalgamation of these goals: "Art can be startlingly fresh, original, new and yet remain as clear, as memorable, as persuasive as a Negro work-song."[32]

Radical modern dance became the scene of this experiment in which white performers alluded to the movement styles of African Americans and of ethnicities making up the population of the Eastern Soviet Union. Particularly in the former case, these allusions were used to assert political solidarity and the CP-USA's policy of antiracism. Hybridity on the Left spelled the unifying power of emotion; for the right, it spelled the racialization of the proletariat.

Either way the working class, as Mark Seltzer has noted, was "deeply embodied."[33] Class itself, from this perspective, provided a way to formalize emotions across ethnic, racial, and national divides. Thus, there are pivotal linkages to investigate between emotion, class, and form.

Although ethnic dance remained a seductive model for politically radical choreographers, the critical problem was how to cultivate movement vernaculars in which an array of ethnic identities coalesces into an image of the working class. How, in other words, could movement vernaculars serve to represent class rather than ethnicity per se. "The problem with folk dance," specified Dudley, "is that it stays folk dance. The reason we went to folk music was because it had a very direct connection to an audience, and it had a direct political statement to make, as in Woody Guthrie's work."[34] The problem of danced ethnicity draws attention to the constructedness of working-class identity, which, far from being spontaneous or natural, required conscious cultivation.[35] Toward the second half of the decade, danced ethnicity was called upon to abstract itself as class. That is, class was expressed abstractly just as essential affect played a structurally similar role for modernist choreographers. There emerged essentialism in the Left's construction of class that is difficult to digest today. But falling out of sympathy with this vision of class should not lead us to misconstrue its original political intent. I argue against such reductionism in chapter 4. The distinction between affect and emotion as modes of embodied feeling should facilitate more scrupulous historical analysis.

The passage of time has desensitized us to the performative nuances that distinguished affect from emotion for audiences of the period. The contemporary political agendas of such distinctions are no longer obvious. It is necessary to re-historicize these dances. Most radical dances survive only in the critically worded image-moment, or in photographs. One important way to re-historicize the dances is through oral history. Although choreographers are not the ultimate authorities on the meaning of their work, their words should be weighted in the analysis. Oral history contributes to an ethics of historical imagination. Given the often-fragmentary remainders of radical performance, journalistic criticism necessarily becomes another indispensable resource. This book is about polemical journalism as much as it is about the dances attacked or upheld in print. Despite extensive recourse to these sources, however, I do not wish to imply that reviews, publicity, and other such ephemera can adequately conjure the absent historical event. Yet print journalism is more than prosthesis. Besides the pragmatics of research into a badly documented area, it recommends itself for "the many ways emotion gets its meaning and force from its location and performance in the public realm of discourse."[36] That is, the glib or articulate texts and images disseminating dance in print media testify to the secondary circulation of embodied feeling. The burgeoning of dance writing and the rise of dance photography and graphics in the thirties indicate that theatrically pro-duced dance was a knowledge-generating practice.[37] Other forms of textual and visual discourse were magnetized to dance and served to increase and di-versify its circulation, bringing a larger audience in urban centers full circle to the sites of performances from which these discourses had originally been generated.

The recognition of such cultural practice and the polemics dance engen-dered on its basis were possible only in an astute and self-consciously articu-late dance community where minute nuances solicited alert interpretation. "Here in New York," wrote newcomer Si-Lan Chen in 1937, "the audience kept in step with every attitude, every subtlety and suggestion in the ideas that were being danced on the stage."[38] My analyses of dance writing seek more than bits of culled information, however vitally important these can prove to be. I also seek the implicit theoretical basis of contemporary judgments. Criticism and visual commentary reveal how dance constituted cultural knowledge. This has helped in turn to rethink genre boundaries that became conceptualized in the 1930s between modern dance, classical ballet, and chorus dancing.

The construction of genre boundaries was crucial to the agon of interpre-tation. The architects of these boundaries were John Martin and Lincoln Kirstein. Martin was a former man of the theater appointed the first dance critic of the *New York Times* in 1926. A champion of modern dance, he was also a significant theorist. Kirstein was a wealthy aesthete and patron of the arts who promoted the Americanization of classical ballet. These two men were apparently opposed by loyalties to aesthetically divergent danced genres. But inasmuch as genres appear to be defined in purely aesthetic terms, their boundaries can also veil the knowledge they contain. Slavoj Žižek has said ideology concerns "the relationship between visible and non-visible, between imaginable and non-imaginable, as well as the changes in this relationship."[39] With Martin and Kirstein, we find ourselves in a realm of the visible and the invisible, in short, in a realm of ideology. I read Martin and Kirstein in chapter 5 as equally ideologically inflected but not, as they are often assumed to be, as ideologically opposed. It is the very vituperative quality of their debate that masks the ideological sameness of their positions.

Let me offer one example of how apparent aesthetic differences can veil ide-ological resemblance. A cartoon published in *Vanity Fair* in 1934 provides a satiric commentary on Graham's defensiveness about chorus dance. The mod-ern dancer is shown performing alongside the fan dancer Sally Rand. Rand's cur-vaceous body steps from behind boa feathers while Graham's angular shapes stretch from a tense, grounded stance. Yet in the accompanying "Impossible In-terview," the two dancers fail to establish essential differences between themselves:

Figure 4: Miguel Covarrubias, "Impossible Interview. Sally Rand vs. Martha Graham" (1934). (Private Collection.)

Sally: Hello, Martha. Still doing the same intellectual strip-tease? Martha: I beg your pardon, Miss Rand, I do not think we have anything in common. Sally: Forget it, kid, we're in the same racket, ain't we? Just a couple of little girls trying to wriggle along. Martha: But my dancing is modern—classical—imaginative. If you leave anything to a customer's imagination, it's because he's near-sighted. Sally: Sure, I come right out in the open. I put my best points forward. Martha: (haughtily): You should learn to bare your soul. Sally: Say, I got to keep *something* covered. Martha: In your dancing, you should seek to interpret. Sally: That's where you're wrong. I always let 'em put on their own interpretation. They like to try to read between my lines. Martha: I don't know what they see in you. Sally: Neither do they. They only think they do. That's why I'm always surrounded by so many fans. Martha: I'm sure you'd be frowned on in the ladies' clubs. Sally: And you'd be a flop in a cooch concession, kid. From now on, we'd better split fifty-fifty. You take the ladies, and I'll take the men. Martha (enviously): For plenty.[40]

The dialogue is "impossible" because it could never have taken place without compromising the common ideology supporting their aesthetic conflict. Although highly cynical about both performers, the author nonetheless perceived that both Rand and Graham functioned within analogous performative economies where the display of what lies hidden—either body or soul—stakes little claim to social reality. The interview is "impossible," too, because the opposition between these highly dichotomous aesthetics is ideologically negligible. Such commonality is another example of the "minimum non-existent" general text. I shall argue that as its substantive ideological struggle, thirties dance culture opposed left-wing modern dance to the chorus line. As a high modernist, Graham masks that authentic tension. The publicized ideological divides generating a false consciousness sufficient to ensure the effective operation of ideology occurred between high modern dance and ballet on the one hand and between high modern dance and chorus dance on the other. The actual ideological divide of consequence was between radical modern dance and chorus dance.

This raises the question of ideology itself as a frequently impugned methodological tool. A few words to plead its usefulness are in order. Ideology is a term germane to the thirties, and its use can thus be justified on these grounds alone. Ideology referred to the organization of social, political, and economic life under the regimes of capitalism, communism, or fascism. These led to particular formations of the relationship between individuals and the social order. This is a simple use of the term justified by the historical context.

A more methodologically complex use of ideology is of a psychological and/or spectacular nature: it concerns the calling of people to the subject positions of their movement, which is a kind of interpellation, as originally theorized by Althusser. I do not conceive the agent of interpellation to be the state apparatus, as did Althusser, but rather actual performances and the movement there deployed. Yet performances are related in many cases to institutional structures at fundamental aesthetic levels. The logic linking those levels is choreographic. Despite interpellation, ideology is shown to operate in a field of subjectivation more than one of subjugation or subjection. Aesthetics and politics as a field of inquiry redefine ideology as actively persuasive rather than flatly oppressive. Yet this is precisely why I find Althusser's thought useful: interpellation posits a process of self-recognition engendered by social address, which could also be considered an effect of spectatorship. All spectators are in a process of becoming themselves. This critical apprehension of interpellation stages ideology as a malleable and competitive operation within culture.

The third sense of ideology engaged with here pertains to danced genres themselves. It is a question of a generic tendency to formalize an organizational logic and to set that logic into visual and kinesthetic motion. Although the term *ideology* has been impugned for reintroducing false binaries of the discursive and the performative, the sources here raise the question of the constant pressure ideology exerted on working bodies. The real choices open to the public during this decade were defined in fundamentally ideological ways. One can even say that ideological interpretation overdetermined the meaning of every action. As modern dancer Fanya Geltman noted: "You were either on one side or you were on the other side. . . . That's what it was, and so you always had your audience. There was no such thing as not having an audience."[41] The very predominance of ideology in this period provides a supplemental context for the centrality of performance to its culture. Performance, too, relies on the presence of audiences.

I survey in chapter 2 the phenomenon of emotional bodies considered from opposing ideological perspectives on the Left and Right, and show how emotional movement itself was an ideologically contested terrain. In chapter 4 the authenticity claimed for class consciousness is traced to the supposed emotional underpinnings of ethnic identities. I propose that the female modern dancer practiced cultural cross-dressing, thus mobilizing associations between femininity and the political emotions of ethnic groups. There are doubtless many other byways through which one could pursue the cultural givens of this period relative to performance.[42]

Part II, "Genre and Class," returns to the broader ideological debates of the thirties. The chorus girl emerges in chapters 5, 6, and 7 as the dominant performative trope of capitalist ideology: spectacle. Here I allude to Guy Debord's theory of the spectacle as the operative term for the incursion of consumerism into everyday life. I return to a possible historical source of Debord's spectacle theory in the kickline of precision dancing, as illustrated in Busby Berkeley's film *Gold Diggers of 1933* and critiqued in the Labor Stage's *Pins and Needles* (1937). Through a reading of Kirstein's American ballet polemic, self-reflexive backstage musical films choreographed by Berkeley, and Lew Christensen's popular "American" ballet *Filling Station* (1936), I argue that chorus dancing and classical ballet shared similar ideological viewpoints in the America of the Great Depression. The much-publicized opposition between classical ballet and modern dance—until recently a linchpin of twentieth-century dance history—was introduced in the dance writings of Kirstein and Martin, where Kirstein defended classical ballet and Martin championed the "new dance." I argue that this polemic obscured the more immediate and ideologically fraught conflict between capital and labor embodied by the chorus girl's opposition to the radical modern dancer. As late as 1991, Graham herself insisted in her autobiography: "I was not a chorus girl or a hoofer."[43] The immediate impetus to this assertion was to de-emphasize her work in the Greenwich Village Follies during the 1920s. But Graham's remark also reveals the uneasy historical relation of dance to class, and by extension to labor.

This book outlines three ideological splits: a split within modern dance (radical versus high modernist), a split between ballet and modern (ideological screen), and a split between radical modern dance and commercial dancing. More broadly conceived, my subject is the performance of work at the intersections of mass culture, political radicalism, and aesthetic modernism. A foundational critique of North American dance history turns on the ballet/modern split as false consciousness. I find this perhaps vulgar Marxist terminology extremely appropriate, and even refreshing, when applied to the sometimes overly aestheticized materials of dance and apprehended at the level of ideological engagement. Such clearly old-fashioned uses of Marxist thought point at once to the dramaturgical impulse behind my historiographic practice and to the presence of dance during this period—again in willfully hackneyed terms—at the level of the superstructure and the base at the same time.

Despite the preceding emphasis on genre boundaries, it should also be noted that the claims of modern dance and ballet to high art status during the thirties were tenuous at best.[44] Also, neither radical modern dance nor chorus dance sought an elite public: radical dance cultivated a proletarian audience, chorus dancing courted a popular audience. These two forms thus competed for the attention of a "mass" audience, but the competition hinged on how this mass would define itself as a function of what it beheld. This was a truly ideological competition, for the forms themselves strove to enlist spectators at the level of their nascent subjectivity. Reciprocally, that subjectivation, when and if successfully assumed, would serve to confirm and validate the generic identity of the performance that had interpellated it into existence. Thus, we confront a situation in the 1930s in which the forms themselves, the manner of address, and the addressees were all in a process of formation. The meaning of mass fluctuated between its class meaning (the working class), its choreographic scale (the dance group), and its statistical scale (mass media audiences).

Evidence of class conflicts between these danced genres can also be traced to high-versus-low debate that pitted professionalism against "amateur" performance. This public debate occurred in the context of the Federal Dance Project and concerned which *genre* of dance qualified as professional work. As part of the government relief effort for unemployed workers under the aegis of the Works Progress Administration, the Federal Dance Project (FDP) was created at a time when radical modern dance was already in full swing. Many modern dancers joined the ranks of the FDP, most notable among them being Charles Weidman and Helen Tamiris, who staged their dances for FDP programs, Nadia Chilkovsky, and Fanya Geltman, who was an effective organizer as well as a dancer. The FDP was originally headed by Don Oscar Becque, who was also a choreographer. The project got started with eighty-five salaried dancers divided into three units, one directed by Becque, one by Tamiris, and the last by Gluck Sandor.[45] As early as 1937, however, dramatic cutbacks threatened the project's existence. The first convening of the House Un-American Activities Commission—then called the Dies Commission—opened hearings into subversive activity in the Federal Theatre and Dance Projects. Hallie Flanagan, the projects' national director, a staunch advocate of experimentation and social relevance in the performing arts, defended them brilliantly.[46] But the Dies Commission's investigation concluded in 1939 with the definitive closing of both projects.

At the Federal Dance Project's inception, the apparently aesthetic conflict between proponents of modern dance and chorus dance took on partisan overtones. To put it bluntly, modern dance seemed aligned with communism and chorus dance with capitalism. Yet a more intricate debate about value in relation to performance also emerged. What did the dancer produce in society such that his or her work merited federal funding? What, asked the Dies Commission, was a dancer's market value? The issues of representation raised by the professionalization debate intersected both aesthetic and political dimensions at the heart of dance as cultural production in the thirties. The issue of value at its core will bring us back to the question of the work of dance at an unprecedented historical conjuncture. If dancers "sell" neither their sexual bodies nor their imaginative souls, do they then produce something "outside" of themselves? What is this thing they produce, and how can market value be ascribed to it? What is the market for human value as political commitment? Why should the taxpayer foot the bill?

As organized protest to safeguard rapidly disappearing dance jobs became necessary, dancers themselves became subjects of public controversy and direct protagonists in labor struggle. Chapter 7 examines modern dancers' roles in these labor actions as well as public response to their political stand on their own behalf. In 1937, controversies over the relation of aesthetics to politics went beyond the concerns of modernism versus radicalism as art practices and beyond dance making conceived as a disinterested activity versus politicking as an interested one. The controversies in which dancers played a concrete role of self-representation reveal another class struggle within aesthetic investments.

Part I **Emotion and Form**

Chapter 1   Organization and Performative Economies of Work

Mechanization, commodification, and metallization are the most frequently cited tropes of communist, capitalist, and fascist performance respectively.[1] The value of each is to characterize a means of production through the psychological effect it exerts on the subject of ideology. From the Western perspective, the communist subject becomes regimented and devoid of feeling, therefore mechanized. From the Soviet perspective, the mechanized domain of work liberates the human qualities of the worker. In whatever way the tropes are interpreted, they fail to elucidate the relation of performance to productive action, a relationship I shall call *organization*. Whether aimed at revolution, management, or entertainment, mass action in the thirties depended on the social organization of cooperative movement on a mass scale. This chapter examines how choreographic rationales influenced the goals of structures administering the organization of the mass, and how choreographic poetics thus came into contact with other social systems. This amounts to the influence of practical consciousness on official consciousness.[2] I use the term *organization* to entail both the aesthetics of social engineering and the politics of artistic genre. Where they meet and overlap is the site of the performative economy.

The working bodies dealt with in this chapter, although restricted to the ideological fields of communism and capitalism, are three: the revolutionary communist agitator or socialist fellow-traveler, the Taylorized worker of industrial capitalism, and the chorus girl of Broadway and Hollywood musicals. (Frederick Winslow Taylor, the father of scientific management, experimented with combinations of time expenditure and the exertion of physical effort among workers in the Pennsylvania steel industry. Workers' movements that are organized and controlled according to his principles of maximal efficiency are referred to as Taylorized.) The revolutionary studies "mass dance" as an amateur group form. The Taylorized worker is trained to economize his gestures in space and time for maximum efficiency. The chorus girl, supplementing Taylorism with an esprit de corps that in reality it lacked, does "precision dancing" through which she imitates the machine or the functioning of the political economy. In neither case is her dance a preparation for productive movement. Rather, she dances a systemic totality that I shall identify as exchange. Her role in the figuration of this totality obscures, not surprisingly, the status of her own performance as work.[3] In order to reflect on the relation of dance to rationalized organizational structures I shall examine the particular tasks designated by each choreographic form. I also ask what the relation of these performances to worker emotion is in each case. That is, what emotions do these forms evoke and what do they attempt to suppress?

Prelude: A New Deal for Spectacle

I begin with a brief overview, the description of a dramatic pageant subsidized by the federal government. Here, the fundamental ideological conflict concerning work and organization is set forth in exceedingly simple yet revealing terms. On 10 June 1936 President Franklin Delano Roosevelt visited Little Rock, Arkansas, to participate in a pageant conceived and produced by the Arkansas Centennial Commission and two artistic branches of the Works Progress Administration, the Federal Theatre and Music Projects. This production, employing "six hundred members of the community,"[4] was a unique instance of the federal government using the Works Progress Administration apparatus for specific propaganda purposes.

America Sings presented a synoptic vision of American history in "a tremendous living mural which will unfold itself very rapidly across a modernistic [outdoor] stage."[5] Its tableaux included "Indian Episode," "March of the Pioneers," "Plantation Life," "Parade of the War between the States," "The Mechanical Age," "World War Parade," "The Aftermath," and "Finale." This last was "of particular interest because it joined the present moment of unrest to a vision of the President's philosophy, personified by his live voice."[6] Roosevelt intervened in this scene to deliver a public address transmitted simultaneously as a national radio broadcast.

"The present moment of unrest" in "The Aftermath" depicted the 1929 stock market crash "accompanied by screaming headlines of the day" and "followed by the wail of the Negro chorus singing 'I Can't Hear Nobody Pray.'" Images of unrest continued into "Finale": "The disorganized mob left by the crash is aroused by a rabble raising speaker urging them to defy law and order, and they form into a violent protest march." Protests, specifies publicity copy, are inherently "unorganized," and thus already a sign of "social dissolution."[7] But "at the height of this march they are stilled by a magnificent voice proclaiming an era of new hope for the American masses and challenging America to cease wailing and to sing again as it has in every crisis."[8] The president's voice organizes the masses who "begin to re-form into lines of usefully employed."[9] After his address, "the chorus swells into 'America,' and then into 'Arkansas,' and the 'Star Spangled Banner' sung by the entire audience."[10]

The resolution of "a violent protest march" into peaceful "lines of usefully employed" evokes two images of labor that haunted America in the 1930s: radicalism and labor efficiency. If radicalism was most readily associated with agitprop performance and the mass dance, labor efficiency evoked images of highly coordinated and stylized motions whose theatrical analogue is the kickline of precision dancing. In what follows, I wish to ascertain not only which figures of organization assumed public visibility as recognizable labels of ideological programs, but also how the choreography configured effective personal and group experience useful in the production and reproduction of competing social formations.

Organizing Spontaneous Action

The vibrant qualities of readiness and expectancy in the proletarian body were central to the politically radical meanings of *organization*. When ignited by the prospect of emancipation, the masses were "organized" emotionally. This could not happen without emotional self-recognition, for organization signified a readiness for action. Each individual was "organized" at the level of his own responsive capacity. Action could only be initiated by large groups demonstrating strength and resolve in their muscular fiber but also emotional intensity in their soft tissue. There is nothing physically uniform about this version of organization beyond a common alacrity to join the collective enterprise.

One theatrical model for organization can be found in agitprop theater. A short text entitled "Basic Principles (1931)" stipulated that agitprop "must awaken class consciousness leading to *organization*."[11] Organization as a "central idea" was not just a cause illustrated by a theme, but a spectacular vision of shifting circumstances and interchangeable roles. Agitprop performance style was characterized by "economy of gesture and motion, this last to permit any worker to take any part with a minimum of rehearsal."[12] Agitprop shunned strict divisions of labor. Roles were not differentiated according to skills, but were relatively interchangeable. Simplicity bordering on stylization favored instantaneous adaptability of each performer to a variety of roles. While transmitting explicit propaganda about worker oppression, the energetic improvisational style of agitprop also invigorated its audience with the expectancy of change epitomized by their own flexibility. Agitprop performers reached out to those not yet in touch with their own radical physical energy. The politically effective concept of organization behind agitprop was thus an accumulation of analogous microcenters of readiness.

Mass dance was a choreographic and pedagogical form providing a more complex organizational model. Jane Dudley described mass dance as an improvisational exercise for anywhere from twenty to fifty untrained performers: "For accompaniment, such instruments as drums, cymbals, piano, gongs, even voice, chants, songs, are valuable, and should be used in order to provide rhythm, and so keep the unity of the movement, and to help build intensity."[13] Dudley may have taught mass dance at the New Dance Group, a studio whose archive holds the only extant photograph of such an exercise. Certainly, NDG students, as described in a press release, qualified as workers:

The heterogeneous character of the New Dance Group membership is apparent from the following occupational classification. This very diversity is an encouraging indication of the very broadening appeal of the revolutionary dancing among the masses. There are: 6 sales clerks, 1 shoe worker, 1 needle trade, 1 food worker, 1 social worker, 1 dress designer, 1 professional housekeeper, 1 dress cleaner, 6 office workers, 1 milliner, 4 students, 1 laboratory technician, 1 artist, 1 hairdresser, 2 beauticians, 1 physical therapy technician, 15 teachers, 2 lawyers, 1 model, 1 chemist, and 1 sailor.[14]

In addition to performers, mass dance classes required a chairman, a dance leader, and a committee. The chairman's role was to lead preclass discussion, and to facilitate postperformance discussion. The dance leader was someone "who can direct large groups of people, who understands the nature of a mass class, and who understands the theme as a revolutionary dance leader."[15] The committee chooses the dance leader, and sees that the leader "thoroughly understands the theme." The committee "can also handle the organizing of the class, the sending out of notices, selecting a studio, etc."[16] These roles insure a bridge between ways of moving and ways of thinking. Further, they indicate

that mass dance was part of a regulated infrastructure. Legitimate questions arise about the level of control of the dancers by the leader figures.

Edith Segal's discussion of the revolutionary dance director and group stresses collectivity over leadership: "The subject-matter is social and is the concern of all the participants in the dance. . . . [It] is therefore not the private property of the director, or even of the group, but that of the audience and society."[17] Segal underplays the potential for authoritarian leadership of the class. The pedagogical goal of the class, as dancer Ruth Allerhand explains it, was the personal experience of group dynamics:

Figure 5: Amateur dancers emerge as intensely individuated subjects in an improvisation for "mass dance." New Dance Group, early thirties. Performers unknown. (Courtesy of the New Dance Group Studio's Archive, New York.)

The group experience is a practical school which teaches something that can never be forgotten, nor taught as eloquently through any other medium. Through union with others, in adjusting himself to the group, he comes to an active discovery of real solidarity. From the individual to the mass! The individual no longer feels that he is the whole, he now sees that he represents the substance. He is not so much a link in a chain, a cog in a machine, as a very alive, very productive cell within a body.[18]

Allerhand's language of organism ennobles individual bodies in the collective enterprise as "the substance," that is, "very alive," and "very productive." Although bodies are pictured as cells making up a larger organism, each cell would seem to have a will of its own. The radical body is vibrantly alive rather than dehumanized. "He actively cuts into space," writes Allerhand of the dancer, "using his body impulsively, he runs, leaps, turns, he creates and composes within space."[19] This description suggests a significant amount of freedom ("impulsively") on the dancer's part to explore patterns of individual energy and choreographic initiative ("he creates and composes").

But the mass dance also trained its participants to think and react beyond the individual. Organization is the gathering of physical and emotional resources in and by the group. Disparate foci begin to converge as the dancers pool a common focus on a world they wish, perhaps for different reasons, to change. When Dudley suggests "the group should go towards a point as though asking for something or demanding something," one imagines that this focal "point" organizes the disparate focus of a large group, investing them with the emotional and physical coalescence of their energetic resources.[20] They move as a whole made up of differentiated parts. Their unity is based on the pooling of distinct personal motives which, together with the power in numbers, lends forcefulness to their collective presence. The amassing of physical and emotional energy within the group is the result of the choreographic directives, which became an effective means of emboldening political consciousness in an improvised situation. "In the mass dance," concludes Allerhand, "the people will find a twofold gain of tremendous significance. The first, the educational development, through which they found themselves and each other, and which has awakened in them a strong feeling of respect and responsibility for others. The second, a group ability to express, to articulate, and formulate what was before only half clear in their own minds."[21] Clearly the group remains a plural entity unified by common concerns. The mass dance teaches the dancers to share resources by contributing to a larger dynamic.

Many modern dance companies and theater collectives in the thirties were called groups, as were the New Dance Group and the Group Theatre. A "group" was also a term for the smallest organized unit of the CP-USA.[22] As the smallest unit of an underground organization, a group was not to exceed ten members. One reads under "Form and Units of Organization" that "groups of the same language within a city or locality shall form a Branch."[23] The organizational hierarchy ascends, from the group as the most basic unit, through branches and subdistricts, to districts that find themselves in "industrial sections regardless of political boundaries."[24] As theorized in the party's *Program and Constitution,* mass action "develops from spontaneous activities of the workers massed in large industries. Among its initial manifestations are mass strikes and mass demonstrations."[25] The group, then, constitutes a collective cell of common cultural traits within the larger mass. Mass dance may well have served as an in-studio preparation for such actions on the group level, even though the *Program and Constitution* does not mention dancing.

Despite the embedded hierarchy of CP-USA, its administrative structure was designed to foster one goal: "spontaneous action" precipitating "the final conflict for power."[26] Mass dance cultivated the physical alacrity and interactive responsiveness needed to cooperate effectively with others in such spontaneous action. Dudley describes preparatory exercises for mass dance that indicate how cooperative motion escaped regimentation to become both personally and socially significant: "In order to give the members of the class an understanding of what it means to move together as a group, a few simple exercises should be given, such as standing together and swaying from side to side, walking together backwards and forwards, sinking down and rising up. These are exercises purely on a movement basis."[27] Other aspects of Dudley's text stress the sense of immediate involvement fostered by mass dance: "Her [the dance leader's] description of the theme, of the movements, must be vivid, must mobilize the members in such a way that they throw themselves into the dancing of the theme."[28] The need for flexibility and improvisation disqualified traditional dance aesthetic conventions: "For this one does not need 'steps.' . . . All that is important is the movement of the group in space."[29] Because of its lack of any traditional technical requirements, mass dance maintains a contradictory relation to party discipline. The *Program and Constitution* states: "All decisions of the governing bodies of the Party shall be binding upon the membership and subordinate units."[30] Yet mass dance allows considerable space for and even presupposes the cultivation of individual responsiveness and personal meaning. "It [the dance] will of necessity be simple," notes Dudley. "It must be moving, especially to the participants. It must have significance."[31]

All of this implies that mass dance provides the sensation of intensely compressed experience characterizing momentous historical events. The moments leading up to and away from action are constitutively different from the moment characterized by action itself, which has the blinding quality of history set in motion. Yet, at the same time, history is set in motion by the group's movement. "The group," writes Segal, "will feel the growth of the movements out of themselves, rather than have them imposed."[32] Segal had also affirmed that the subject matter belonged neither to the director nor to the group, but to the audience and society. Thus, the movements of the collective grow from individual bodies and move outward toward society at large: they never become commodified. To the choreographers, neither the subject matter nor the movements realizing it in dance belong to those dictating from above. Rather, the study of dance is the study of historical agency. This is particularly true of Segal's account, in which the choreography should be "based on the collective discussion."[33]

According to the *Program and Constitution,* mass action should result in the experience of union and the spark of "new tactics and a new ideology."[34] Mass action is followed, as in the dance class, by group discussion and questions. Action itself, however, is not only the *Program and Constitution*'s telos, but also its blind spot. One cannot predict what may catalyze action, nor which new ideologies will be set in motion. The desired result of spontaneous action is a new collective identity in which the individual is subsumed but not submerged. The spontaneous experience of this union discovered in movement was the educational goal of mass dance in movement culture, a lesson that cannot be explained, taught, or inculcated. Each individual discovered it in his or her particular experience of movement with the group. The role of the class was to render that experience conscious. "No doubt," notes Segal, "it is easier and simpler to dictate each movement and see it executed immediately, but there is a danger in cutting the group off entirely from the creative process. There must be a give-and-take attitude on the part of the director and the group, with the final word in the hands of the director."[35]

The practice of mass dance projects a different image of "the political emotion embodied" than that sketched out in *The Romance of American Communism.* The thumbnail sketch of Boris Edel, devout Communist, emphasizes "the gift for political emotion highly developed, [but] the gift for individual empathy neglected, atrophied."[36] He experiences humanness only as an idea. The very process of mass dance training and performance entails a kinesthetic empathy that is surely the radical physical basis for any further idea of empathy.

Emotional Equilibrium

By the 1930s, political emotion embodied became a concern of scientific managers. André Philip's research into American labor in 1927 was already cognizant of a necessity at the rank-and-file level to sublimate the worker's creative instincts. Philip cites psychologists who believed signs of labor unrest to be "morbid symptoms indicating the repression of certain fundamental instincts that must be fulfilled at any price."[37] The worker's creative instinct, affirmed Philip, had been "brutally repressed," (161) necessitating a successful counterstrategy of sublimation.

It is possible to divert the worker's creative instinct from the individual work to collective work; if one fully informs the worker about factory production, and of his role in national economic life, if one explains in detail his function in the creation of the total work, one will probably not have removed the repulsive and monotonous character of his work, but one will have given him the feeling of useful collaboration.[38]

Yet industrial capitalism had clearly subverted the individual's freedom of movement. It was at this level that the notion of creative instinct was broached; however, there proved to be no effective way to sublimate the creative instinct. Whereas mass dance managed to accommodate the individual contribution, the fact remained that extreme division of labor repressed desire. The by-product of this repression burst forth as emotional reaction. Emotion takes on the lineaments of a dangerous frustration that disrupts the reproduction of the status quo in the industrial context.

Scientific management's tactical response to the emotional problem of the worker was prevention. The worker became the subject of psychological observation. To counteract radical emotion's power to forge social and political community, a research industry grew up around workers' emotional dysfunction.[39] "Scientific" studies show management's attempt to survey and regulate workers' emotional vicissitudes. The author of *Workers' Emotions in Shop and Home* recommends that the term *crisis* replace the general psychological concept of *stimulus:* "When we consider the ordinary day-by-day activities of human beings," he writes, "there can be little doubt that the word crisis connotes more clearly the inaugurating influences of human reaction than other words."[40] Emotional embodiment, in other terms, is a crisis for scientific management, and for that reason, emotion is political. Emotion requires surveillance: "It is the wise executive or foreman who keeps eyes and ears open for any signs which may help him to determine how his men will react to any crises which may be ahead of them."[41]

Case studies measured worker depression ("lowered emotional or physical state"), neutral or nonemotional state, and high emotional or physical state against an array of possible domestic and social crises. The stated goal was to maximize worker productivity with respect to "physical capacity" and "emotional resistance."[42] The implicit concern was to avoid "the psychological tides and storms which result in strikes."[43] By studying workers' relationships to their personal, social, and emotional afflictions, the "psychosomatic approach" presupposed the worker's fundamental instability.[44] Corporate research contemplated the worker as in either passive quiescence or abnormal excitability. The best management could hope to achieve was temporary emotional equilibrium.

Both mass dance and scientific management conceived of the worker's body and emotions—the two coalescing in a body in motion—as artistic material to be shaped. In 1922 Henry Ford proclaimed the industrialist to be an artist in the laws of personality: "If a man wants a field for vital creative work, let him come where he is dealing with higher laws than those of sound, or line, or color; let him come where he may deal with the laws of personality. We want artists in an industrial relationship. We want those who can mould the political, social, industrial and moral mass into a sound and shapely whole."[45]

Antonio Gramsci saw in this pretension to artistry the necessity for industrial capitalism to reinvent the worker as body and self devoid of emotion. In his "Americanism and Fordism" essay, written in the early thirties, Gramsci noted a discrepancy between capitalist ideology and the proletarian body: "There is an inherent conflict between the 'verbal' ideology, which recognizes the new necessities and the real 'animal' practice, which prevents physical bodies from effectively acquiring the new attitudes."[46] Although government and industry subscribed to an emotionless or emotionally flat but profitable concept of organization, it recognized the inevitably volatile emotional nature of workers' temperament. Scientific management could only represent worker emotion as a negative factor to be overcome by resistance or be pacified. The fact remained that emotions could be neither expunged nor transformed. Short of being able to reinvent "the new man" as a working machine, Gramsci reformulated the goal in terms of the automation of the worker's body itself: "The only thing that is completely mechanized is the physical gesture; the memory of the trade reduced to simple gestures repeated at an intense rhythm, 'nestles' in the muscular and nervous centers and leaves the brain free and unencumbered for other occupations."[47] Gramsci perceived the desire of industrial capitalism to sever emotion from performance by seeking a nonaestheticized, yet still formal, reduction to gestural givens. The gesture that "nestles" in the worker's muscular and nervous centers, however, leaves his mind free to wander: "One walks automatically, and at the same time thinks about whatever one chooses."[48] This disconnection between movement and mental concentration poses the problem of distraction and, from a different point of view, the ideological necessity of entertainment (the art of distraction) in its specific relationship to the problem of the worker.[49]

Dancing Management

Although "dance was a working person's activity,"[50] as Graff points out, neither male nor female industrial workers attended precision dance classes in their leisure hours. What then does it mean to say the performative embodiment of the auto worker, or any such industrial worker, was the chorus girl? It is important to recognize that chorus dancing not only represents labor efficiency, but constitutes in itself labor efficiency *in* dancing. It is very easy to ignore the fact that that the chorus girl was a worker herself in the Broadway and Hollywood entertainment industries. Yet among dancers, chorus girls were, it seems, the slowest to organize.[51]

In chorus dancing we confront the displacement of the Taylorized male body by the female dancing body of the chorine. Siegfried Kracauer asked in 1931: "What is it that they [chorus girls], like an image become flesh, embody?" His answer was: "The *functioning* of a flourishing economy."[52] According to Kracauer, the chorine does more than replicate the disciplines of work: she represents an overall functioning. She takes on a greater semiotic burden than the amateur mass dancer and the Taylorized worker. This obliges us to further define the movement of an economy as what Alfred Sohn-Rethel calls the "abstract and purely social physicality of exchange."[53] To follow this thread, we must recognize not only where the chorus girl came from, but also what her destination became in the Great Depression.

The most frequently cited choreography of industrial capitalism was precision dancing. The kickline, in particular, was burned into twentieth-century cultural memory by the British Tiller Girls and immortalized in Kracauer's 1927 essay "The Mass Ornament."[54] It entered the American cultural imaginary under the auspices of the Ziegfeld girl, whose image was broadly disseminated during the 1930s in backstage musical films, which took the production process as their theme. The tradition of chorus dance in America was developed and refined in New York by impresario Florenz Ziegfeld for his Ziegfeld Follies, which ran from 1907 to 1932. The end of the Ziegfeld era in the early thirties also marked the end of the chorus girl's reign in live spectacle and the beginning of her presence in the Hollywood backstage musical film. The Ziegfeld girl is transmitted to posterity, as Linda Mizejewski shows, through the cinema of the thirties and forties.[55] Busby Berkeley's cinematic treatment of the chorus girl introduces important differences with stage performance. Although Berkeley does depict stage performance, the role of dance is minimized. The chorus girl's function in the popular imagination during the thirties necessitates combining an awareness of the choreographic and performative aesthetic of the Follies tradition with her visual and narrative representation through cinematic means.

Taylorized Choreography

The chorus girl exemplified the emotional equilibrium that Taylorist management sought in workers. In chorus dance, emotions are restricted to cheerfulness at carrying out the routine. Kracauer remarked that "their faces were made up with an optimism that nipped all resistance to economic development in the bud."[56] Cheerfulness becomes a figure of pacification. The chorine's demeanor, athletic strength, and collective discipline fostered a positive and entertaining image of unskilled labor under the regime of machine culture. In contrast to the mass dance just discussed, chorus dancing afforded no opportunities for creative adjustment to others' impulses. The movement of the ensemble was strictly regulated.

On the stage, the concept of the chorus "routine" characterizes this form of choreography. Although the routine allows for variation from number to number, it limits all movement to an immediately reproducible format framed by an entrance and an exit. Some movement vocabulary is borrowed from classical ballet, especially the high kicks. Choreographer Ned Wayburn advised the aspiring chorus dancer: "If you are being taught a dance routine and a stage direction is given you must be able to turn to that direction without stopping to think about it or hardly realizing what you are doing."[57] Every aspect of chorus movement was to nestle, as Gramsci had foreseen, in the muscular and nervous centers of the body, such that variations could be introduced almost without thinking. A scene from the backstage musical film *Ziegfeld Girl* shows two chorus dancers kicking their legs in rehearsal while maintaining a private conversation. Like the operating of a machine, chorus dancing could be considered automated labor. The impression of machine-like precision that eyewitnesses emphasize should be taken quite seriously. "When they raised their legs with mathematical precision," noted Kracauer, "they joyfully affirmed the progress of rationalization."[58]

This approach also testifies to an extreme atomization of movement vocabulary. Carefully defined divisions of labor organized dancing in a Follies routine. Subgroups of the chorus specialized in particular branches of choreography. The "pony teams," for example, were never entrusted with solo work. The most individualized group was the showgirls, but they tended to walk rather than dance. There were five groups in all, each performing a limited subset of the chorus work.[59] Although the audience might not perceive specialization because the performers looked interchangeable, it narrowed each dancer's range of movement options. Such organization limited the dancing body to specialized tasks on the model of scientific management. More routines could be set more quickly when dancers were made to specialize in "piecework." Thus, an image emerges of the chorus girl's performance showing her to be both disciplined and distracted. That is, her ever-present mask of cheerfulness takes the audience's attention away from her discipline, but the internal emotional range permitted by this mask is also a sign of her own potential distraction. Her mind is elsewhere. Her performance configures high physical efficiency with low emotional intensity ("lowered emotional state"); it is not fully free of a dialectic.

The Exchange Scene

All the more reason to embed this scene in the act of exchange. Scientific management prescribed the maximally efficient relation of the worker to his instruments, his task, and his coworkers. Taylor aimed to condition the worker to yield the maximal output of work possible short of exhaustion.[60] As Sohn-Rethel points out, this amounts to "human labor made into a technological entity, homogeneous with the machinery."[61] Kracauer described the chorus line in strikingly similar terms:

Anyone who has ever taken a pleasure trip on a steamer has surely at some time or other leaned over the inside railing, his back to one or another sea, and looked down onto the ship's shining engines. The girls' poses recall the regular play of the pistons. They are not so much of a military precision as they correspond in some other way to the ideal of the machine. A button is pressed and a girl contraption cranks into motion, performing impressively at thirty-two horsepower. All the parts begin to roll, the waves fall into their cycles. And while the machine stamps, shakes and roars like a sawmill or a locomotive, a smile drips a steady supply of oil onto the joints so that the cogs do not suddenly fail. Finally an inaudible signal brings the mechanical action to a stop, and the dead whole automatically decomposes itself into its living parts.[62]

For Kracauer, this is essentially a dead performance whose organic basis is only visible through a phenomenon of decomposition. It is as if the real-life chorus girl behind the mask were buried in layers of decay, from which she returns to life as merely a "living part," rather than a whole human being. This speaks to the inorganic aspects of her organization (a theme developed by Kracauer as the mass ornament) and most pertinently to her profound disorgan-ization—a sign of her emotional decay. When one considers the chorus dancer as a worker in her own right rather than only an allegory of productivity, one becomes aware of her commodification, and of the commodification of her work. Mizejewski has shown how the chorus girl's performance in the Ziegfeld Follies was often combined with the display of commodities such as elegant clothes. Ziegfeld and later Berkeley standardized her physical appearance to commodify her. There occurred a blurring of her bodily commodification with the appurtenances her body paraded. Where did one stop and the other begin? These problems have been addressed by feminist critique and can be extended. They take place within the dialectic Gramsci foresaw in which the worker would no longer be required to concentrate during the execution of disciplined action.

Consider the opening scene from the film *Gold Diggers of 1933*. "We're in

Figure 6: The production number "We're in the Money," a fictional musical show that folds early in Busby Berkeley's Gold Diggers of 1933. *(Gold Diggers of 1933 c. 1933 Turner Entertainment Co.*

the Money" takes place in an empty theater where chorus girls, parading around in oversized silver dollars, rehearse for an upcoming show. Their earrings, necklaces, capes, and brassieres are stitched through with coins. "The long lost dollar has come back to the fold," intones Ginger Rogers. "With silver you can turn your dreams to gold." In its extravagant improbability, "We're in the Money" makes a metastatement on chorus dancing in the Great Depression. From the theater history perspective, it emulates the extravagant Broadway production numbers of the twenties, with an essential

difference. The chorus girl performs not only the commodification of sex but also the fascination of the commodity itself as spectacle. Her glamorized body makes the commodity work both in and as the activity of exchange. She performs neither sex nor the commodity per se, but rather "the exchange abstraction."[63] The action of exchange is definitive for a flourishing economy and thus gains symbolic importance in chorus dance. For Sohn-Rethel, the movement of commodities as they are exchanged implies an abstraction of time and space because they are supposed to maintain their value by avoiding any use during exchange. For this reason, commodities exist outside the world in the moment of exchange, and thus exchange partakes of abstraction. The chorus girl performs currency in its effective circulation and the abstract human labor distilled in it. Her dance thus embodies both "the form and the substance of value."[64] She stands for both the commodity (its form) and what the commodity commands in monetary terms (its substance). Yet her substance is rendered in the form of money, and her form is determined by sexual commodification. "We're in the Money" uses women's bodies to reverse the collapse of the exchange nexus during the severest year of the Great Depression.[65] How is this shown?

Film scholar Martin Rubin has noted that "We're in the Money" establishes "strong links between money and sexuality."[66] Patricia Mellencamp has written of the "sexual economics" of *Gold Diggers*.[67] One could say, indeed, that "We're in the Money" illustrates what Guy Debord has called "the other side of money": sex as the "abstract equivalent of all commodities."[68] I propose that abstraction is the scene in which sex itself is commodified as exchange. In order for this to happen, the chorus girl's body must circulate and be simultaneously in suspension.

For Sohn-Rethel "exchange serves only a change of ownership, a change, that is, in terms of a purely *social status* of the commodities as owned property."[69] He characterizes exchange as the suspension of use: "Wherever commodity exchange takes place, it does so in effective 'abstraction' from use. This is an abstraction not in mind, but in fact. It is a state of affairs prevailing at a definite place and lasting a definite time. It is a state of affairs which reigns on the market."[70] The abstraction of use is necessary to the social act of exchange. The chorine's use is suspended by the fact that she is herself both the goods and the measure of value regulating their own exchange. In dancing the role of money, she does more than equate sex with money: she embodies the contradiction of money itself, the coin as material object which is at the same time the abstract measure of the value in the exchanged object. Although the dancers do not literally become immobilized as do Sohn-Rethel's commodities, the emphasis on their relationship to space has the effect of erasing time. A chorine's performance is visually suspended in an unreal spatial dimension. Such departures from realistic spatial coordinates is typical of Berkeley's mise-en-scène. The camera abandons the realist representation of the stage and theater for what Lucy Fischer calls "plastic abstractions."[71] Rubin refers to this spatial abstraction as the consistently impossible or contradictory character of musical numbers in relation to the dominant, realist narrative discourse of the film.[72] One obvious example is the reappearance of Ginger Rogers at the end of the line of dancers across which the camera pans, making her seem to be in two places at once. The ambit of performative glamour occurs at precisely this unreal site where moving bodies appear as free-floating objects. The abnormally enlarged close-up of Rogers's lips singing the song in pig latin both underlines and palliates the unreality, as if it were merely a gag. In general, the most "ornamental" far shots in Berkeley production numbers are intercut with close-ups assuring the viewer that the mass ornament is "performed" by real people. These are the visual tools of exchange abstraction, signaling not only a departure from the representation of reality, but the suspension of use which is the condition of commodity exchange. The chorine's body is suspended—from its place, from its dance, from use. Yet we are continuously distracted from the meaning of this suspension by expressions of cheerful and accommodating dancers doing their work.

Critics have recognized this objectification of the chorus girl's body as "image." Lucy Fischer describes the chorus girl in another Berkeley spectacle as "the image of woman as image."[73] Reciprocally, Debord characterizes spectacle as "capital to such a degree of accumulation that it becomes an image" (section 34). It is true that the actual choreographic routines of the Ziegfeld days have been suppressed, leaving only a similar staging and a look reminiscent of chorus dancing. This "image," cut off from the "live" performance and its danced movements, renders the commodity's stillness in the instant of exchange. With respect to real bodies in motion, the image invokes the "quality-less condition" of the commodity abstracted from its use value and existing in timeless suspension.[74] Equally related to the loss of qualities is the loss of the sense of time. The chorus girl as worker and performer is subject to what Georg Lukàcs calls the becoming space of time: "Time sheds its qualitative, variable, flowing nature; it freezes into an exactly delimited, quantifiable continuum filled with quantifiable 'things' (the reified, mechanically objectified 'performance' of the worker wholly separated from his total human personality): in short, it becomes space."[75] Thus, the commodification of the chorus girl is exactly parallel to the commodification of the worker. Suspension from use in the moment of exchange is shown by the chorus girl's being "moved around in time and space in accordance with [her] character as a commodity rather than a use-value."[76] One thinks of her display on revolving floats, staircases, and other architectural set pieces. As an entertainment industry worker, she is likewise in an alienated relation to her work, which fact is emphasized by her inability to experience time or space organically. Either the camera moves or the ground on which she poses moves; she herself has lost the art of movement.

The following description of exchange exemplifies the Berkeleyan number at its most accelerated level of unreality: "Abstract movement through abstract (homogeneous, continuous, and empty) space and time of abstract substances (materially real but bare of sense-qualities) which thereby suffer no material change."[77] The chorus girl is taken up by the cinematic apparatus and restaged in an abstract space-time. What her "image" permits us to understand is the contradiction that characterized her qualities under Ziegfeld. Her sexuality was asexual; her lascivious appeal was wholesome. It is only in the suspension of potential use values in the abstract moment of real exchange that such contradictory attributes can be recuperated.

Although "We're in the Money" is only one among many production numbers in the Berkeley canon, it is paradigmatic of Hollywood's response to what Kracauer called the situation of "girls and crisis" in the thirties.[78] By crisis Kracauer meant the Great Depression, which lent an air of implausibility to the girls' purported enthusiasm. "We're in the Money" is an implausible visual recuperation of an already implausible performance—a double fantasy made to appear artistically plausible by Berkeley's "impossible" production values. As resolved into the exchange abstraction by cinematic means, the chorine's body was very likely also industrial capitalism's response to Gramsci's formulation of the dialectic and its solution to "political emotion embodied" as crisis. But analyzed as both commodification of labor and suspension of use in the exchange abstraction, the chorus girl's performance—grasped as both spectacle and work—performs its own ideological analysis.

Chapter 2 **Essentialized Affect and E/motion**

Chapter 1 compared the choreographic and emotional attributes of ideologically opposed regimes of mass organization. This chapter turns to the physically legible shape of emotional qualities. Here it will not be a question of the exploitation or restriction of embodied feelings, but of stylistic differences in physical expression. The field of study is no longer communism and capitalism necessarily, but nuances of self-presentation within modern dance. As an introduction to this material I draw on literary and cinematic depictions of emotion in relation to radicalism in the work of Richard Wright, Michael Gold, Ralph Ellison, and Pare Lorentz. This digression into literature and film serves to underline that the radical subject of the thirties experienced emotion in relation to gender, ethnicity, race, and class identifications. The high modernist subject, on the other hand, tended to universalize and nationalize feeling as what I shall call affect.

Reconstructing Radical Emotion

When novelist and essayist Michael Gold, editor of the influential left-wing publication *New Masses,* called the radical promise of the thirties "the romance of tens of millions of men and women," he was proclaiming a proletarian avant-garde that neither modernism then nor postmodernism later were to embrace.[1] Although modernism is frequently considered aesthetically "radical," it is less often politically radical. Aesthetic modernism often positions form as the most effective artistic consideration and thus sublimates and/or universalizes particular emotion. In this way, modernism tends to blur issues of identity grounded in a situated politics. Gold's romance implies an indulgence in sentiment, even sentimentality, foreign to modernist formalism.

Gold's contemporary Joseph Freeman called the thirties "a *trauma* . . . an emotional block."[2] Whether they viewed the period as success or failure, both agreed on the seminal role of emotion—passion or trauma—in thirties cultural experience.

FRANKO: Did that period mark you in any way emotionally?
DUDLEY: Yes, I think it did. It drew me to certain subject matter, and to treating subject matter with a certain kind of emotional intensity.[3]

This book argues for the enduring critical and emotional heritage of thirties radical culture, one that gains visibility with the waning of postmodernism. Alan M. Wald, a leading literary historian of American left culture, has pointed out that artistic creativity on the American Left was more preponderant than critical theory.[4] An important aspect of such creative work was emotion explored in relation to social and political realities.

With the advent of McCarthyism and the Cold War in the early fifties, left culture went underground. We have become desensitized over time to the performative nuances that could generate distinctions between kinds of embodied feeling in the 1930s. The political failure of the Left brought about a de facto quarantine of the radical decade's cultural artifacts as "documents." Because radical performance reflected socially motivated concerns, it was believed to have relinquished aesthetic values.[5] James Agee said the documentary project was, with respect to photography, "to pry intimately into the lives of an undefended and appallingly damaged group of human beings."[6] This concept of subject matter and mode of treatment stuck. With respect to aesthetic modernism, radical culture in the thirties acquired the status of a curious document with minimal aesthetic value. Elaborate interpretation seemed off-limits in critical accounts.

A tendency remains to consider the proletarian subject abnormally reduced and pathologically lacking in subjective and objective aesthetic agency. There is a myth that the subject's suffering can be documented but not rendered with lasting artistic values. This view reduces radical bodies and emotions to unreflective, nonanalytic, and thus inexorably contingent artistic and social practice. Documents of the oppressed may elicit pity, but they short-circuit the contemplation of form required by artistic expression; hence the argument that left-wing radical art did not qualify as art because it could not transcend the immediate givens of its own historical context as subject matter and conditions of production.

On these grounds, the radical decade was long considered either untheorizable or just not worth the trouble. Discredited for intellectual vacuity and political naïveté, radical art could be maligned as well for its ethnic origins. Characterized politically rather than aesthetically, radical art fell through the cracks between avant-gardism, aesthetic modernism, and socialist realism. Art criticism's derogatory view of popular emotion viewed radical art as lacking in intellectual merit, and the radical sensibility further lost favor as the politics that motivated it were forced underground. Ultimately it was incompatible with the postmodern "waning of affect."[7]

Structures of Feeling and Aesthetic Reduction

In examining the cinematic work of Pare Lorentz and the literary work of Richard Wright, Michael Gold, and Ralph Ellison, I assume that information about literary and cinematic bodies is relevant to historical performing bodies for the purpose of reconstructing radical emotion. The role of emotions has not gained wide recognition in the historiography of North American radicalism which has recently become a terrain of conflicting epistemological claims. One historical approach stresses what Raymond Williams calls "official consciousness."[8] It examines radicalism as fixed, locatable in documents, and thus institutionally definable. This position has gained momentum from the partial opening of archives in the former Soviet Union.[9] Some New Left historians propose "practical consciousness" as a felt politics, encompassing a "particular quality of social experience" in "specific feelings, specific rhythms."[10] We could add: in specific physical expressions, gestures, and signs of emotional behaviors. This study favors the "practical consciousness" afforded by dance, theater, film, and literature.

Performances lent form to radical emotions, and form is, among other things, a repository of social specificity. To encompass the formal aspects of lived experience whose history normally eludes notation, Williams posits the analytic notion of a "structure of feeling." This term is valuable because the conjoined appreciation of emotional and formal properties it suggests opens up the signifying potential of radical art.[11] "Structures of feeling" are bodily, aural, or visual traces that allow us to recover aesthetic elements in a past culture that was immediate rather than traditional, specific rather than universal, corporeal rather than ideal. Emotion was material; its embodiment as either political action or performative activity was consonant with a materialist vision of the world.

The term radicalism itself pertains to root or roots, "to that which is central, essential, fundamental, primary, or the source and origin of any phenomenon."[12] Emotion is one of radicalism's key elements; the other is body.[13] They are fundamental not because of any essentialism, but because they have undergone a social reduction. Modern dance of the 1930s frequently showed existence reduced to its material base as an emotional body. It resembles the modernist aesthetic reduction to essentials without the purity of modernism's grasp of essence. The transmission of feelings in and to bodies was an act fostering social depth with both subjective and ideological ramifications.[14]

Dance relieves us, therefore, of the historical defeat of radicalism's immediacy, or this immediacy's flip side—literalism. The term "structure of feeling" is, in fact, so relevant to dance as to be almost tautological with it. Williams understood *experience,* the term he considered before settling on *feeling,* as "embodied, related feelings."[15] The necessary relation of the fleshly body to its markers of identity and subjectivity lends feeling its structure from experience, through performance, to interpretation. This feeling is practically unmediated in that its passage from life to the stage entails no studied adaptation. By the same token, it is already theatrical when we first encounter it.

The social glue holding form and emotion together is authenticity, which also permits the individual to identify with the group as well as to represent the self and group seemingly without mediation. Rena Fraden has called authenticity "a political, aesthetic, and cultural category" of the thirties.[16] The emotional experience of radical culture bridged authentic ethnic experience with a nascent class consciousness which drew upon discourses of authenticity to precipitate a felt politics. Jane Dudley's testimony goes to the heart of the convictions about authenticity that linked audience and performer in the 1930s:

DUDLEY: I know we all felt we were in the middle of something that had a lot of promise, that was fermenting. Sometimes three thousand people came to a modern dance concert.

FRANKO: Did you feel your audience bonded with you?

DUDLEY: Yes. That was very important part of the thirties and forties. We felt we were dealing in the subject matter that the audiences needed and wanted to see on the stage, in theater and dance.

FRANKO: How did emotion serve that?

DUDLEY: The thing that sticks in my mind was a certain fervency, a certain conviction that what we were doing was important, that we weren't dancing about ourselves but about things that other people needed to have danced about, and it was important to reach our audiences. I think one of the tragic things about what happened later was this separation between the audience and the artist.[17]

Locations of Left Authenticity

The most explicit claims for the authenticity of radical sentiment were made in autobiographical ethnic fiction. Richard Wright's concerns about race, social injustice, and writing, for example, evoke relevant intersections between politics and emotion, which allow us to develop the cultural locations of authenticity in ethnic identity. In his *Black Boy (American Hunger),* a novel chronicling the writer's own development from childhood in the South to young adulthood in Chicago, Wright confronts racial oppression with radical politics. The hero's coming to terms with racism in America is both enabled by his joining the Chicago John Reed Club and forged in a critical response to that same experience. His "hunger for a new way to live" was a physical and emotional response to deprivation:[18] "I knew now what being a Negro meant. I could endure the hunger. I had learned to live with hate. But to feel that there were feelings denied me, that the very breath of life itself was beyond my reach, that more than anything else hurt, wounded me. I had a new hunger."[19] His new hunger, based on a drive for the expansion of "feeling," becomes a writing project: "I strove to master words . . . to make them mount into a rising spiral of emotional stimuli, each greater than the other, each feeding and reinforcing the other, and all ending in an emotional climax that would drench the reader with a sense of a new world."[20] Wright describes the mastery of words as modeled on a performative process—"a rising spiral of emotional stimuli"—culminating in "an emotional climax." Emotions channeled through art engendered not only the confidence to protest, but also, as in Negro spirituals, the vision of a "new" world.

In his novel *Invisible Man*, Ralph Ellison evoked a similar complexity of emotions in connection with the Negro spiritual and the modern dance:

As the organ voices died, I saw a thin brown girl arise noiselessly with the rigid control of a modern dancer, high in the upper rows of the choir, and begin to sing a cappella. She began softly, as though singing to herself of emotions of utmost privacy, a sound not addressed to the gathering, but which they overheard almost against her will. Gradually she increased in volume, until at times the voice seemed to become a disembodied voice that sought to enter her, to violate her, shaking her, rocking her rhythmically, as though it had become the source of her being, rather than the fluid web of her own creation.[21]

Although Ellison explicitly associates only the singer's posture with the tense physicality of the modern dancer in the 1930s, this entire passage speaks of movement's role as a contradictory but powerfully connective force. It seems to violate the singer's private self, but also to activate her personal energy and her resolve to project "the source of her being" toward a perhaps hostile world. In the process of singing, she appears overwhelmed by her own agency—its emotional force tending to objectify her body by issuing forth, and then turning back on itself from without. This is a potent image of the relation of emotion to expressive culture that, not accidentally, makes the young singer appear to Ellison like a modern dancer. Above all, the sounds she emits are not to be "of her own creation" but are nonetheless objectively present to her. This also indicates the power of emotion to bypass representation.

Wright's protagonist is ultimately unable to reconcile class warfare with the social and personal pressures attendant upon African American identity. "Politics," he concludes, "was not my game."[22] He leaves us, as Mark Naison has said, with "a landmark statement of anti-Stalinist liberation."[23] Yet Wright doesn't sever emotion from politics: "it was only in the realm of politics that I could see the depths of the human heart."[24]

The emotional impetus for personal identification with collectivity also arises in Michael Gold's novel *Jews without Money*.[25] Gold's tie to community staked its claims to authenticity in childhood experience. "Mother! Momma!" he exclaims melodramatically, "I am still bound to you by the cords of birth. I cannot forget you. I must remain faithful to the poor because I cannot be faithless to you! I believe in the poor because I have known you. The world must be made gracious for the poor! Momma, you taught me that!"[26] The protagonist's compassion for the poor and downtrodden originates in his maternal identification. Gold's novel, which relates his childhood spent on Manhattan's lower East Side, ends with the protagonist sinking deeper and deeper into perdition, one sign of which is a growing religiosity: "I developed a crazy religious streak. I prayed on the tenement roof in moonlight to the Jewish Messiah who would redeem the world."[27] The Messiah arrives on the novel's last page as the Revolution: "A man on an East Side soap-box, one night, proclaimed that out of the despair, melancholy and helpless rage of millions, a world movement had been born to abolish poverty. I listened to him. O workers' Revolution. . . . You are the true Messiah."[28] Behind the patriarchal Jewish Messiah and the Communist Party stands Gold's mother. From despair to radicalization, his sentimental education leads from maternal identification with Judaism to class consciousness. Wright, Gold, and Ellison chronicle how emotions rising to consciousness transmute into political commitment.[29]

The Gender of Radical Emotion

The connections just described between emotions and politics evoke associations with the feminine, yet the iconography of the worker in American visual culture privileges the male body.[30] But dance does not follow the lead of visual culture in this sense. Only three choreographers, to my knowledge, deployed the male body to represent labor. Edith Segal's *Unite and Fight* (1930) staged a white male and a black male discovering worker solidarity under conditions of labor oppression. Stacey Prickett relates that "the dance depicts three successive stages in the development of labor and technology: in the first we're shown primitive tasks; in the second, a tree was felled with a double saw; and in the third, workers collapsed from the speedup of an assembly line."[31] Ballet choreographer Lew Christenson created *Filling Station* in 1938 to a libretto by Lincoln Kirstein. It featured a gasoline attendant performed by a classical *danseur noble,* bringing ballet technique in line with American popular culture. The transparent shirt and overalls by Paul Cadmus underscored a homoerotic subtext to the Americanization of ballet, a theme which took precedence over the depiction of labor.[32] Ted Shawn created *Labor Symphony* for his all-male company in 1934.[33] Shawn depicts a shift from the heroic male body at work to a mechanized body heralding the end of skilled labor in the work process. Shawn combines issues of labor and technology with homosocial cooperation.

The first three sections of *Labor Symphony*—"Labor of the Field," "Labor in the Forest," and "Labor of the Sea,"—show eight bare-chested men in cooperative efforts. Their work is rendered by mimetic gestures such as sowing, hoeing, threshing, and hauling. The mirroring of these movements by paired couples and their repetitive quality render the obvious iconography progressively more abstract. Moments of deliberation and repose are also mimed. The final section, "Mechanized Labor," is essentially a machine dance in which the men perform the movement of interlocking mechanical parts. The notion of cooperation itself becomes mechanized in that the overall pattern of the dance demonstrates the movement of the dynamo without human agency or subjectivity. This is achieved in part by covering the performers' arms in dark sleeves to permit the interlocking patterns to emerge clearly. Despite the dehumanization of the final section, however, it is always the male body that is on view, exhibiting its ability to represent through dance these shifts in the ethos of labor. In a certain sense, *Labor Symphony* was a presentation of dance as a form of skilled (male) labor.

What "Mechanized Labor" eliminates is the quality of individual effort, repose, and mutual support, as well as the previous demonstrations of the male body arduously stretching, pushing and pulling, exerting itself to the limits of

Figure 7: Ted Shawn's company posed in Labor Symphony (1935). (Courtesy of the Dance Collection, New York Public Library for the Performing Arts at Lincoln Center, Astor, Lenox, and Tilden Foundations.)

its physical strength. Instead, each body forms a relay in a chain of movements that emerge purely at the level of pattern. There is a clear suggestion here of Kracauer's mass ornament made up in this case of male rather than female bodies. Yet the male body also seems displayed more narcissistically in this section than in the previous ones. Bodies move through space with less assertiveness and energetic pulsing, and thus they appear more objectified. The confinement of the group in a smaller central space on stage with two framing figures on either side allows the gaze to appraise bodily morphology with more attention than in the previous sections. Bodies frequently spin in place rather than lunge or jump. The machine dance ends with the dancers scattered across the floor like disparate and dysfunctional parts of a broken mechanism. This final moment underlines the loss of human and homosocial community.

Labor Symphony does not address the loss of work as unemployment, but alludes rather to what George Chauncey has called the exclusion of homosexuality from the public sphere in the 1930s.[34] In fact, the works of Shawn and Kirstein constitute an exception to this rule. The spectacle of male labor on the stage with its eroticizing potential was nonetheless not widespread. For one thing, male dancers were less plentiful than female dancers. The cultural stereotypes that classed emotional behavior as feminine and expressive—emotional —rather than masculine and rational—scientific—were likely the same that disqualified dancing as legitimate work for males. The gendering of art practices was inverted by the gendering of labor. The radicalization of labor feminized the male body just as did the act of dancing. Dancing and radicalization seem in this way to be on equal footing.

Paula Rabinowitz has explained why male literary figures of the workers' movement, such as Michael Gold and Joseph Freeman, cultivated a macho identity: "Literature and the body were coded as feminine while history and the body politic were masculinized. . . . More broadly, the institutions and apparatuses that the [Communist] Party had fostered to encourage the proletarian aesthetic held within them this same (gendered) contradiction—between word and deed—for all its active participants, regardless of their class or gender."[35] To compensate for this labile gendering of left culture, radical male intellectuals frequently characterized radical female artists—particularly if they were modern dancers—as emotional rather than rational. When Michael Gold wrote of Isadora Duncan that she "was a Red, but not a real revolutionist," he evoked the gendered split between expressive and rational culture: "it was all emotion with her," Gold concluded, "glorious and erratic."[36] Similarly composer Alex North wrote of his companion, dancer and choreographer Anna Sokolow, with less explicit criticism but a familiar tone, that her "ideas about what was going on—the problems in society—were emotional rather than intellectual."[37] Despite the male intellectual's tendency to consign emotion to the feminine sphere, emotion was fundamental to radical culture and foundational to the radical ethos. Wright, Ellison, and Gold all explained radicalism through the emotional experience of ethnically marked environments.

Modern dance, unlike women's fiction, did not function as a "secondary zone."[38] Dance differed from literature in this important respect that it contained no "(gendered) contradiction" between aesthetics and politics; this fact is crucial in grasping dance's cultural centrality to the left and to politics in general during the 1930s. The female body in motion was culturally coded as both history and the body politic. Consider that modern dancers were engaged in deeds, not words.[39] The energy, alacrity, and stamina they evinced as well as the live contact they sustained with a sympathetic audience narrowed the gap between performance and political action. Jane Dudley has said, "I think one of the problems with this period was finding the means of stating the ideas. The ideas were more important than the expression of them. The expression of them was really pretty naive. . . . I know that I was always a very compelling performer. I had a sense of that, of real belief on stage. And I'm sure that carried a lot."[40] Modern dancing displayed political energy, and sometimes this energy relied for its transmission more on the charismatic skills of the dancer than on the narrative or formal structures underlying the choreography.

I propose to add to Rabinowitz's assertion as follows: "the body" was one thing; "the body in motion" quite another. History and the body politic were not masculinized in modern dance in the same way Rabinowitz shows them to have been in literary culture. The radical body in motion was feminine and always political, and therefore always already racialized.[41] Radical emotions grounded in the experience of Eastern European Jewry and in African American culture could thus be more effectively represented by the female than the male body. The female body's emotional expression enacted a positive valorization of a position of weakness, whereas the male body represented a negative embodiment of what, in other circumstances, would be a position of strength. Modern dance gendered labor feminine. For Catherine A. Lutz, "Western discourse on emotions constitutes them as paradoxical entities that are both a sign of weakness and a powerful force."[42] This discourse must be seen to extend to emotional performances and its representations.

It follows that radical modern dance did not limit women to conventional and restricting gender roles. Unlike radical theater, men were not cast in modern dance as the breadwinners (except in Shawn's work), and women were not icons of maternity and domesticity.[43] Both sexes were presented, rather, as protagonists of social turmoil and social change, as well as satirists of the old or-

Figure 8: Female consumers marching for fair electric rates in Arthur Arent's Power *(1937), a Federal Theatre Project Living Newspaper in the Seattle production, directed by Florence Bean James. (Billy Rose Theater Collection, New York Public Library for the Performing Arts at Lincoln Center, Astor, Lenox, and Tilden Foundations.)*

Figure 9: Jane Dudley in "Dream World Dora" from her Middle Class Portraits *(1935). Photo: Leo Hurwitz. (Courtesy of Jane Dudley.)*

der. The female soloist in particular destabilized gendered understandings of production and reproduction. She performed in the fluctuating metaphorical zone between production as cultural reproduction and biological reproduction as cultural production. This was in keeping with performance's mandate to rehearse what had not yet historically taken place. The metaphor of new culture birth contains a pun on the term "labor" as giving birth to rather than producing. By the same token, the expectancy of emotionally vibrant proletarian bodies could be purposely interpreted as a "condition," like pregnancy, with which to pathologize the worker in a feminized and racialized identity.[44]

Reproduction as Social Pathology

Pare Lorentz's film *The Fight for Life* (1941) examined the problem of infant and maternal mortality in Chicago during the Great Depression. The United States Film Service, established by Roosevelt under the jurisdiction of the National Emergency Council in 1938, produced this documentary. The mission of the Film Service was principally educational, although the documentaries it produced were screened in movie theaters alongside commercial features to large audiences.[45]

Tenement mothers in *Fight for Life* become the allegory for a proliferating radical subculture that modern science and the New Deal government ostensibly undertake to save from extinction as they conscientiously survey and document its development.[46] Although the film narrates scientific advances in hygienic childbirth, it also stages Anglo-Saxon male doctors as agents of surveillance opposite expectant immigrant mothers. The ethnicized mothers are allegories of a proliferating proletariat ready either to erupt or else to collapse. They frequently do both, first by giving birth and then by dying. Most striking in this allegorical layer of *Fight for Life* is how the "real thing" becomes the dying thing as it desperately attempts to give birth. Both the power and the weakness of radicalization emerge in this conjoining of radical body and emotion as childbirth under the cold, watchful gaze of science. It is the power and weakness of the feminized, ethnicized, and racialized proletariat.

The opening delivery room sequence is meticulously choreographed. Lorentz wrote extensive "Music Instructions" for the entire film, but he specified that the first sequence would be "rigidly edited to metronome time" because it was "the one sequence that needs synchronization, and not interpretation of any kind, save through an exact beat."[47] The opening sequence transpires wordlessly, and its choreographic qualities are thus enhanced. The sound of two hearts beating is superimposed on the soundtrack: the mother's heart beats slower than that of the unborn child's. Doctors circulate busily in the operating room like futuristic

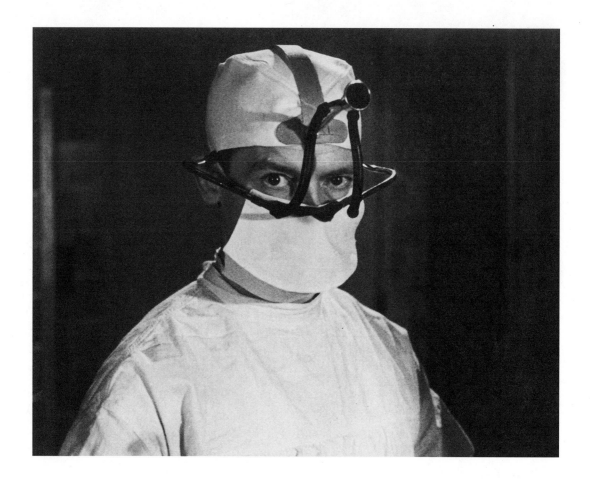

Figure 10: The obstetrician's alienated stare in the delivery room sequence of Pare Lorentz's The Fight for Life. (Reproduced from the Collections of the Library of Congress).

insects peering out from behind masks with strangely protruding headgear. They scrutinize their female patients coldly. The patients return their gaze with alienated passivity.

The expectant woman is shown as a powerless being, pacified, inert, and moribund, but also brimming with confused emotions. Yet her glance also prefigures a science-fiction aesthetic: the expectant woman as alien being. The birthing of her offspring occurs as a silent drama in response to which she silently expires—dispossessed of her own labor. The doctors—"men against death," says the film—enter the field of obstetrics to discover in the Chicago tenements a morose world of poverty and squalor—"tainted blood and cracked hearts." Like director Harold Clurman pacing the nocturnal streets of New York with playwright Clifford Odets, these doctors discover the Great Depression as an underworld.[48] Like the social scientists who studied workers' emotional dysfunction for big industry, the doctors provide a social analysis of a medical condition ("they're hungry") and a medical analysis of a social condition ("the verdict of life and death was

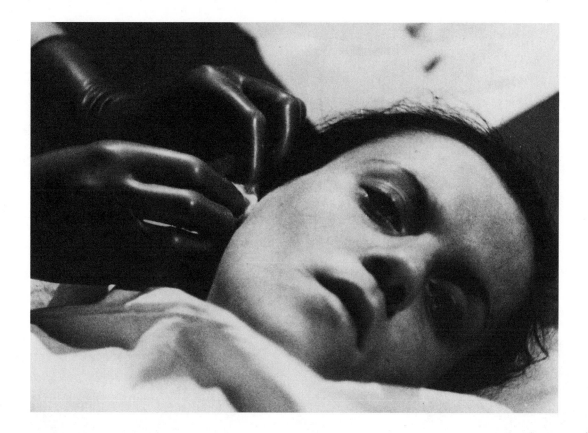

written in the chemistry of her blood"). This analysis is set forth through the internal monologue of one young doctor who, having lost his patient, walks pensively through the Chicago night. In *Fight for Life,* the maternal body is repre-

Figure 11: An expectant ethnicized mother in Pare Lorentz's The Fight for Life. *(Reproduced from the Collections of the Library of Congress.)*

sented, like the radical body, as an emotional body of unpredictable moves— by turns helpless and threatening. These expectant bodies lead the doctors to ponder a pandemic of birth and death, which is also the allegory of a social pandemic. Even in a film whose social awareness is linked to a specific health issue, science and government manipulated the phenomenon of working-class emotion in representations that feminized and racialized the proletariat.

Affect and Emotion

I distinguish between two or more modes of emotional expression in dance in order to recast the form-versus-content cliché frequently imposed on political art of the thirties. An ideological divide within modern dance (and within aesthetic modernism itself) supported at least two kinds of feeling projection: affect and emotion. What I shall call *affect* is traditionally accounted for as

Figure 12: Individual emotional life existing within class consciousness: Tamiris and company in "The Individual and the Mass," from Cycle of Unrest *(1935). (Photograph by Bouchard © by Diane Bouchard. Dance Collection, the New York Public Library for the Performing Arts, Astor, Lenox, and Tilden Foundations.)*

physiological, if not anatomical, processes, linking it to volition as well as to visually expressive meaning. Affects are attributes of the self-possessing individual. Emotion, by contrast, is transpersonal and trans-subjective: it moves between persons—e/motion.[49] In modern dance of the thirties, affective movement transmits the essence of a feeling whereas emotional movement transmits specific, temporally contingent feelings.

The artistic goal of expression is frequently linked to universality and sanctions the performer's *impersonality*—her ability and intent to embody a feeling's essence. Martha Graham danced mourning in her solo *Lamentation* (1930) without the inference of particularized suffering. Even the gender of Graham's enshrouded figure, seated on a bench, remained unspecified, while her costume's elastic stretch broadened her gestures toward the visually abstract. Graham's impersonality in this solo did not connote lack of charisma, but rather a displacement of personal—especially facial—particularity. This displacement entails a degree of abstraction, which Graham designated as *individuality.* "While the individual becomes greater," she noted of her dances, "the personal becomes less personal."[50] Emotion, by contrast, sanctions personality, which was more likely to appear colloquial, popular, or ethnically marked.[51] The rejection of individualism does not entail the erasure of subjectivity. Helen Tamiris's "The Individual and the Mass" from her *Cycle of Unrest* treated this theme directly. "Tamiris," wrote the *Daily Worker,* "satirically depicted a character who superciliously disdains to become part of a proletarian group. This dance was an integrated composition expressing the sterility of individualism."[52]

In Talley Beatty's *Mourner's Bench* (1947), a black man and a bench occupy the stage. Although this solo stands chronologically outside the period under discussion, it is worth mentioning for its apparent commentary on *Lamentation.* Beatty pounds the bench with his fist, a gesture of emotional specificity that Graham would never have included in her piece. Beatty's solo is about a bench where slaves were allowed to mourn, a place chosen by their owners for mourning their dead. This reference to social history in Beatty's choreography transforms the bench and the dancer's relationship to it into a historically specific instance of human suffering.[53] *Mourner's Bench* was about a situated reality of mourning. This reference to social history in Beatty's choreography transforms the bench and the dancer's relationship to it into a historically located instance of suffering. *Mourner's Bench,* as its title indicates by focusing on the object, is about a situated reality of mourning. *Lamentation,* its title naming the action and its choreography rendering the essence of lament, is about mourning as an eternal condition. The presence of emotion in dance implies that "form is time-bound. It originates, dies and changes within time."[54]

"Essence. That's the word. Essence means a lot to me," writes dance photographer Barbara Morgan of her remarkable documentation of Graham's work in the thirties: "Both Martha and I knew that when we got ready to do something—I to shoot and she to dance—we had to become the thing we meant to project. When I had my camera ready, and she had made herself the thing, before we got to work we'd sit about fifteen feet apart and meditate—and then we'd become that thing. Then we'd try to make it emanate."[55] To "become that thing," as Morgan expresses it, is to vacate the place of a historical and historically bounded self. When German dance critic Rudolf von Delius lauded Mary Wigman in 1914 for achieving a dance form that transcended personality and its depiction, he asserted of this new art that "everything historical falls away as totally uninteresting."[56] This is another indication that the forces transcending personality were also meant to transcend history. For Graham and Morgan, this was apparently the work of (modern) dance. As early as 1929, Graham's *Heretic* explored tensions between an individual and the group. Fredric Jameson has interpreted the defense of the individual in these terms as the "blind zone(s) in which the individual subject seeks refuge, in pursuit of a purely individual, a merely psychological, project of salvation."[57] In broad strokes, this project marks a divide between Marxism and modernism in the thirties. Yet to reject the psychological project was not to empty the social of personal agency. This is what justifies the split between affect and emotion proposed here as a hermeneutic tool. If impersonality and individualism connote a form of psychological inwardness with an ambiguous relationship to social consciousness in the thirties, then social consciousness assumes the forms of personality and its individuation without individualism. The rest is oversimplification, or, in the most derogatory sense, ideology.

The divide between affect and emotion in choreography was frequently perceptible in narrative terms, but it was also evident in the dancer's self-presentation. Left-wing dance critic Edna Ocko registered the following complaint about many of Graham's dances in the thirties: "By isolating her theme from contemporary references, *and then stripping it of human, emotional qualities,* Miss Graham makes unsuccessful her efforts to communicate with the very people for whom she is creating."[58] For Ocko, Graham's commitment to a modernist expression of individuality was evident not only in her choice of themes, but more importantly in her performance of emotional remoteness. More than anything else, it was Graham's ambiguous relationship to current events that elicited this sort of critique.

The point is not whether Ocko's opinion about what made a "good" dance was any more correct than Morgan's, but that Graham's work was evaluated and debated during the 1930s from ideologically fraught positions. More importantly, the ideologies in question not only were manifested at the obvious thematic or narrative level, but shone through the performative nuances of the dancing itself. Although working-class audiences did not have aesthetic expertise, emotional and bodily nuances were the material of their daily experience. This overlap of everyday experience and aesthetic perception explains why modern dance was popular during the thirties with working-class audiences. It also explains why ideological implications easily accrued to danced movement, such that the critical treatment often turned, consciously or unconsciously, on the ideology of feelings. Emotion, as distinguished from impersonality, was neither self-expression nor amateurism, but the idiom of left sensibility. Graham was preoccupied with abstraction and essence, and these were not, on the whole, politically radical qualities.

Janet Mansfield Soares has presented evidence of the significant role Graham's accompanist, manager, and lover, Louis Horst, played in cultivating the choreographer's modernism. Soares quotes Horst: "Your materials must be sublimated to form and stylization or symbolization into a work of art. Until that takes place, it is only self-expression."[59] The argument is still made that the political school was amateur and the modernist school professional. But Horst made it sound as though expression and self-expression were the sole alternatives. When the full cultural context is restored, however, Horst's omission of emotion is revealed as partisan. Moreover, along with expression, Horst favored a psychological tone or neurotic tension. Sophie Maslow's choreography, for example, was not sufficiently neurotic in tone for Horst's taste, and he told her so.[60]

By mid-decade, the discrepancy between workers' activist dance and the increasingly schooled performance of modern dancers trained by second-generation choreographers Graham, Humphrey, and Holm was evident. Each school taught and continued to develop the movement vocabulary of its founding leader, and thus vocational competency in dance began to look less and less like a working-class pastime or a militant activity. The aesthetics of modernism that inspired Graham and others led to the development of technical performance standards which, in Graff's view, were incompatible with the social motivation of radical choreographers:

The Workers Dance League mandated political content, but that content was not easily framed within the emerging modernist aesthetic. How to dance the oppression of the working class, the exploitation by a capitalist society, the threat of fascism, and the horrors of racism, yet not depend upon mimetic action? On one hand was the Marxist concept of art as a literal reflection of reality, on the other, the modernist project that demanded the viewer's participation in the creation of meaning.[61]

Graff here evokes the form-versus-content divide that would place modernism in a self-sufficient, aesthetic realm. The advent of new and impressive technical standards in modernist dance contrasted unfavorably with the lack of consensus over politically radical movement vocabulary. Prickett notes that a hallmark of radical dance was eclecticism.[62] Connections between radical modern dance and folk dance forms were being discussed, and the need for a truly popular dance idiom debated. Graff posits a disparity between modern dance and worker's dance more substantial than that of technique alone. It pertained to the aesthetic goals of choreography: "The principles of modernism—abstraction and distortion—complicated the social message."[63] Is this not to say that it was difficult for good dance to have political significance, and difficult for political dance to be good?[64]

all that is good is diff.

In a similar line of reasoning, Prickett points up the paradox of Nadia Chil-kovsky's solo *Homeless Girl* (1934). This solo, which emphasized the sensitivity of the oppressed, was a celebrated left-wing dance precisely because of its moving qualities. Henry Gilfond wrote in the *Dance Observer,* "Propaganda or no, it moved and projected itself across the footlights; it carried a significance that could not be bound by its limiting title."[65] Yet Prickett sees this as a contradiction inherent to dance solos as radical expression. For Prickett, *Homeless Girl* "exemplifies the paradox of the solo form used to communicate an ideology which is predicated on the individual as a social being."[66] Here we have the absolute dichotomy of the personal and the social as a critical precept. It is only by making distinctions between kinds of projected feeling that we can see how radicalism rejected individuality, but sustained subjectivity and individuation.

The relation of modern dance to politics (and of realism to modernism) is more accurately reflected, to my mind, in a letter that radical soloist Si-Lan Chen received in 1937 from her brother, graphic artist Jack Chen:

The modern dance must necessarily be at first mainly of a realistic pantomimic nature, while some of the best dancers will be able to devise movements and combinations of movements that will be able to suggest the modern ideas and feelings without resorting to absolute naturalism (pantomime) and that will be even more effective perhaps than pantomime because of their unexpectedness, and because suggestiveness is able, particularly with an intelligent, intellectual, and accustomed audience, to move them more deeply than pantomimic movement, because the suggestive symbolic movement can have so many connotations, can rouse up so many varied associations. The trick is I think obviously to find that happy medium between the two—realistic or pantomime gesture and the "sublimated," suggestive gesture or movement that gives the greatest freedom in compositional possibilities, that can arouse the most intense and deepest thought and emotional associations in the audience.[67]

Chen's theory suggests that a crossover potential existed between left humanism and modernist radicalism. He implies that radical dance would grow more sophisticated as dancers and audience underwent parallel development. Jane Dudley's thoughts about her own compositional methods during the thirties also mirror a departure from the pantomimic: "What we learned to have was a transference of the feelings those ideas created in us, and translated them into movement without an ideational, concrete story line as much as a feeling line. And only when you use words could you make it more concrete."[68] Dudley points out how modes of projected feeling intercede between "form" and "content" in complex ways. Graff does concede that when Jane Dudley and Anna

Sokolow, both of whom were members of Graham's company, performed their own dances, "for a brief period some radical dancers could satisfy the demands of both dance and politics."[69] But it was not technical sophistication per se that allowed Dudley, Sokolow, and Si-Lan Chen, among others, to bridge the conflicting demands of art and politics.[70] The ethics of affective versus emotional embodiment were equally crucial, if not more so. Radical emotion in Sokolow's *Strange American Funeral* (1935) and Dudley's *Time Is Money* (1934) powerfully conveyed the worker's experience as victim.

Graff's assertion that "what established their [left-wing artists'] art as revolutionary was content" is potentially misleading in my view despite the fact that it reflects a belief generally held at the time. The perception of movement as emotional or affective was indispensable to the audience's recognition of its revolutionary or bourgeois qualities. These were recognizable modes of social being. The old cliché of form versus content—humanist art versus leftist art—just won't do. For example, it doesn't account for the fact that Graham's *Primitive Mysteries,* a dance assumed to be in the disinterested, qualitative sphere rather than in the aesthetically indifferent sphere of propaganda, had a politics. Abstraction and distortion not only complicate the social message, they also convey a social message of their own. Distortion, moreover, fits just as well into the aesthetics of worker victimization as into the Horstian quality of neurotic twistedness. Dance does not become political only when the choreographer adopts politically legible content; the cultural politics of dance are always embedded in form. This is especially so when those cultural politics relate to the everyday actions and postures of people's lives. Political content can and did have identifiably formal properties, and dance is an art that renders visible such levels of otherwise invisible formality. Although both affect and emotion were quite possibly dependent on technical facility for their ultimate theatrical effectiveness, both also had political content by virtue of their formal properties.

A left-wing faction of American modern dance, made up in part of Graham's students and company members, proposed emotion in their work as a performative alternative to impersonality or psychological latency. Their dances were characterized by socially specific emotions rather than by essentialized affect. Yet Dudley and Sokolow did not make a clean break with Graham and Horst. From 1935 on, Dudley was artistically committed to Graham while still being a left-wing artist in her own right.[71] She has never viewed the situation from a crassly political standpoint.

You know, I hate to say it, but from my feeling at that time, the "decadent bourgeois" Martha Graham—in *Chronicle* (1936), for example—had some very good movement material. You see, the problem was these people [some radical choreographers] weren't dancers, and they didn't have enough movement in their bodies, they didn't have enough vocabulary, enough training, they didn't know how to come up with it. . . . I think one of the problems with this period was finding the means of stating the ideas. The ideas were more important than the expression of them. . . . Anna Sokolow and her group were the most ready for the challenge that was offered to us.[72]

Sokolow became independent of Graham by the later thirties, although she remained close to Horst, with whom she had studied choreography. These artists' personal relationships to Graham and Horst complexify the relation of dance to politics in the thirties.

Nevertheless, the contemporary situation is relatively clear in the critical writing. Graham was heckled by left-wing critics who wanted her to move from what they perceived to be coldness and abstraction toward more palpable, and therefore emotionally political, commitment.[73] They called for emotional aliveness from Graham's work, and asserted that this quality could only be aroused by authentic political commitment. I do not believe that this debate was sheerly opportunistic, as Agnes de Mille reported in her biography of Graham.[74] We know that not every cultural worker was a party member during this period, nor were all dance concerts the CP-USA sponsored limited to disseminating party line.[75]

That choreography by Dudley and Sokolow was not accused of aloofness speaks to its political situation. Despite Dudley's advocacy of Graham's art and of the professionalism fostered by Graham's training, a relation between emotional performance and politically radical convictions is evident in her work. I focus on affect and emotion in choreographic analysis to bring theoretical definition to the performative alternatives of the period, but with the caveat they be understood, not as eternal aesthetic categories, but rather as historically grounded and culturally contextualized ones. Specific choreography can illustrate the differences between essential affect and e/motion in concrete historical terms.

In chapters 3 and 4 I shall argue that the acknowledgment of e/motion as a structure of feeling distinct from essential affect can have ethical consequences for the interpretation of specific works. My discussion of the work of Asadata Dafora and Si-lan Chen serves to underline the fact that a plurality of embodied expressions with differing cultural motives held the decade's stage.

Chapter 3 **Metakinetic Interpellations**

> Ideology must figure as an organizing social force which
> actively constitutes human subjects at the roots of their lived
> experience.[1]
>
> Terry Eagleton

How do individuals apprehend their identification with a nation, class, or ethnic group as "lived experience" in the sense intended by Eagleton? How do organization and expression—to use the most general terms employed thus far—produce ideological effects? Given that the ideological effects are lived, what is the relationship of ideology to authenticity? Since bodies are at the root of lived experience, it can be shown that dance works with the same materials from which the organizing social force of ideology must be drawn.

Subjects are constituted by self-recognition in the process of aesthetic perception. I propose to analyze Eagleton's "organizing social force" exerted by dance as the transference of "feeling" in the double sense of sentiment and sensation. John Martin theorized the empathetic process of this transferal as metakinesis, and Louis Althusser theorized the ideological process of self-recognition as interpellation. The theories of the American dance critic and the French Marxist philosopher are complementary. Just as metakinesis implies transfer of identity, so interpellation implies visceral address.

Interpellation

Interpellation designates the process whereby people become enlisted as subjects of ideology through the experience of self-recognition.[2] Interpellation, specifies Althusser, "can be imagined along the lines of the most commonplace everyday police (or other) hailing: "Hey, you there!" The hailed individual, turning around in response to this call, "becomes a *subject*. Why? Because he has recognized that the hail was 'really' addressed to him, and that it was *really him* who was hailed (and not someone else)."[3]

In relation to this encounter, consider the following description of Hemsley Winfield's choreography for his solo *Negro* (1931): "A Negro comes out very nonchalant. Music that accompanies his walk is a very slow blues. The music is low and played as a slow opera. Music changes and becomes barbaric and more negroid. The figure fights against this music, but finally succumbs. The figure moves, becomes heathenish and uncouth, and he becomes negro."[4] In Winfield's *Negro,* the music interpellates the dancer, who refuses at first to recognize it. When he succumbs to its insistent address, however, the response is to adapt himself to a stereotype, and in this way to become a subject of ideology. *Negro* staged interpellation as spectacle; that is, it showed that authentic identity for one individual could appear as ideology to another. Because *Negro* functioned in this way as a metacommentary on interpellation—characterizing ideological effects rather than exercising them—Winfield seems to have understood only too well the decade in which he would have been a major player had he not died of pneumonia in 1934.

I propose that performance could also "call" audiences to subject positions; this is to say that interpellative address in the thirties took the expressive form of dance. Physical expression thus gains a political dimension, and interpellation contains useful aspects of a theoretical model, providing that subjectivation can be distinguished from the power of punishment in Althusser's theory.[5] More recently, Jacques Rancière has proposed the dividing up of "feeling" (*le partage du sensible*)—understood as the domain of sensual and affective address—as another way to theorize ideological effects of an aesthetic nature.[6] Setting aside the issue of interpellation, the division of works of art—aesthetically and generically—into visual and performative experience itself has an impact on identity formation. Such artistic divisions of the sensual world serve to displace the overtly authoritarian agency of the police in Althusser's dramatization.

The division under examination here between 1931 and 1935 is between the publicly projected feelings of affect, emotion, and possession in Martha Graham's *Primitive Mysteries* (1931) and *Frontier* (1935), Jane Dudley's *Time Is Money* (1934), and Asadata Dafora Horton's *Kykunkor, or Witch Woman* (1934).

Dafora, Dudley, and Graham each created dance that induced an audience to identify themselves with Pan-Africanism, emotional Marxism, and nativist modernism.[7] Their dances rendered these "isms," however, not in blatantly ideological terms, but as ways of moving in divided experience.

Metakinesis

One confirmation of the idea that the domain of lived experience available for division in the 1930s was composed of the "totality" of moving and being moved—"feeling" (sensation/sentiment) rendered by movement as substance —is to be found in the writings of contemporary dance critic John Martin. He theorized modern dance as "the externalization of emotional states in terms of physical action," and he delineated the efficacy of projected emotional states in relation to the socius.[8]

In a series of essays appearing in the *American Dancer* between 1936 and 1937, Martin stated his preference for the term "expressional" to "modern" and emphasized thereby that modern dance adapted its physical expression "to the emotional needs of our own time." This emphasis on emotional need made "modern" dance—for Martin was a fierce partisan of modernism— "once again a useful, contributory element of living."[9] With these two fundamental elements, emotional need and emotional communication, Martin's rhetoric seems aligned with the politically radical tendencies of the thirties. Yet Martin's articulation of modernism allows him to introduce considerable ambiguity into his terms, as does Graham's.

In *The Modern Dance* in 1933 he named the transferential process "metakinesis," by which he understood the physical transfer of feelings across bodies. Consequently, the reception of modern movement required internal mimesis, or an "inwardly gesticulating audience."[10] The spectator's brain should "translate the sensory impressions received from the dancer's performance into motor terms and the corresponding emotional states which automatically associate themselves therewith."[11] Interpretation would require self-observation and analysis. But the actual workings of this process of reception and interpretation, which was tied to the irrational imperative, condemned metakinesis to a particular history of distortions. It left space for a particularly irrational idea according to which successful metakinesis universalized the personal and essentialized the irrational.

What is labeled irrational is emotional movement itself, and this aspect of Martin's theory introduces irrational associations between personal and national identity. The rationale for this practice was "the conveying of some concept of what the artist believes to be *universal* truth, but which transcends his powers of statement in the conventional terms of words."[12] Critic Paul Love also articulated this contradictory idea: "Since he [the dancer] seeks to externalize the essence of his individual humanity, he must, in the process, achieve a universality; that is, his dances, as the expression of individual personality, will be but the 'intimate concrete appeal' of universal personality."[13] Although Love was arguing in this instance for the artist as spokesperson of personal rather than national consciousness, the equality of universal truth and inner compulsion suggests somewhat eerily that metakinesis and nationalism were parallel routes to self-recognition. Their convergence is irrational.[14]

This parallelism explains why Martin's conditions for empathetic transfer are so elusive. For a dance to meet his aesthetic criteria it cannot be too personal; that would amount to indulgent self-expression and result in a frustrating illegibility. Yet it should also not be obvious, for this would compromise the inherent complexity of feelings and prove shallow. My most personal truth, the dancer should proclaim, has personally unique qualities translated in terms of my particular movement qualities. Although each dance is as different as each body, the individual's dance—the individualistic dance—is a key to the shared subjectivity of nationality. One touches here upon the equality between extreme individualism and nationalism. Shared nationality becomes the basis of metakinesis, the empathetic transfer of physical qualities. Without (shared) nationality, there can be no empathy.

What makes this theory modernist for Graham is the fact that nationality remains at the level of a construct, an incomplete project. "She [Graham] often makes reference to the 'new race,'" wrote Blanche Evan, "which she says, must be direct, concise, unsentimental."[15] In typically modernist terms, Graham weds the new with the archaic, both of which stand outside of history. Like Martin, she endows the term "primitive" with a particular meaning: "We are weaving a new fabric, and while it is true that we are weaving it from the threads of many old cultures, the whole cloth will be entirely indigenous. The dancers of America may be Jewish and Spanish and Russian and Oriental, as well as Indian and Negro. Their dancing will contain a heritage from all other nations, but it will be transfigured by the rhythm, and dominated by the psyche of this new land."[16] An alert radio interviewer pressed Graham on the terms with which she related modern dance to national identity:

INTERVIEWER: The allusion to you as an "American" dancer is not necessarily to make it clear that you are American-born, Miss Graham. As I understand it, the expression dictates that you have evolved a characteristically American idiom in the dance. Now, when La Argentina, for instance, danced, only one glimpse of her costumes sufficed to inform us that she was a protagonist of the Spanish dance. What is there about the physical appearance of the stage, and more particularly, your costumes, which indicate that your dances are American?

ANSWER: It is hard to define the American characteristic. It is less easily recognized than the Spanish. My dances are not easily recognized as American from my costumes because we have no traditional costume. It must be recognized as American either through its subject matter or through a tempo, rhythm, and attitude toward space which is peculiar to America and, while not so quickly recognized, is unlike any other country on earth.[17]

In this interview, Graham retreats to the position that national identity is "not so quickly recognized" and describes access to it as "a certain quality of movement." Identity is not located so much in a style as in a quality. Similarly for Martin, metakinesis tracked movement not just from the dancer's body to the spectator's body, but from personal to national identity. But the substantive transfer escaped unequivocal interpretation. It is the identity of the art's subject matter with its medium as essential substance as postulated by modernism that consolidates this point of view.

Graham's Nativist Modernism

Dressed uniformly in long dark jersey "woolens," twelve women march slowly on stage as a disciplined group, shepherding Graham, who stands out in a white dress with large panels creating planes of volume about her face like halos. This slow processional entrance establishes the stage as a ritual place rather than a showplace, which was one of the most innovative aspects of Graham's *Primitive Mysteries*. It showed an intentional disregard for differences between theatrical and real time, which enhanced the impression of a communal performance. The footfalls of the group entering and exiting between each section of the dance also established an unhurried and deliberate rhythm, placing the spectator in an expectant, but likewise meditative, state of mind. Unlike the earlier *Heretic*, the group no longer represented an oppressive force for the individual, but rather framed Graham, a kind of animating icon in their midst, with devotion.

In the first section, "Hymn to the Virgin," Graham as soloist circulates between groups who frame her reverently in *tableaux vivants*. They perform a number of seeming rituals structured on repeated patterning such as passing between lines of women, touching their hands as they kneel beside her, and leading them around the stage. The women always act as a group; Graham always acts as an individual. "Crucifixus" is more mysterious and foreboding, ending with the famous "bison jumps" in a circle around the immobile Gra-

Figure 13: Martha Graham and Bonnie Bird in
Primitive Mysteries *(1931). Photo: Paul Hansen.*
(Courtesy of the Dance Collection, New York Public
Library for the Performing Arts at Lincoln Center,
Astor, Lenox, and Tilden Foundations.)

ham. In "Hosanna," Graham herself is relatively immobile, and in the process of becoming an object of worship.

Primitive Mysteries launched the modern dance movement in earnest by providing its first recognized masterpiece. Under the subheading "A Spontaneous Outburst," Martin related the cathartic opening-night audience response: "The majority of the house burst into cheers. It was not just a scattering of 'bravos,' . . . but was the expression of a mass of people whose emotional tension found spontaneous release."[18] Without using the term in this review, Martin relates a successful case of metakinesis as the collective recognition of Graham's "emotional blossoming." It is metakinetic in that it takes the form of the release of emotional tension. Martin omits any analysis of his own participation in this process. The review is frustratingly elusive. It focuses on formal qualities Martin had dismissed in earlier columns as irrelevant to the expressional dance. He rates the composition of *Primitive Mysteries* "among the choreographic masterpieces of the modern dance movement" but interprets it simply as an "evocation of the childlike religious elevation of a primitive people." He thus implies that the dance evokes primitive culture as childlike rather than explaining how such "religious elevation" was adapted "to the emotional needs of our own time." *Primitive Mysteries* seems to prefigure Martin's theory, and therefore to enter into metakinetic transfer with it, evoking thereby his irrational approval.[19]

At this *locus classicus* of historical modern dance in 1931, Martin obscured the "useful, contributory element" determining his preference for the term *expressional,* and thus placing his emphasis on the role emotion should play in modern dance. In the remainder of his review, he links Graham's style to that of modern painting and sculpture, despite the fact that he had rejected modernism on this basis in earlier columns as superficial.[20] Most important, Martin's account of a seminal case of metakinesis in modern dance history fails to explain what prompted "the expression of a mass of people whose emotional tension found spontaneous release."

I do not claim to be able to answer this question myself, but I would like to further explore how Graham theorized the relation of expression to social community. She asserted in 1932 that "primitive sources . . . though they may be basically foreign to us, are, nevertheless akin to the forces which are at work in our life."[21] The primitive, present as a source of movement, is understood as a socially shaping power. Graham identified such sources as "rhythms," form-bestowing cultural influences. African American choreographer Katherine Dunham expressed a similar idea in reversed form: "The rhythms of the human body . . . are in constant competition with the cacophony and disharmony which are the fruits of our industrial age."[22] Although Graham was not engaged in such a contrast in *Primitive Mysteries,* she did choose to make reference to traditional society. Rhythm is the term for Graham that translates the archaic past into the contemporary present, and is thus the element of her vocabulary that deserves the most concerted attention.

Doubtless influenced in the early thirties by Mary Austin's *The American Rhythm* (1923), Graham claimed that rhythms embodied "the sum total of one's experience." She emphasized in this way that movement qualities are determinant for identity, and thus also for community—*Primitive Mysteries* shows us a community able to walk to a single rhythm without any rhythmical cues. Yet during the Great Depression, the group or mass had radical political connotations that Graham did not address until the later thirties. Later works such as *Panorama* transform the tribe into the urban group. *Primitive Mysteries* with Graham's lone and impassive figure proposes social embeddedness without social engagement. Surrounded by her dance company, she is both leader and icon. The material opens onto a self-referentiality that renders its meaning ambiguous.

Graham evolved toward a more actively social stance in the course of the decade. Yet even when she produced her solos on the Spanish Civil War in the later thirties, modernist critics reasserted the principles of universality, attempting to dispel the specter of her social engagement. Of her *Immediate Tragedy* (1937), for example, Martin warned: "Lest there be something of the suggestion of 'propaganda' or of mere timeliness about a theme deriving from the Spanish Civil War, let it be said at once that this will be a moving dance long after the tragic situation in Spain has been brought to a conclusion. For it has completely universalized its materials."[23] Even as Graham perceived a connection between her movement vocabulary and disturbing events in the world, Martin's warning reveals how deep was the ideological split between modernism and social engagement in the dance world.

Austin, whom Graham and Horst visited in New Mexico in the early thirties, was influential in Graham's way of conceptualizing her work. In her study of Amerindian poetry, Austin said rhythm transmitted the common impulses of subjectivity as "an affection of consciousness." She maintained that rhythm arose "fortuitously in the environment" and was realized as "activity of an organism"; once embodied, it could exist "as distinct from our intellectual perception of it."[24] In *Primitive Mysteries,* Graham seems to have imagined a community whose mutual connection was "deeply" rhythmic in the way Austin intended. Certainly the dance was not rhythmic in any obvious sense and was in no way a reconstruction of Amerindian dance.[25] One could, however, infer that the mysterious rhythmic connection between Graham and the dancers was based on something sensed in common, on the basis of which they walked together, and assumed symmetrical formations of a perfect geometry.

The emotional tie to rhythm, making it an effective common ground for community in Austin's work was called affect. Affective rhythm is less a metrical than a qualitative mode in which gestural norms stamp physical presence with identity. It denotes, in Graham's terms, "a certain quality of movement." In the complex of issues revolving about modern American identity, the place of affect in Graham's work is more significant than any particular instance of rhythmicity. More important, because rhythm is a theoretical reference in Graham's choreography for the figuration of American culture as "new" while also relying on the figure of the earth, ground, or territory, affect shifts uneasily between universalist and nationalist senses. The term universal is bounded by a particular sense of the term national.

This is an even more patent development in Austin, who further defined affect by differentiating it from emotion. She distinguishes between the two as authentic depth of feeling is distinguished from contingent experience. In this way she effectively endows affect with a class politics: "The difference between the mob-mindedness created by the modern agitator and the tribal-mindedness of the Corn Dance is the difference between rhythms that are merely poetic and those that are rhythms of poetry. It is the difference between rhythms that produce an emotional *effect* and those that are spiritually *affective*" (24). Distinguishing between affect and emotion in this way, Austin also introduces class into her discussion of ethnic identity. "Mob-mindedness" refers to working-class identities. The rhythms of national identity are viscerally opposed to those of the masses, whose emotional rhythms, she seems to say, may have an effect but lack truth. Affect, by contrast, stems from the "autonomic centers of experience" (7); that is, while emotion may also be physical, it lacks the depth of truth. The modernist dance critic would say it lacks universality. Austin represents national identity in this way as distinct from social disturbances—strikes, for example, which were an important feature of the thirties—that are devoid of the "organic rhythms . . . recapitulated from generation to generation" (8). Social disturbances, in fact, can only be considered the consequence of emotional upheaval, and emotions are linked as with Taylor to social instability. Social protest, in other words, is not only shallow but also antinationalist; it is disconnected from the land as the source of affect.

Through such assertions, national identity is not severed from modernism's experimental form, but instead becomes fully entrenched within it. This is how American identity could be characterized during this period by modernists as "a form" still in development and hence "lacking in tradition as the American experiment itself" (10). When Graham wrote "the psychology of the land is to be found in its movement," she was envisioning national subjectivity on an organically affective basis, that is, as an identity that traveled from "the land" through the subconscious to the autonomic nervous system.[26] So Martin could both propose and defend its irrationality. Yet the modernist could still consider the discovery of American forms to be a subjective and original process. The derivation of a common "quality of movement"from the autonomic nervous system is oddly suggestive of Gramsci's proposal, discussed in chapter 1, that the worker's movements should not just be learned, but should "nestle" in the muscular and nervous systems. Graham too, stressed discipline and the rigorous development of technical standards for modern dance. As one of her students, Blanche Evan, wrote in a series of articles on Graham's pedagogy in *New Theatre:* "[Graham] has created a dance scene wherein only slaves to professional discipline can hope to survive. She has shown us what the dance demands in actual physical labor."[27]

We are returned here to the ideological sameness within difference of Graham and Rand in the Covarrubias cartoon. Could the sameness masked by the stark contrast between modernist high seriousness and commercial entertainment suggest aesthetically unlikely analogies between concentration and distraction? Be that as it may, Austin most likely enabled Graham to understand how to be both nationalist (or nativist) and modernist at once. The spontaneous outburst at the first performance of *Primitive Mysteries* was doubtless a metakinetic response to Graham's artistic realization of this dual identity.

One more word about Austin: she attributes the merely "effective" or "emotional" rhythms to the modern agitator, "the tribe of modern industrial workers," and the African. In *The American Rhythm,* she warns against emotion as "letting in the Congo, and Mumbo-Jumbo" (33); she credits African influence with "spiritual disintegration" through "bond-loosening, soul-disintegrating, jazz-born movements" (32). Graham followed suit, calling "the Negro dance" a "rhythm of disintegration" but "the Indian dance" "a rhythm of integration."[28] Although it was not distinguished by its rhythms, *Primitive Mysteries* referred to integrative impulses of physicality and proposed a danced model for what Austin called "affective group-mindedness" (36). "We as a nation," Graham said, "are primitive also—primitive in the sense that we are forming a new culture."[29]

But *Primitive Mysteries* was, for all intents and purposes, a work of the twenties. By the mid-thirties, "mob-mindedness," or class consciousness, had emerged into national prominence and become identified with the plight of workers, among them African Americans. By 1935, Graham reformulated the nationalist presuppositions of *Primitive Mysteries* in a new solo, *Frontier.*

Frontier is also Austinian in that it historicizes the relation of the American body to the land. The immigrant of 1930s primitivism becomes the American nineteenth-century settler. Graham dances a lone woman confronting the

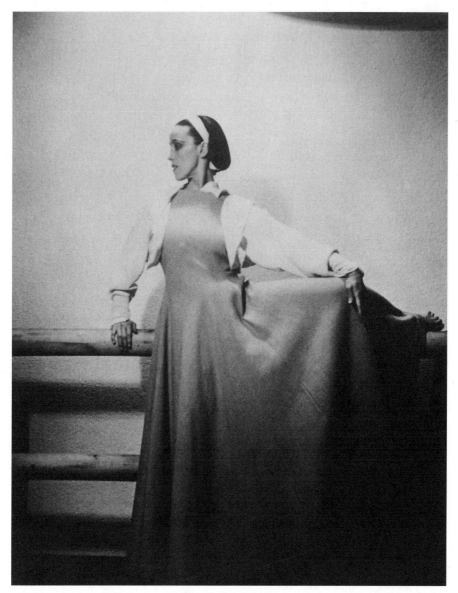

Figure 14:
Martha
Graham in
Frontier *(1935).*
Photo: Paul
Hansen. (San
Francisco
Performing Arts
Library and
Museum.)

prairie before her fence and interpreting "the land" by measuring herself against its challenging expanse, evoked by Isamu Noguchi's hanging V-shaped rope, whose ends reach aloft, out of sight. From an ideological perspective, Graham performs a white, Anglo-Saxon primitive and a woman doing "a man's work." Although resolutely antifascist, her own "racial" identity was important to Graham during this period, probably for professional reasons. A 1936 program identifies her as "Born Pittsburgh of New England-Dutch Stock."[30]

Although Graham's movements avoid mimetic images in *Frontier,* they are more mimetic in this piece than in *Primitive Mysteries*. One can discern an alternation of seriousness and playfulness, as well as a suggestion of rearing children (indicated by cradling an imaginary nursling in her arms). She likens her body to the land by lying across the fence, reaching to the horizon's limit with fervor, and outlining the perimeter of her space by gliding along its boundaries. She traces formulaic and repetitive patterns: from upstage toward the audience, along the diagonal from upstage to downstage, and in a square pattern on the circumference, always facing front. The term frontier indicates a boundary, and Graham moves literally within a boundary yet also aspirationally beyond its purview. The fence suggests a square or rectangular enclosure, but the hanging rope suggests a vector breaking out of that boundary and extending over the audience. The dancer aspires to the unsettled expanse for which she demonstrates appetite. Her movements are predominantly erect and vertical in their orientation, but her focus is aggressively forward. Despite Graham's enormous interest in floor work during this period, in the whole solo she descends only once to the floor. Another important aspect of her technique, the contraction, often an indicator of emotional complexity, is little in evidence. She is an erect and vertically stretched body on the move.

Frontier is purposefully repetitive, suggesting a didactic quality. Performed repeatedly are the almost militant slicing of the air with arm and leg as she approaches the audience head-on, the diagonal and undulated "running" step, or the playful sideways jumps with cocked head. These steps are also stressed for their rhythmic content, and they establish themselves through methodical repetition as identity markers, emblems of an "affective state."[31] Just as modernist features of movement (the floor work, the contraction) are minimized, so the sense of "rhythm" is deployed more literally. Horst devised a musical score that shifted abruptly in rhythmic pattern to match the relatively isolated motifs of the dance, but the sense of montage was not conveyed by these shifts. Graham's choreography uncharacteristically follows the music frequently, introducing something like a folk element. A film of the work shows that she used her mouth in a subtly anticipatory opening motion.[32] Graham's performance style, to borrow Austin's phrase, is "a state of acute, happy awareness" (99) which Austin named as the "primitive state of mind" (28). Graham shapes *Frontier* as "spiritually affective" rather than "emotionally effective." The political nature of the dance lies in how the soloist projects her energy into and beyond the plot of land on which she dances. She seems to be drawing strength from the land: she does not so much explore the land itself as she does its confines, projecting the affections she draws from it as a statement of conquest. Graham wrote, "All of life today is concerned with space problems, even political life."[33]

Given that Austin's distinction between affect and emotion opposes the communities of nation and class, a comparison with politically radical modern dance will be useful to delineate the aesthetics of radical emotion as something more than the shadow of affect.

Dudley's Emotional Marxism

Bearing weight, exerting effort, internalizing stress, and asserting defiant presence exemplified a style of experiencing and reacting to capitalism and racism in radical modern dance. These bodies rocked heavily against the ground, pressed against invisible forces, thrust and hurled themselves through unoccupied space, stood rooted with resolve, or drew themselves up in high spirits. These were qualities that Taylor attempted to stylize beyond recognition. The proximity of "modern" American movement to work and labor was immediately aesthetic before it also became overtly thematic. Embodied movement came to be seen and felt as political and social rather than purely personal or suprapersonal. Whereas conscious appetite in Graham feeds instinctual (affective) identity, hunger for Dudley awakens radical negativity leading to revolutionary emotion.

In Dudley's *Time Is Money* (1934), an oppressed figure weaves in and out of a circle of light in center stage while a speaker outside the circle, looking in, recites a poem by Sol Funaroff about labor as suffering.[34] There is no musical accompaniment. The structure of the composition is a montage. The dance's rhythms are fitful rather than continuous. Dudley noted, "I think [Fritz Lang's film] *Metropolis* was a very important image I worked from—when the workers go to work." The speaker intones: "Time! Time! Time! The skin to bone of workers, wives and kids."[35]

FRANKO: You performed *Time Is Money* (1934) yourself, right?
DUDLEY: Yes, that's right.
FRANKO: So *Time Is Money* was originally for a female soloist.
DUDLEY: Yes.
FRANKO: Because when I looked at the 1993 tape of the reconstructed dance with Tom Warfield it was this male worker.
DUDLEY: That's right.
FRANKO: And then the voice of the interlocutor in the reconstruction was female.
DUDLEY: I never thought of the question of whether I was a man or a woman. I thought of the content of the words. Now, I must tell you that when I asked Tom Warfield to do it [in the 1993 reconstruction] I considered it a much better dance. I'll tell you why: because I think there were many more images which I used which I might not have known about at that

Figure 15: Jane Dudley in The Dream Ends *(1934), a solo that was a study for* Time Is Money. *(Photo: Leo Hurwitz, courtesy of Jane Dudley.)*

period when I was doing it in 1934. The idea of a homeless person picking garbage out of a trash can, the limp.[36]

Because the structure of both the choreography and the poetic syntax is montaged, sometimes a verbal image evokes a gesture, while at others the gesture seems to call forth the word. A difficult productivity—a work *against* time—not the rhythm of the land, generates the evolution of this dance. In this process, which is one of contradiction, "the worker sinks to the level of a commodity and becomes indeed the most wretched of commodities," as Marx noted in *The Manuscripts of 1844*.[37] What the chorus girl accomplished with such apparent ease in "We're in the Money" is here revealed as a gargantuan task in which commodification equals death. The smiling chorus girl is the inverted figure of this travail: a figure of mortification: "Labor in which man alienates himself is a labor of self-sacrifice, of mortification," says Marx.[38] He claims the political economy becomes defined by its ability to create precisely this contradictory situation.

The dancer's rhythms are repeatedly accelerated by work. Dudley says, "There is one section where he starts to work and then he gets feebler and feebler and he collapses. That image was there from the very beginning." At times, the dancer also hobbles on the outskirts of the harsh center-stage light, energy flagging, but then returns again under the light's central beam. She attempts to physically articulate machine-like alacrity of arm and head with a collapsed and trembling frame, alternating energetic resolve with withered frailty. *Time Is Money* relates the reduction of subjectivity to a material base turning on barely sustainable bodiliness. "It is only as a *worker* that he continues to maintain himself as a *physical subject,* and . . . it is only as a *physical subject* that he is a *worker.*"[39]

In the dance's final moments, she sets forth in the audience's direction, breaching the voyeuristic relation that circumscribes her as victim. This time, rather than circle the pool of light, she breaks out of it. This change is accentuated by the speaker's changing position too, so that the final image does not grow from the preceding one, but occurs in isolation, as had all the others. Now facing the public outside the circle of harsh work light, she appears strong and demanding but also newly self-contained. The entirety of her physical and emotional self-assumption comes into focus. No longer striving, she looks out, then down briefly at her own fists clenched at hip level, then again out at the audience, with an expression of both shock and awakening. Stopping to confront her audience, and bringing the dance to a halt, the dancer appropriates time as essential to the *performative* economy. This moment is diametrically opposite to the scene of exchange abstraction in Berkeley's "We're in the Money." The reappropriation of time corresponds to the reclaiming of qualities in experience. This meaning of the gesture is, however, less evident than the defiance required for it to emerge as a gesture.

DUDLEY: I am sure I did something very defiant at the end, but I don't remember whether it took the shape of coming forward at the audience. I don't remember whether I thought of a breaking the shackles image which is what I use in the reconstruction.

FRANKO: That's a very Marxian image of coming to consciousness.

DUDLEY: (laughs) Yes, that's right.

*Figure 16: Tom Warfield in Jane Dudley's
1993 reconstruction of* Time Is Money
*(1934). Photo: Angela Taylor. (Courtesy
of the photographer.)*

FRANKO: It fits so well into the theory of working class oppression.

DUDLEY: That's right. It absolutely did. And one of the interesting things about that period, of course, was the naive going from Depression to defiance, and to victory: a pendulum swing that a lot of playwrights and dancers were into.[40]

The working body in *Time Is Money* has no rhythm of its own: it struggles against another tempo, the engineering of time. At the dance's conclusion the dancer stops engineered time by stepping out of its domain. Now that she has "broken the shackles" of what Marx refers to as passive bondage, the dancer's senses "become directly in their practice [active] theoreticians."[41] All this is suggested in the dancer's facial expression in that final moment. One could say that she discovers the domain of what the young Marx called "essential activity": "Poverty is the passive bond which causes the human being to experience the need of the greatest wealth—the *other* human being. The dominion of the objective being in me, the sensuous outburst of my essential activity, is *emotion,* which thus becomes here the *activity* of my being."[42] The state of "activity as suffering, strength as weakness" triggers a consciousness of its "other," which Marx calls "the dominion of the objective being in me," "essential activity," and, most importantly for my argument, "*emotion.*" Emotion frees activity to be "essential," and this liberation occurs as an outburst. The worker ceases to become a subject of labor by discovering his "objective" being, which is the theoretical creation of his senses. This is ideology in reverse. This revolution in and of the body turns on the pivot of emotion as the realization leading to spontaneous action. Within the context of modernism, it comes to define the "substance" of movement, yet within radicalism it is allowed to belong within the social world.

As Paul Ricoeur shows, objectification is a positive alternative to alienation: "It is the meaning of work as such that we deposit our meaning in something exterior."[43] Here, however, the external objectification of meaning is emotion. It is not merely a form of reaction, but is actually understood as "essential activity," that is, another sort of work that is noninstrumental: the very opposite of commodification. "The *Manuscripts,*" further notes Ricoeur, "are of interest not for any depiction of the concept of ideology but rather for the elaboration of the opposite concept, for what is the concrete basis of human life as opposed to the ideological construct."[44] The dance configures self-objectification in that it rejects worker subjectivity by sensuously theorized (that is, performed), noninstrumental movement. Dance and revolution are the only two human endeavors that can replace the political economy with a performative economy. Inasmuch as it results in the objectification of self, the labor of dance is emotion: the only product movement produces without engaging subjectivity in contradiction. Its only claim to the status of product is its mode of objectifying the self. The work of dance, understood in this sense, is the only objectifying activity that avoids bodily commodification while still producing effects with consequences for relations of production.

Without accepting Austin's pejorative view of emotion per se, I nevertheless retain her terminology to argue for its qualitative distinction between two cultural performances of identity. Politically radical modern dance replaced high modernism's aesthetic reduction to affective qualities, understood as formal, with its own reduction to emotional qualities, understood as objective. Affect leads to nation; emotion leads to class. The realization of self-consciousness as a new awareness that the self is a social as well as personal being is a thoroughgoing emotional event. Far from being a sign of limiting subjectivity, then, emotion is actually the very condition of objectivity, and precisely in this capacity it is to be distinguished from affect. Put otherwise, emotion is the theatrical sign that the dancer has become both the subject and the object of (his or her own) knowledge. But this becoming must be understood as a historical event. Thus Joseph Freeman required that proletarian literature address "specific experience which arouses specific emotion in specific people at a specific moment in a specific locale."[45] Unlike the specificity of experience, emotion, people, moment, and locale, affect is essential precisely because it stands as if outside of time. It is the link between modernism and bourgeois self-definition. As Agnes Heller writes, "The significant individuals of the bourgeois class lived and reflected their feelings not only as historical feelings, or as class feelings, but they also inseparably generalized and formulated these same feelings anthropologically as 'eternal human' feelings and experiences."[46] Because Dudley's *Time Is Money* spoke to issues of identity in terms of class rather than of nation, we can accept the relevance of Austin's terminology and conclude that Dudley's choreography was emotionally effective rather than spiritually affective.

"Drums in the Blood"

When Asadata Dafora Horton's African dance-drama *Kykunkor, or Witch Woman* burst onto the New York dance concert scene in 1934, it was unanimously acclaimed as the most exciting event of the year. Dafora's presentation of West African performance culture participated in the Pan-African movement's focus on the relevance of African culture to African Americans, but also to American cultural nationalism. Parenthetically, pan-national identity might also enable African Americans to call for freedom and reform in an international

KYKUNKOR

THE WITCH WOMAN
AFRICAN DANCE DRAMA

Figure 17: Asadata Dafora on the souvenir program cover of Kykunkor *(1934). (Billy Rose Theatre Collection, New York Public Library for the Performing Arts at Lincoln Center, Astor, Tilden, and Lenox Foundations.)*

context apart from the Communist Party.[47] It is in this context that I shall discuss the intense critical and popular interest Dafora generated. Dafora's work stood outside the institutional constraints that determined identity ideologically in the thirties. Yet his intervention in the affect/emotion dichotomy played on both sides of the equation (land and race) while speaking to a broader range of subjects than had perhaps been the case until then.

Dafora was a native of Sierra Leone who had been educated in England, taught African dance in Berlin in the 1920s, and sung at La Scala in Milan. In 1929 he came to America, where he formed his company Shologa Oloba (Dancers and Singers) and began training its members in African performance arts. A souvenir booklet for *Kykunkor* relates that the company performed some dances in 1933 at the Red Press Bazaar at Madison Square Garden, where Anne Kennedy, business manager of the Unity Theatre, first noticed it. This led to an invitation to perform at the Unity on East Twenty-third Street, and spurred the development of *Kykunkor.*

Contemporary dance scholars disagree on the historical significance of *Kykunkor.* Lynne Fauley Emery writes that the dance-opera "revealed the potential of ethnic material to black dancers, and herein lay Dafora's value as a great influence on black concert dance."[48] Thomas de Frantz considers Dafora's work exoticism. "Though Dafora confirmed the great theatrical potential of West African dance for American audiences and African-American dancers, his success set in motion a critical formula which emphasized the exotic novelty of the black body on the concert stage."[49] Both scholars address the posterity of Dafora's work, but it is still worth noting that in the wake of the Harlem Renaissance, classical African cultures were recognizable as expressions of cultural nationalism. As George Hutchinson explains:

Modernist African American art would draw from both sources [African American folklore and classical African cultures] in the process of its own "impure" and "cosmopolitan" development of "cultural racialism." The desire to "recapture" the African heritage and promote pan-African consciousness coexists with pride in African American culture as both "mixed" and uniquely "American"—in fact, with a commitment to American cultural nationalism.[50]

As Alain Locke noted, *Kykunkor* was "an entirely new and healthy adaptation of the pure African tradition of ritual, dance, costume and music" that would place a foundation "deep into the earth under modern Negro music and modern Negro dance."[51] If one takes account of the important theoretical place of classical African culture in African American modernism since the 1920s, one must concede that, whatever trends *Kykunkor* may have encouraged in subsequent concert dance, it nonetheless contributed to the interpellation of subjectivities in the context of cultural nationalism. It also contributed to the concept of dance modernism. Dafora's production merits historical analysis in the context of thirties performance because Dafora presented the black body at that time, not as exotic, but as cultural. What interests me here is less the apprehension of the work as exoticism by white critics than their reception of the work in terms of metakinesis and interpellation. *Kykunkor* was unique, not just for its exposition of African arts, but also for the success with which it reached an audience broader than that of either modernism or the radical Left.

Billed as an "opera," *Kykunkor* presented a choreographic and musical narrative of West African village life. Despite New York concertgoers' familiarity with the narrative structure it employed, the dance style and its relationship to the uncommon percussion appeared as unusual as *Primitive Mysteries* and garnered as much if not more attention. Black dance critic Leonore Cox aligned Dafora with Winfield and the Hampton Institute Dancers as "pioneers in modern and concert dancing," as distinguished from "jazz dance or primitive dance."[52] She thus established "ethnic dance" as an integral part of modernist experimentation, a direction in which Katherine Dunham and Pearl Primus would continue. For this reason, the analysis of the choreography was to be put on the same level with that of Graham's and other modernist innovators.

Dance critic Edwin Denby analyzed Dafora's movement qualities as follows:

The feet are light and quick, and move from the ankles. The torso is bent forward slightly, the chest is open and the shoulders, relaxed. It is in the arms chiefly that the dance ornamentation takes place, and they can move with extraordinary speed, and with great precision, without looking strained. When they fly out the force of the gesture is toned down just before the end so that the movement remains graceful and the gesture does not break off. There are spinal movements and head movements too, but they play a lesser role.[53]

There is nothing in this description that marks the dance as exotic. To the contrary, Denby attempts to analyze a series of new effects possible to the modern dancing body. *Kykunkor* was nevertheless publicized as authentic African dance and music, and although all the instrumentalists were African, some of the performers were New Yorkers.[54] Dafora himself not only played the bridegroom, but also directed and choreographed the entire production. Since *Kykunkor* was performed in West African dialect, this involved the coaching of African American dancers and singers in unfamiliar material.

Against a background of secret feminine ritual, two kinds of possession occur in *Kykunkor*. A male intrudes upon the liminal female space to choose a bride; the female liminal space avenges itself upon him through the agency of the witch woman, whose evil spell possesses Bokari's body, rendering it uncon-scious.[55] The broader context is that of an intertribal courtship disrupted by the witch woman who, it is noted, "has been sent to spoil the wedding by a jealous rival." In the most dramatically impressive scene of the work, a witch doctor, performed by Abdul Assen, exorcised the evil spirit from the bride-groom's prostrate, hypnotized body and revisited it upon the witch woman by forcing her to imbibe it from a cow horn. The witch doctor, in other terms, is the performative site of transfer between two bodies, and what is transferred is death. I shall argue that what we have here is a staging of metakinesis itself in the realm of magic, and a dramatization of the effects of interpellation as hyp-notism, unconsciousness, and death.

The contest between witch woman and witch doctor introduced the theme of possession, which captured the critical interest of most white commentators. "Nothing," wrote one critic, "could be more thrilling than his incantation over the senseless bridegroom. Here is passionate emotion of immense power."[56] "It was at this point," wrote another critic, "that the presentation became rather over-whelming. The witch-doctor began his incantations with shrill laughter . . . he danced and shrieked, moaned, cursed, wrestling in an awful agony with the spirit of evil."[57] Passionate emotion accelerated to become an overwhelming experience raises the question of what sort of involvement was being solicited from the audience. Who was becoming possessed? John Martin summed up these characteristics when he wrote: "It is, indeed, this possession that gives the performance its unique quality."[58]

Black commentators, on the other hand, viewed the work as a welcome corrective to distorted representations of Africa:

How different the customs of that land appear on the stage from the depressing tales which missionaries bring back! No unclothed savages preparing a juicy stew of some hapless fellow man. No listless natives wallowing in filth. Instead, here are a beautiful black and brown people, colorfully clad in gay raiment of brilliant hues—gold, green, crimson and white—riotously dazzling against the background of their dark bodies.[59]

Rather than focus unduly on the possession scene, black commentators viewed *Kykunkor* as a totality. Similar reactions were also reported among white spec-tators in the souvenir booklet: "Quiet and composed and very well dressed off-stage, he [Dafora] listens to dressing-room visitors who express their enthusi-asm for his work and their amazement at the revelation that Africa may not be so 'barbaric.' 'Barbarism?' he murmurs, 'but there are lynchings in this country. And voodooism? But that is a real religion, practiced as any other religion is practiced.'" These comments of Dafora's clearly indicate his awareness of the

political force of his work. Leonore Cox also praised the work's folk origins while situating it within Martin's understanding of the sublime: "This [Negro] dancing began as an emotional expression. The Negro felt an uncontrollable desire to say something for which he had not words, for which indeed there are no words."[60] Cox also took *Kykunkor* as an occasion for reasserting the idea of metakinesis as "a relationship between the internal and the external with the development of which the artist can readily transfer his own emotions to the consciousness of the audience."[61] Just as Cox had situated Dafora within modernism, so she linked *Kynkunkor* to a metakinetic logic of transfer. Dafora's work becomes inscribed in this way within the modernist and radicalist context. The parable of the work may be that the witch doctor provides an antidote to ideological possession. The witch doctor is an agent of repossession, and the frenzy of emotion in his procedure is one that both recalled other effects of modern dance and also exceeded them. Transfer becomes transformation; identification becomes possession.

Figure 18: The first appearance of the witch woman in Asadata Dafora's Kykunkor (1934). Dafora is center. Photo: Maurice Goldberg. (Dance Collection, New York Public Library for the Performing Arts at Lincoln Center, Astor, Lenox, and Tilden Foundations.)

Metakinetic Interpellations 81

Kykunkor both narrated an event of a possession and extended the notion of metakinetic transfer beyond Graham's nativist fiction and Dudley's Marxist genealogy. Here was a work that spoke of nationalism and social protest with neither the transcendental and formalist commitments of conservative affect nor the specific program of radical emotion. Yet both registers were implied in the possession it recounted, virtually enacting it upon its audiences.

Houston A. Baker Jr. has described possession as a discourse with transferable meanings: "*Possession* operates both in the spirit work of voodoo and in the dread slave and voodoo economics perpetuated by the West. What is involved in possession, in either case, is supplementarity—the immediately mediating appearance, as spectre or shadow, of a second and secondary 'self.'"[62] Baker's reference to supplementarity is warranted in this discussion. The second or secondary self evoked by possession could also be the "objective self" of *Time Is Money* or the autonomous communitarian self of *Primitive Mysteries.* The secondary self can also be considered a self to come. Despite the acclaim Dafora's work garnered, the white establishment denied its power of interpellation. That is, by conceiving it as possession, they testified to its power but simultaneously attempted to distance it. Martin seemed to confirm the power of possession as transfer but also denied the possibility of its interpretation: "The effect of watching such authentic frenzy," he wrote, "is impossible to describe."[63] Interestingly, Martin refers here neither to what was seen, nor to the audience reaction, but to the "effect of watching." Why could it not be described as metakinesis? Because possession is the mediating appearance of metakinesis as interpellation. What Martin's admission of descriptive impossibility before the effect set aside was the theoretical necessity to grant universal truth to this particular metakinetic transfer. Remember that for Martin dance transcends the artist's "powers of statement in the conventional terms of words" in order to present universal truth. What does universal truth mean in a cultural context removed from the representation of America? Dafora raised the issue of cultural specificity with respect to universal truth. *Kykunkor* exposed the ideological basis of metakinesis in the latter's relation to national identity. Like Winfield before him, Dafora was staging interpellation as well as a commentary on interpellation.

The place held by dancing the African cultural totality blocked the deployment of an awakening to radical negativity as in *Time Is Money.* Instead, Dafora's emotion asserted (pan-)national identity fully reliant on rhythmic appeal. The appeal of rhythm to affective identity and its role in the discovery of emotional identity were both short-circuited. Although rhythm was a more evident artistic procedure in Dafora's dance than in that of Graham or Dudley, it escaped the ideological claims of Austin because it was entirely performative. The compelling rhythmic power of the drumming was both supported and

undercut by the dancers' improvisatory techniques. Margaret Lloyd explained: "There is no timing, as we understand it. The dancer catches the rhythm from the drums; that is, the drums start, the dancer follows, and then they work together in a sort of flexible rapport, so that no two performances are ever quite alike, for there is always an element of improvisation."[64] Rhythm and bodies in flexible rapport suggested a danced alternative to affective rhythm even as the formalism detected by Denby's trained eye constituted a new variety of modernism.

Figure 19: A rehearsal of Dafora's Kykunkor, *possibly at the New Dance Group. Dancers (left to right): Alma Sutton and Bess Samuels. (Courtesy of the New Dance Group Studio's Archive, New York.)*

Dafora thus proposed a redefinition of dance modernism in tune with Pan-Africanism, and avoided in this way linkages the Communist Party hoped to cement between American blacks and the American working class.[65] At the same time, *Kykunkor* contained a lesson for the left in that it triumphantly demonstrated how broad the appeal of a certain rhythm could be to the mass audience coveted by the Communist Party.[66] Owen Burke wrote in *New Masses* that "[there is] a folk quality in Negro dancing and a freedom of movement, a spontaneity and a joy in performance that have got to be acquired by the more sophisticated concert dancer."[67] It is unclear whether Burke meant the "bourgeois" or the "revolutionary" concert dancer, but it is possible he meant both. It is sure, however, that *Kykunkor*'s success made some reflect on what rhythm really meant. It clearly had a complex emotional harmonic, as noted by another critic: "The drums beat an incessant rhythm, weaving a curious pattern in percussion, and the singers chant and moan. Weirdly lovely is the effect, for the soft syllables of the tribal dialect melt into the slurs and melancholy cadences of this peculiar scale."[68] When one considers *Kykunkor* as an intervention into the mid-thirties discourse of affect, emotion, and rhythm, the inordinate focus on possession by white critics becomes explainable. Dafora effectively rewrote the affect/emotion dichotomy inherent in Martin's metakinetic formula such that a white audience succumbing to *Kykunkor*'s power of interpellation described that power as possession. White audiences, that is, read themselves metakinetically into Dafora's narrative.

Hallie Flanagan seems to have realized this occurred. When praising the Federal Theater Project's later adaptation of *Kykunkor*'s dances in *Bassa Moona* (The Land I Love), she renamed possession "drums in the blood," and interpreted their presence as a good omen for the popular national American theater that was never to be. "I hope," said Flanagan on the radio, "our audience will never be without that beating of drums in the blood which is the prime necessity for any theatre."[69] Flanagan pointed to the project of a people's theater as emotion and affect conjoined: "drums," non-Western impetus to improvisation, but "in the blood," reaching the "depth" of affect without racialized exclusions based on essentialized geographical influences. The project of a national theater was to redefine popular American identity, and what Flanagan called "black magic" was suggested to be the fulfillment of the Federal Theatre Project's socialism without revolution. *Kykunkor* suggested a different model through which national identity might be identified not with land or with blood, but with drums that endowed emotions with formal rigor, aesthetic inevitability, and improvisatory freedom.

Given the power of Dafora's interpellation of his public in 1934 and the critical insights into his practice as a potentially revolutionary if nonviolent one, it is worth exploring how left-wing dancers represented "blackness." This is the subject of chapter 4.

Chapter 4 **Cultural Cross-Dressing as Class Construction**

Having surveyed three versions of cultural authenticity as political subjectivation, I now turn to an ethnically hybrid dancing body particular to mid- to late-thirties left culture. I ask to what use the Left put the representation of racial identities in dance movement. If the proletarian body on stage was a "racialized" body, what role did race actually play in its staged depictions? To examine the question of references to other cultures—particularly to black culture—by left-wing modern dancers, I draw upon the following examples: the solo work of Si-Lan (Sylvia) Chen (a dancer of Chinese and French-African ancestry), Helen Tamiris's *How Long Brethren* (1937), and Jane Dudley's *Harmonica Breakdown* (late thirties).[1] I ask how left-oriented racial impersonation evoked political content and what changing concepts of class these experiments reflected. Following Alan M. Wald, I call such impersonation in the left-wing milieu "cultural cross-dressing."[2]

The Internationalist Context

Modern dance soloist Si-Lan Chen was the only radical dancer during the 1930s to have worked consistently both in the Soviet Union and the United

States.[3] Although some American modern dancers (Anna Sokolow among them) visited the Soviet Union during the thirties, none stayed there to work. Soviet dance was unresponsive to contemporary developments in American and German modern dance. Si-Lan Chen appears to have been the exception to this rule. She was also one of the few radical soloists of the period with extensive classical dance training.[4]

Chen crossed in her own person African, Chinese, West Indian, and East Asian ethnicities and nationalities. She was born in Trinidad and raised in England, but also lived in China and the former Soviet Union before coming to New York in 1937. Thus she embodied, or nearly embodied, the ethnically diverse subject positions depicted in her dances, and this was atypical for the period. She tended toward terse character depictions the press described as pantomimic. A 1932 review from Moscow remarks on mimetic qualities: "No longer is she merely a dancer. She has become a pantomimist of rare ability. Her dancing, in some instances, is overshadowed now by her talent as an actress; yet one, without the other, would be incomplete."[5] In 1939, John Martin wrote: "She moves with a crisp and engaging clarity, and if occasionally she sins on the side of literalness, at least she is never obscure."[6] Chen's international background combined with her artistic and ethnic diversity—her composite identity as black, Chinese, Soviet, New Yorker, modern dancer, and ballet dancer—make her both a fascinating figure in her own right and an informative point of comparison for the issue of cultural cross-dressing in thirties modern dance. By virtue of her life experience and complex ancestry, she had more specificity at her command in the depiction of ethnic particularity than other modern dancers of the period.

Her Chinese ancestry led her to explore the Beijing Opera form, and to choreograph a number of solos utilizing traditional Chinese dance.[7] "The Partisan," a section from her *Shanghai Sketches* that depicted "a peasant fighter against the invader," was choreographed after a Beijing Opera sword dance. Her African ancestry led her to create a dance in 1932 on racial prejudice in the United States, *The American Negro (a protest)*. While living in the Soviet Union, she studied traditional dances of Turkistan and Uzbekistan, which were later distilled in *From Soviet Asia*, as well as in the "Uzbek Girl" section of her *Three Modern Women*. Traditional dances of Trinidad, the island on which she was born, also entered her repertory. In New York she shared concerts with modern dancers Anna Sokolow, Dorothy Bird, Miriam Blecher, and Lily Mehlman, with whom she felt close artistic ties. Many of these concerts were benefits for Chinese medical relief in the second Sino-Japanese war. "The pupils of Martha Graham, my contemporaries," she wrote in a newspaper article, "are certainly among the leading group of younger dancers. Their school is

much more formal and abstract to the type of dancing I do, but our aims are similar."[8] Another article underlined this fact: "Her dances, she insists, are too modern to be abstractions. 'They are as realistic as I can make them. Realism is needed today to arouse my people.'"[9]

Figure 20: Si-Lan Chen in Shanghai Sketches *(1933). (Jay Leyda–Si-Lan Chen Collection, Tamiment Institute Library, New York University.)*

One gathers from reviews that her dances were short and succinct. In an interview in the *Daily Worker* she explained her reasons for avoiding longer compositions: "'In the Soviet Union,' she explains, 'my dances were of necessity always short, terse, to the point. Four or five minute dances are unheard of in the Soviet Union. The worker expects above all clarity of expression and economy of means. He would be very impatient with a long dance that presented variation after variation on the same theme.'"[10] Chen's awareness of feminist issues might also be attributed to her international background. An unidentified clipping reports on her lecture "Soviet Women" in Shanghai in 1935: "Miss Chen, who recently returned from a five-year stay in Moscow, stated that education plays a foremost part in life there. Marriage is simple, but divorce is getting more difficult now that the family is becoming more solid. There is no alimony for a wife, only support for a child, who always, in case of divorce, belongs to the mother, although the father must pay one third of his income for its support."[11] Publicity styled her as the modern Chinese woman or the new woman of the awakened East. Publicity copy describing *Three Women* situates that dance within a feminist consciousness:

Her suite of *Three Women* is expressive of her modern tendency. There is the Uzbek girl, vivacious, vital, who has thrown off the yoke of colonial exploitation and is free to live and be the equal of man. (This dance was composed on the basis of national Uzbek dance movements while Miss Chen was travelling in the East.) Her "Soviet Girl" is sturdy, independent, serious with the seriousness of youth. The suite ends with a satire on the flighty jazz-baby, the gold-digger of Western civilization.[12]

The "Uzbek Girl" should be thought of in tandem with Sophie Maslow's *Two Songs about Lenin* (1934). Inspired by Dziga Vertov's film *Three Songs for Lenin*, Maslow's dance used folk music brought back from the Soviet Union by Alex North to depict the religious devotion to Lenin of ethnic minorities in the east. In a subtle and mediated sense, it explored the relation of revolution to ethnicity outside the American context.

Since Chen herself embodied many of the subject positions explored by her dances, her artistry throws a different light on the ethics of cultural cross-dressing in thirties modern dance. Because of her experience in China and the Soviet Union and her awareness of women's causes conjoined with her awareness of racial prejudice, Si-Lan Chen's thinking on the relationship of modern dance to subaltern cultures and feminine identity is particularly relevant. Most noticeable in her approach is her impatience with the context of nationalism. She viewed the traditional dances that she studied and practiced as languages of the oppressed. In a manuscript about folk art, she notes: "The policy of czarism towards the national minorities in the Russian empire was very similar to that which the Nazis have toward the conquered people of Europe."[13] In a long article she published in the British West Indies, she explodes the notion of "national" dances: "The average person speaks about Russia as one country and one national group. Actually, when they say Russia they mean the Soviet Union and when they say Soviet Union they mean the Union of Soviet Socialist Republics. This area covers more than one-sixth of the world. Within its borders there are at least two hundred different national minorities, and the

Figure 21: Si-Lan Chen, probably in Woman in War *"depicting the transformation of women from passive victim to active heroines" (1935). (Jay Leyda–Si-Lan Chen Collection, Tamiment Institute Library, New York University).*

Republics that make up the Union are as numerous and consist of races as different as those of Western Europe."[14] Although Chen's life was unique and in many respects privileged, it allowed her to speak out about cultural appropriation. She did this in terms of what now would be called humanism: "Our task can now be directed towards joining the efforts of the many who today believe that human beings can become united regardless of race or nationality. We can achieve this in the themes upon which we base our dances, in our closer knowledge of the folk dance of the world's peoples, and presenting this material with intelligence and art."[15] Although the concept of union in this project is today politically passé, Chen transmits important information about historical elements of left sensibility. The fragile notion of class was buoyed up by internationalism, and justified in this way cultural cross-dressing. The very performance of dances of differing ethnic traditions by one and the same person on one stage carried a strong political message, but this message was indistinguishable from the formal organization of the dance as a "comprehending of life": "Our task today is the resolving of the problems of life, the incarnation of life itself in the form of the dance. Art in general, and in particular the dance, is an instrument for the comprehending (the *organizing* of our consciousness) of life."[16] Here, as elsewhere in the materials of the left tradition from the thirties, the term organization takes a prominent place even in the most personal contexts. Yet Chen also reflected on the tensions between dancing and organizing, understood as political action: "To involve ourselves only with organizing seems to me just as much an escape from facing real issues, as those of us who escape from the realities of life by ignoring what goes on in the world. It is a nice safe and a little superior feeling to be busily involved with organization of one sort or another, it is easier to do that than it is to get into a studio and do a little hard work on dance composition."[17] The act of dance composition itself could be inherently political in that organizing consciousness and comprehending life were simultaneous and interrelated endeavors.

The Minstrelsy Effect

Helen Becker, an American dancer of Russian Jewish ancestry, took the stage name Tamiris. She was of an earlier generation than most politically radical dancers of the thirties and was not an alumna of the Denishawn School like Graham and Humphrey. Tamiris's solo concerts won her artistic recognition as early as 1928, though she bypassed the high modernist paradigm shared by most second-generation modern dancers, who would not have danced *Negro Spirituals* a year before the stock market crash. She became the outspoken director of the Federal Dance Project, for which she had lobbied in Washington.[18]

In a recent article on Tamiris's group work *How Long Brethren,* Susan Manning characterizes the effect of white female dancers performing to Negro spirituals as "metaphorical minstrelsy."[19] A Federal Dance Project production, *How Long Brethren* had a black chorus singing spirituals in the theater boxes, and an all-white, all-female company dancing to them onstage. The spirituals were drawn from the Gellert-Siegmeister collection *Negro Songs of Protest.* Hallie Flanagan, the national director of the project, praised *How Long Brethren* as "a powerful social document on freedom from racial prejudice." In particular, she experienced it as the presentation of a composite identity made up of voice and bodies: "One could not tell where music became movement, where black voices became white bodies."[20] A similar image emerges here of solidarity on the international model.

Manning questions why black dancers did not perform Tamiris's work for the Federal Theatre Project. She argues a racial exploitation for which the term *metaphorical minstrelsy* becomes the critical pivot. The evocation of minstrelsy requires careful consideration. Graff admits that "it is tempting to criticize Tamiris's efforts from today's vantage point," but she also argues a cross-racial identification in *How Long Brethren:* "Revolutionary dancers identified with Negroes because they believed they were members of the same class and because Negro protest songs echoed their determination to take control of their economic lives."[21]

Tamiris's politics, even if out of date by today's standards, should be legible in immanently aesthetic terms. Otherwise, an organically danced politics is impossible. Yet at the same time, the reconstruction of those aesthetics must rely on a historicization of the context, without which we can only imagine *How Long Brethren* in a hypothetical present—that is, in nakedly aesthetic terms. The fruitful conjunction of politics and aesthetics depends for its validity on this double operation.

How are we to understand the notion of minstrelsy as metaphorical? Metaphor suggests a selection of corresponding elements of meaning whereby is brought to the surface a magical and essential equality not visibly shared between two entities. A metaphor says that A is like B, but it also suppresses the comparison in favor of equality: A is not *like* B, A *is* B. The contradictory force of metaphor provides it with its energy, but the apparent distance of "metaphorical" minstrelsy from actual historical minstrelsy is still a teasing one.

Let us recall three important historical points about minstrelsy: (1) it was a working-class male performance phenomenon; (2) it focused on the derisive mimicry of the black body; (3) it was performed to burlesque minstrel songs whose origins are uncertain. None of these conditions are met by *How Long Brethren,* which was danced by women in a modern dance idiom without caricature, and to spirituals, songs of sorrow whose element of protest was discovered in Gellert's fieldwork. It is therefore not obvious which performative units of meaning could be the vehicles for the metaphor making an essential linkage between two such different entities as left-wing modern dance and minstrelsy.

Perhaps minstrelsy is itself a metaphor for a certain political intent. Manning argues that the white, middle-class dancers of *How Long Brethren* were actually engaged in a process of self-legitimization as female dancers in a new art form. They had no concern for the African American population with whom Tamiris's choreography was designed to express political solidarity; their concern was rather for their own cultural status. She refers to this status as feminist: "The metaphorical minstrelsy of 1930s modern dance legitimized a feminist staging of the white female body."[22] The "shifting contours" of white women's politics in the thirties has recently received attention from scholars. For example, the National Consumers League, run principally by women, combined feminism, union rights, and antiracist policies.[23] One should not assume that middle-class women were politically unengaged or ineffective. Also, the apparent conjunctural politics of choreography should not be extended indiscriminately to the dancers. The women who performed in the premiere of Graham's *Primitive Mysteries,* for example, were by and large the same radical individuals discussed throughout this book.

Manning associates the final exit ("marching into a red dawn") in *How Long Brethren* with a socialist position on social change: "In historical context, the political connotations of the ending are clear: it is the socialist-inspired mass, not the individual, that must take the lead in effecting social change." While the red dawn unmistakably suggests radical aspirations, what is troubling is the socialist and communist politics that are set at odds with some feminist consciousness, because this casts female modern dancers of socialist or communist persuasion as racist, or protoracist feminists. This claim is supported by "the unspoken assumption that the Euro-American body could represent black experience, while the African American body could only represent black experience." The issue of representation is at the core of Manning's argument.

How Long Brethren should also be considered in the context of the Popular Front in which internationalism gave way to issues of nationalism on the Left. The African American performer Paul Robeson sang in Earl Robinson's "Ballad for Americans" (1935): "You know who I am. I am everybody who is nobody; I'm the nobody who is everybody. The etcetera and the so forth that does the work." "Are you an American?" the chorus asks him. "Am I an American?" replies Robeson, "I'm just an Irish, Negro Jewish Italian French and English Spanish Russian Chinese Polish Scotch Hungarian Litvak Swedish Finnish Canadian Greek and Turk and Czech and double check American."[26] Here, multiple ethnicities are perceptible within the aggregate conveyed by Robeson's singular African American voice and body. His strategy—essentially that of Popular Front "ethnic Americanism"—was to counter racism with a vision of racial and national hybridity and, since "Ballad for Americans" was originally a WPA project, multiethnic nationalism. This case should be compared with *How Long Brethren* since it also involves a radical artist and a federal project. Robeson himself was an avowed communist demonstrating that the communist subject did present himself or herself as a racial composite. Graff points out that "the Communist Party, seeing Americanization as a means to spread Communist values to the American working class, initially discouraged ethnic identification, but it later came to support a form of American radicalism defined by ethnicity."[27] The multiethnic pluralism of the Popular Front was struggling to find a language that could be translated into performative terms. This language was, more often than not, to be found within the African American tradition. "Paul Robeson's concerts," writes Michael Denning, "were, for his audiences, an embodiment of this Popular Front vision. By singing songs from around the world, he created a symbolic federation of national folk musics anchored in the African American spiritual."[28] One way to depict the multiethnic makeup of America was to represent the dance and music of the peoples. This is a simple historical fact that should be taken into account in any assessment of cultural cross-dressing.

Manning also makes the case that Tamiris, like Graham, fashioned the female modern dancer as universal subject. This transcendent subject would have nothing to do with any ethnic identity. This was a premise of dance modernism, and its "feminisms" can be seen to derive from its universalizing aesthetic. But, given the antiracist politics of the CP-USA in the thirties and the "ethnic Americanism" of the Popular Front, "speaking for" oppressed African Americans was not construed as appropriating identity from black subject positions. To say that it did so in these particular historical contexts is to indulge in historically unwarranted revisionism.

The distinction between affect and emotion sketched in the previous chapters can help to clarify this situation. Which of these two aspects of modern dance aesthetics was really at work here: the affective or the emotional? From the topical subject matter of *How Long Brethren* it is arguable that Tamiris did not position herself or her dancers as universal "affective" subjects, but rather as emotional subjects of class. Impersonating ethnicity within this class perspective, they expressed solidarity among workers across racial and ethnic lines. This is, of course, indicated by the exit into the red dawn.

Manning problematizes the casting of *How Long Brethren*. Still, her analysis overlooks historical ties between the CP-USA, the Popular Front, and the fight against racism in America during the 1930s. As Alan M. Wald has written, "The Communist Party itself during these years [between the early thirties and the mid-fifties] was the most successful multi-racial class struggle political organization ever built on the U.S. left." "Its great theme," he adds, "was anti-racism."[29] The two causes that sealed the historical relation between the Communist Party and African Americans were the cases of the Scottsboro Nine and that of Angelo Herndon. Both are amply documented in Philip S. Foner and Herbert Shapiro's *American Communism and Black Americans*.[30] The public figure most representative of this relationship was Paul Robeson. The question of the all-white casting of *How Long Brethren* should be addressed to the Federal Theatre and Dance projects rather than to the CP-USA or the Popular Front. The institutional history of the projects must be balanced against that of the Communist Party and Popular Front. Despite the progressive leadership of Harry Hopkins and Hallie Flanagan, institutionalized racism did exist in the national administration of the WPA.[31]

Hallie Flanagan wrote that the Federal Theatre Project "presented the widest range of productions, talents, tastes, attitudes, races, religious and political faiths. It was everything in excess. In short, it reflected the city."[32] Yet the administrative structure of the project in New York, one of its major fields of operation despite its national scope, was fragmented into "units" that reflected the linguistic and ethnic conclaves of the city. Segregation thus was built into the projects' administrative structure. For example, the "Negro unit" of the Federal Theatre Project was located at the Lafayette Theatre in Harlem. The Living Newspaper unit, which operated all over the city, was the most experimental and controversial, but the majority of other units were identified according to cultural community within the metropolis. The logic was to serve particular communities, but the possibilities for segregation were easily veiled by this structure.

One can and should differentiate between the administrative structure of the FTP, which favored segregation in the WPA projects, and the CP-USA's well-publicized stand against racism and for working-class interracialism. As Mark Naison writes, "the Harlem CP-USA gradually evolved toward a policy that insisted on the complete integration of blacks and whites in every aspect of Party life. . . . From 1929 on, being a black communist in Harlem meant meeting, studying, protesting, and socializing with whites."[33] Would not the dancers of *How Long Brethren* have adopted the Popular Front line? Dudley remembers that "the corps who were on the WPA were Party Members."[34] Both Tamiris and one of her dancers, Fanya Geltman, suffered later at the hands of McCarthyism. Geltman relates: "They had me down—I had the FBI across the street from my house where I still live, parked day and night, day and night."[35]

Manning's argument about FDP dancers' opportunistic feminisms hinges on a publicity photo of the *How Long Brethren* cast posed in an orderly row with legs partially exposed, each head resting on the shoulder of the other. This photo, she claims, resembles that of a chorus line, and was exploited as such by the publicity department to attract attention to the production. Yet she also maintains that the casting of white women in the work draws on "the emergent convention of 1930s modern dance that a collective of female dancers could figure the body politic rather than compose an eroticized chorus line."[36] So to resist being identified with a chorus line, further argues Manning, modern dancers had to engage in "metaphorical minstrelsy" to "legitimize their challenge to traditional images of the female dancer."[37] That is, they not only must Americanize themselves with metaphorical blackface, but they must also politicize the chorus girl image, for which metaphorical blackface also acts as an antidote. Their Americanization is atypical because it is feminist, and it operates on two aesthetic fronts.

The photo in question could not, I believe, have evoked a chorus line even

Figure 22: The performing company of the New Dance Group: Nadia Chilkovsky, Miriam Blecher, Fanya Geltman, Edith Langbert, Pauline Shrifman, Grace Wylie. Compare these faces with those of Ziegfeld girls. (Courtesy of Jane Dudley.)

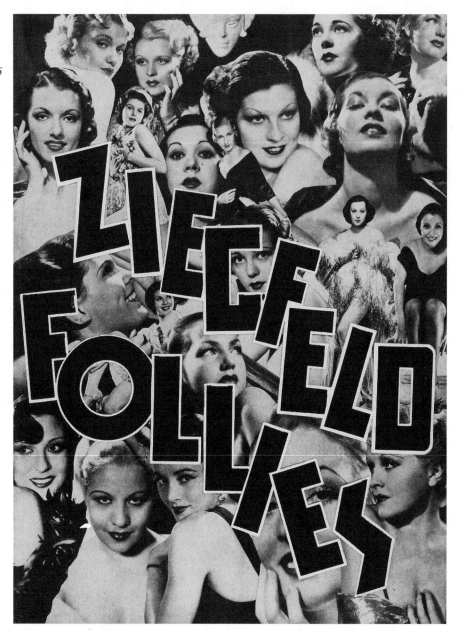

Figure 23: The parade of faces. Souvenir program for the 1936 Time Marches On. (Shubert Archive, New York.)

for the most casual observer. He or she had only to note the complexion of these women's faces, the morphology of legs, and the material and style of costumes to realize this was no chorus line. Unlike radical modern dancers who were predominantly dark complexioned, Eastern European, and frequently Jewish, chorus girls of the Ziegfeld tradition disseminated in Hollywood films throughout the thirties were predominantly standardized Anglo-Saxon types. More important, Manning's interpretation implies that the whitening of the female Jewish body through its metaphorical blackening was sufficient for a

Figure 24:
ILGWU
publicity: "Our
Races Are Many
—Our Aims Are
One," from the
Twenty-Fifth
Anniversary
Book of Local
'91. Frequently
used for racist
purposes, the
composite por-
trait is refash-
ioned here as
a response to
racism. (Cour-
tesy of UNITE
Archives.)

dancer to achieve cultural legitimacy—Americanization—on the model of popular culture while avoiding the popular culture model of "feminine" performance. What appears improbable is that this popular culture model, subverted through a racist detour, would serve to facilitate the modern dancer's challenge to the capitalist order, including its racist injustices.

A challenge does not legitimate itself if it is to remain a challenge, and when the challenge to the capitalist order addresses the repudiation of its systematic racism, it is hard to see how Tamiris or any other politically radical artist of this period would sacrifice fervent political convictions for the presumed artistic authority of assimilation. This conclusion would be so fundamentally unethical as to disqualify any serious political commitment among radical artists of this period. Legitimizing authority was acquired by the Left through the authenticity of experience grounded in childhood memories that provided access to emotional depth as its talisman in the social world. Association or pastiche did not acquire it.

Manning draws on Michael Rogin's analysis of Al Jolson's blackface performance in the 1928 film *The Jazz Singer*.[38] The problem is that Rogin's theory does not travel well into the modern dance field of the 1930s. Although Jolson, like Tamiris and most of her dancers, was Jewish, to ascribe the same strategy of Hollywood celebrity-building to the countercultural New York modern dance community of the thirties is a red herring. A radical modern dancer could not have sought cultural authority in the same manner as a movie star.[39] It was not in keeping with the radical ethos of the period that a challenge to the existing order would necessitate legitimization in the terms of popular culture. This challenge—one of the fundamental ideological challenges of the decade—becomes a screen in Manning's account for Jewish assimilationist strategy.

Communists, Jews, and blacks were lumped together by the radical Right as the common and indistinguishable enemy. This was particularly true in the southern strongholds of racism and was a reaction to the new phenomenon of organized labor there. To which mainstream America would urban, socialist, Jewish women be attempting to assimilate in a communist-inspired work on the oppression of African Americans, even without the actual participation of African American dancers? What Manning misses is the emotional impact of racial solidarity in the left-wing tradition and thus the background of communist culture taken seriously. Unlike the CP-USA, "blackface did not engender a single interracial political working class alliance," says Rogin. But he adds, "The Socialist and Communist movements of Central and Eastern Europe constituted the major political effort to overcome nationalist xenophobia and incorporate separate peoples into a single political community."[40] The overwhelming majority of "white" modern dancers came from this Central and Eastern European background, making it likely that they shared this outlook.

Radical modern dancers were not engaged in immigrant Americanization because modern dance was not a "popular" form. If anything, these dancers raised the specter of Eastern and Central European Marxism. Clearly, one problem is that Rogin's thesis about popular culture is based on a comparatist perspective: "The Jewish/black alliance worked better for American Jewish assimilation than did the Jewish/worker alliance for European Jewish cosmopolitanism."[41] The terms of this comparison do not include socialist Jews of European origin in America whose concern was not social climbing and assimilation but radical politics and social change. Rogin is also not alone in describing minstrelsy as a male activity: "white over black parallels man over woman . . . and capitalist over worker."[42] Is the Jewishness of the dancing female socialist sufficient to transform both her gender and her class? In other terms, is Jewish identity sufficient to turn a worker into a capitalist, a woman into a man? Is Tamiris a Jolson? Is the Federal Dance Project in New York interchangeable with Hollywood?

Radical modern dance as a metaphor for minstrelsy raises the question of the ethics of cultural cross-dressing in thirties dance performance. However out of date it would appear by today's standards, it served a progressive purpose then. We do not need to adopt a modernist view on the timelessness of art to reject it as a contemporary option; this is a part of the past that is not usable. However, as Ramsay Burt has argued in *Alien Bodies*, there are qualities of affinity and autohypnotic identification in modern dances of the thirties and forties. "What is at issue here," Burt writes, "is not the act of appropriation . . . but the underlying ethics of the act."[43] The "convention that enabled the Euro-American body to circulate identities marked as culturally other" was not a convention at all in the context of left-wing dance. Cultural cross-dressing was grounded in the ethos of class-consciousness, a place where identities meet. Although the strategy of cultural cross-dressing, the hybrid, or the composite is inappropriate to the present-day fight against racism, it demonstrated respect for difference without leading to differential racism in the thirties.

Class Breakdown

Jane Dudley choreographed *Harmonica Breakdown* for herself between 1938 and 1941 to a plaintive harmonica, vocal, and washboard composition composed and recorded by Sonny Terry. The *Oxford English Dictionary* cites the following meanings for "breakdown": "a ruinous downfall, a collapse; a fracture or dislocation of machinery resulting in a stoppage; a dance in the peculiar style of the negroes." These definitions wed psychological distress to labor and race, but they also refer to minstrelsy: "the peculiar style of the negroes."

Dudley has said that the danced character was inspired by a scene in Leo Hurwitz's *Native Land*, a film that develops a powerful correlation between racism and antilabor forces in American culture:

A group of sharecroppers had a meeting, and there was this absolutely beautiful, tall, skinny black man with hollow cheeks and huge, sad eyes. In the film, he came out of the woods as a white vigilante hit him in the back from behind. Shot in the leg, leaning up against a bank of trees, he couldn't move. A white sharecropper came to his rescue, and together they started down this long dusty road, as the vigilante stepped out with a shotgun and shot him again. He fell forward into the dusty road. The image of that man was one of the qualities I used.[44]

Figure 25: The sharecropper in Leo Hurwitz's film Native Land. *(The Museum of Modern Art Stills Archive.)*

The reference here is to the "Two Men Dead in Arkansas" sequence of *Native Land*. What Dudley doesn't mention is that the white sharecropper is also shot, and dies hanging on a barbed-wire fence. One moment of the dance seems to mime the shot in the back, but the dancing figure does not die as in the film: the dancer survives and perseveres. She strides from place to place on the stage in a way that makes her appear tied down to it in an attempt to escape humiliation and wounding. "This 'gotta keep on going,'" Dudley explained, "was like the effort that just living might mean to black people."[45]

The specificity of the image rendered it problematic to proponents of modernist universalism. Although John Martin praised the dance as beautiful, he also categorized it as "grotesque," "colloquial, even vulgar."[46] These comments mirror negative remarks about minstrelsy itself. At the same time, one cannot help but wonder whether universalism was precisely the desired, and missed, effect. Lois Balcom, reviewing the New York premiere in 1941 for *Dance Observer,* noted that "*Harmonica Breakdown* was notoriously humorous throughout."[47] Dudley acknowledged the veracity of this report: "People

Figure 26: Jane Dudley in Harmonica Breakdown. *Photo: Barbara Morgan. (Barbara Morgan Archives, Hastings-on-Hudson, N.Y.)*

often laughed at *Harmonica,* which I never danced in any way for comic effect. I was always surprised by that."[48] The vocabulary is resolutely modern, but unconventionally so. The contraction is broken down into a series of rhythmic microimpulses. The apparent comicalness of the figure at the time of the solo's first performances is hard to come to terms with, since Balcom also notes no "recognizable gestures nor the hints of burlesque." Dudley clearly did not place herself in any literal or mimetic relation to her material:

FRANKO: In your video about *Harmonica Breakdown,* too, you described yourself dancing the role as "in defiance of the white man, although I am white."

DUDLEY: Yes that's right.

FRANKO: So you staged yourself as black in some way in *Harmonica Breakdown?*

DUDLEY: It wasn't really the dance of a black woman for me. I don't know what to say about that. Of course, it came so closely out of the music of Sonny Terry.

FRANKO: *Time Is Money* could be danced by a male or a female.

DUDLEY: Originally, it was a solo of mine. I think it's much stronger as a role for a black man.

FRANKO: But *Harmonica* could not be danced by a man.

DUDLEY: Probably not. I think it would lose its flavor. In *Harmonica Breakdown* I may have felt that I was almost like a black man, I'm not sure, but I thought of it as the travail and effort of living, and it was built straight out of the music. So whatever inner line I worked on came as a result of the structure of the music.[49]

Dudley makes two interesting remarks here. One is that she in defiance of the white man although she is white. The second is that as a white woman she may have felt she was a black man (evoking the image from Hurwitz's film). These are crux statements on the figurability of the solo. But in neither case is Dudley occupying a "concrete" subject position.

This conception of her performance is faithful to the music. Dudley described Terry's voice as "a distortion where you never really picked up the words." What we have here is a psychological exploration of cultural cross-dressing signaled by the shadow of gender instability. Dudley combined the double sense of breakdown as dance with psychological and physical breakdown in words. What may also be breaking down in the solo—in the same sense as the contraction is broken down or Terry's words are broken down—is class as a viable entity. There is a terrible violence behind this breakdown, though it is distanced by the act of dancing. But the dancing itself occurs in montage structure because images of slavery emerge. Although montage is not as structurally obvious as in *Time Is Money*, it still regulates the dissemination of images in *Harmonica Breakdown*.

Dudley used the contraction—a breath originating in the pelvis and lower back rendering concave the upper and lower spine—to suggest the experience of psychic and physical collapse. Opposed to this collapse was the walk, which served to separate one image from the other. What is shown in a series of montaged moments are different physical states, which break down a body resisting them with enormous tension. For example, there is the trembling dynamic of the contraction, mirrored by the shivering foot: "In one section where I'm hunched, standing on one leg, I scratch the leg like an old hound dog with his tail between his legs, a skinny, old bony hound dog."[50] There is also the trembling of the legs with the two fists clasped together: "A whole section was built on defiance, like a cakewalk, as though I spit on the person over my shoulder, as though I snapped my finger at him."[51] The cakewalk collides with the image from *Native Land* of being shot in the back. In the end, "I remember going

down to the floor, and the feeling was, 'I just don't know. I can't figure life out'—that sort of feeling, not despair, but resignation, I guess."⁵²

Figure 27: Jane Dudley in Harmonica Breakdown. *Photo: Barbara Morgan. (Barbara Morgan Archives, Hastings-on-Hudson, N.Y.)*

Harmonica Breakdown was performed by a radical white middle-class woman and presents strong images of racial oppression, notably of slavery. It suggests that class could be understood as a montage or composite representation of ethnic and sexual identities, a kind of class vernacular. This feels particularly true of the run in place toward the end of the solo, which has a characteristic quality that can nonetheless not be pinned to any ethnicity. It projects retreat and resourcefulness, avid energy and uncertainty, space without home. In this passage, Dudley touches on a popular energy that escapes narrow definition. *Harmonica Breakdown* suggests that by the late thirties the danced representation of class was accruing modernist procedures: it aspired to subsume characteristic particularities beneath one "transcendent" subject position, not that of any recognizable individual. It attempted to capture a popular sublime through montage. Yet it also suggests a crisis in the representation of the proletarian body. The referent of minstrelsy was unavoidable and was freighted with a different working-class performance tradition.

The adaptation of a white middle-class dancer's body to attitudes and gestures of working-class black (and possibly male) identity does suggest some relation to the operations of minstrelsy. If Dudley does not impersonate the black male's image from Hurwitz's film, she does locate working-class identity between a white female body and a black male's voice and physicality. The conflicting motifs of bringing together (harmonica) and falling apart (breakdown) by dancing (*breakdown*'s other sense), implicit in the dance's title, inform the composite. They further suggest that suffering and adversity eat away at gender, leaving a sexually undetermined core of a person. Yet the problem for radical modern dance was the loss of the will to specificity with which it had started.

Cultural cross-dressing on the concert stage in the late thirties and early forties created a collage similar to Paul Robeson's in *Ballad for Americans*. It reminds us that class was a creative and formal rather than a naturalistic construct. The compositional tendencies of modern dance to allude to, compress, and overdetermine meaning provided the aesthetic school for a dance about class. As in any dance class, danced *class* was a cultural location where movements could be imitated and interiorized in a visual and auditory montage, a syntax of layered identities. The "work" of class in modern movement encompassed the internal hailing or interpellation of one ethnic and/or gendered identity by another. But this interpellation was encoded on the stage rather than between the stage and the audience. Spectatorship was becoming more mediated, indicating that class itself was no longer unequivocally recognizable. This is not to say that class now presupposed homogeneity, but rather to stress that the performative construct of class precluded any mandate to represent ethnicity or gender as self-sufficient units of identity. Evaluating *Harmonica Breakdown* solely in the light of current political agendas risks missing the original political intent, an intent not contained autonomously in the aesthetic "object" as it might be reconstructed, but constructed of its own historical logic.

Part II   **Genre and Class**

Chapter 5 The Ballet-versus-Modern Wars as Ideology

> "Is a Rockette a little rock? Or, is it a little rocket? Is it
> *little?* . . . Later: Someone has just told me that a Rockette is a
> little Rockefeller."
> James Waring

The apparently agonistic task of the most prominent dance critics of the thirties was to establish modern dance and ballet as legitimate theatrical genres. Although forms of ethnic dance were classed with modernism, hoofers were generally absent from serious critical discussion. This chapter explores the unacknowledged triangulation of genres with respect to the ballet-versus-modern wars. The aesthetic ideologies of mainstream dance criticism and theory in the 1930s were represented by the writings of Lincoln Kirstein, the philanthropic promoter of American ballet dancing as popular spectacle, and John Martin, the journalist who championed modern dance and theorized metakinesis. Their ballet-versus-modern wars have been bequeathed to posterity as representative of authentic ideological strife in dance history. This chapter deconstructs the meaning of these wars, and thus clears a space for more ample discussion of the chorus dancer.

The ballet-versus-modern wars were an ideological phenomenon (in the derogatory sense) in that they camouflaged both the more meaningful tensions within the modern dance field and the "impossible" bond between high modernist and show dancing.[1] Chorines become disavowed models for ballet as a commercial project and modern dance as a critical project. Themselves displaced, they also serve to displace. The chorine is the shadowy supplement of art dance. I understand the supplement to be an element which, although structurally absent from a discourse, participates nonetheless at its defining core.

My analysis turns on the way Kirstein manipulates notions of the popular, and Martin notions of abstraction. Kirstein's project of an American ballet promotes a popular entertainment medium to a high art status while maintaining the forms of classical ballet. Martin critiques the political motivation of radical modern dance for its use of "abstraction," distancing it thereby from the sources of experience that animate nonacademic dance. Such polemics and their attendant critiques occur in passages of their writing where the ideological stakes are high. Although these are not wholly typical of the critics in question, they are noteworthy for the particular critical moves that negatively materialize the figure of the chorus dancer. The texts are taken from Kirstein's polemics on ballet, and Martin's reception of a work by leading modern dance choreographer Anna Sokolow.

Americanizing Ballet

While radical modern dance tried to address the masses during the 1930s, classical ballet in America also sought a broad popular base. Self-ordained apologist and well-endowed patron of the new American ballet Lincoln Kirstein competed with an influential leftist culture for the idea of a "mass audience."[2] Refusing to imagine his desired spectators as snobbish or elite, Kirstein hypothesized that the average American consumer of popular culture could become a balletomane. If only ballet could be made to reflect the clichéd content of movies and newspapers, everyday folk would want to see it. The Russian ballet then dominated American touring circuits, and the flamboyant Russian style was associated with ballet art in the American mind. Kirstein denounced the Russian ballet hegemony vigorously as "the Great Conspiracy" that robbed his American ballet project of its own rightful audience. In polemicizing homegrown ballet versus foreign imports, Kirstein focused on the necessity to eradicate a certain kind of ballet, viewed by a certain kind of public, and performed by certain kinds of dancers. His overarching argument was to retain the integrity of "international theatrical dancing"—the four-hundred-year-old classical pedagogy of dance technique. The ballet idea for Kirstein was trans-historical and "absolute." He not only asserted that ballet was a timeless, al-though still evolving, training method for theatrical movement, but also pro-jected that ballet was capable of absorbing and abstracting elements foreign to its own basic sources, such as movements from non-European cultures as well as themes or musics not associated with ballet history. Retaining its integrity, ballet assimilated elements foreign to its own European balletic logic.[3]

Although Kirstein salvaged American ballet's social relevance, its technical adaptability, and its modernism, he was tied above all to a classical *form*, and was committed to argue that the technical basis of that form could be adapted to fit unusual content. Thus the importance in Kirstein's mind of "popular vaudeville, revue-dance, and popular jazz or swing music" for the develop-ment of American ballet.[4] These styles could be sufficiently abstracted by the classical form to fashion an aesthetically acceptable if ersatz popular culture. Since the subject matter of American ballet was to be drawn from popular cul-ture, the forms of elegance and personality associated with dance classicism would have to be modified. Kirstein called this modification "grafting."

The presumed affinity of classical ballet for American popular perform-ance culture is not a purely conjectural construct on Kirstein's part. Ballet in America has a history connecting it with popular culture. In the Ziegfeld film *Glorifying the American Girl* (1929), chorus girl Gloria Hughes (Mary Eaton) auditions for the Follies using the outdated shuffling numbers she learned from her aging vaudeville partner. Fearing rejection, she pleads with the re-hearsal director to show what she can "really do." Given another chance, she performs an impromptu ballet variation in pointe shoes which succeeds in landing her a starring role in the Follies. As I interpret this segment, classical ballet was a way of moving the chorus girl never studied, but rather discovered as a native resource in herself. Classical ballet, in more general terms, belonged to the chorus girl's mythical cultural capital. The permeability between ballet and show dance testified to by this myth lent credibility to Kirstein's project for an indigenous American ballet. Yet, in his writing, he presents it as an idea without historical precedent.

One can point to other precedents for this cultural affinity. The balletic choreographic tradition of the Follies was linked to popular ballets of the late nineteenth century such as *The Black Crook* (1866) just as "nineteenth-century ballet spectacles had engendered the image of the American chorus girl."[5] The chorus girl was a figure of popular American culture linked to the call girl, but also to the "ballet girl." Behind the American ballet dancer stood Lydia Thomp-son's British Blonds, the Gibson Girls, the Tiller Girls—all of whom, like Anna Pavlova, toured the States—not to mention the Ziegfeld Follies, which began in

Figure 28: A 1931 Ziegfeld Follies production number in which pointe shoes, the hallmarks of classical ballet, are combined with feather boas, the hallmarks of burlesque. (White Studio. Billy Rose Theatre Collection, New York Public Library for the Performing Arts at Lincoln Center, Astor, Lenox, and Tilden Foundations.)

New York in 1907. There is also a high art connection to the Follies—Michael Fokine, one of Diaghilev's Ballets Russes choreographers who settled in America in 1919. Fokine's first commission in the new world was to choreograph the musical *Aphrodite*. In 1922, Fokine contributed two numbers to the Ziegfeld Follies.[6] Pointe shoes and feathers are trappings of *The Dying Swan*, his legendary 1905 solo for Anna Pavlova, as well as of the Follies soft-focus girlie spectacle of the early thirties. During the 1930s, Kirstein's ultimate protégé, George Balanchine, devised choreography in New York for the Ziegfeld Follies of 1936 and in Hollywood for the film *Goldwyn Follies* (1938), as well as for Broadway musicals. Kirstein does not emphasize these facts, looking instead on commercial work by European choreographers in American theater as a mild dilution of their authentic values. What he never calls into question, however, is the cultural continuity of practices underpinning this conjuncture. More is at issue here than the locations of display. These, it seems, were fairly loose; they permitted Martha Graham and Harald Kreutzberg to present modern dance at the gala opening of Radio City Music Hall in 1932. The historical interconnection of classical ballet and commercial theater dance, however, was something entirely different: it testifies to a collusion not only of occasions and locations but also of practices—both technical and thematic—with a settled historical basis in American performance. Classical ballet had existed in American musical theater since the late nineteenth century. The first permanent American ballet company was the Radio City Music Hall Company established in 1932 as an adjunct to the Rockettes.[7] Ballet modernism in the European tradition of Kazian Goleizovsky, Vaslav Nijinsky, and Bronislava Nijinska was a latecomer to American theaters. Balanchine's first independent concert presentation, at which *Serenade* premiered, was in 1935.[8] In his attempt to invent American ballet in the thirties, Kirstein overlooked the fact that it had already been invented. His mission actually was to institutionalize it.

The Goldwyn Follies provides a miniature allegory of what Kirstein was after. A European film producer (Adolphe Menjou) overhears a typical American girl (Helen Jepson) accuse his work of artificiality. Realizing that she is a natural taste arbiter, he hires her to advise him on what the American public really wants. In one episode, they sit in a darkened theater and sound stage watching the filming of Balanchine's choreography for *Romeo and Juliet*. The American girl complains that Romeo and Juliet should be married and live happily ever after. Menjou immediately requests the proper changes. In the choreography itself, the Capulets and the Montagues are all women, but are represented by different dance styles: ballet and show dance. Each group performs a short sequence of choreography and is then supplanted by the other. While this stylistic difference seems to be motivated by a conflict between the two families, it also works visually as a counterpoint between the classical and the modern, the old and the new. These different styles of dance are also protagonists. The curtain opens on what looks like a tenement: laundry hangs from clotheslines extended from building to building over the stage. But when the laundry is brusquely drawn in, a small Italian village is evoked. Similarly, the dancers are dressed in modern attire until the love duet when the two soloists appear in pseudo-Renaissance garb. The rewritten ending shows show dancers and ballet dancers together, bumping, grinding, and pirouetting in modern dress as the laundry lines return. What this choreographic sequence demonstrates is not only the necessity of updating classical ballet to commercial show dance standards, but also the ease and facility with which this can be accomplished. The American public wants them to live happily ever after.

The connection between commercial theater and classical ballet in American culture remains, nonetheless, implicit in Kirstein's argument; it was the unspoken foundation for his recourse to American popular culture in the creation of new ballets. Classical American dancing needed, in Kirstein's view, to

Figure 29: The Rockettes as pajamaed workers (1936). The photo legend reads: "Luncheon: the girls eat their meals in the theatre cafeteria—in pajamas if they wish. Here are Betty Sasscier, Ruth Sproule, and Dorothea Frank over their coffee cups." (Dance Collection, New York Public Library for the Performing Arts at Lincoln Center, Astor, Lenox, and Tilden Foundations.)

display American character, and it could develop this through what he called "American character dancing" as represented by "vaudeville or musical-comedy" as well as ballroom dancing.[9] These dancing images were widely disseminated in Hollywood films, where Kirstein found another element of national character assimilable to dance classicism—the dancer's personality, or personal style: "Our style springs from the personal atmosphere of recognizable American types as exemplified by the behavior of movie stars like Ginger Rogers, Carole Lombard, or the late Jean Harlow" (201). More precisely, Kirstein imagined these celebrities as able to "establish a direct connection, approaching personal intimacy, or its cinematic equivalent, with their audiences." The example that came first to his mind in "Blast at Ballet" was that of Follies performer Helen Morgan, "perched on her piano" (201).

Initially the exorcism of foreign influence from national ballet venues was more urgent to Kirstein's project than his rivalry with another homegrown theatrical movement: modern dance. But despite the time and energy he spent attacking European ballet imports, no one did more than Kirstein to popularize the idea of an ideological schism between classical ballet and modern dance. Given the situation just outlined, he did this for reasons as much of political expediency as of aesthetic investment. "Modern dance," he wrote "was a radical revolt from" classical theatrical dancing, "so violent at its outset that the base was rootless" (254). For Kirstein, this meant that modern dance disqualified itself as legitimate theater. To deny theatrical legitimacy to modern dance masked the historical continuity between ballet and American popular culture, one in which ballet was subservient to the popular, rather than the other way around. It masked, in other terms, the low culture status of American classical ballet. Kirstein diverted attention from the "commercial" status of dance forms to issues of their legitimacy, arguing on this basis modern dance's absence of theatricality; without theatricality, no legitimacy. Although frequently applied to Martha Graham, this flawed argument was the set piece of his public debate with the dance critic of the *New York Times,* John Martin. Martin's key term in this context was not "theater," as Kirstein insisted, but rather "spectacle." Martin attributed the qualities of spectacle to ballet and the qualities of ritual to modern dance.[10] The spectacle implies personal attendance at impersonal, visual, "historical" events that represent the decline of ritual and festival *communitas* in human experience. Although Martin did not fully develop the ramifications of his critique of spectacle on behalf of modern dance in either anthropological or political economy terms, such a critique was implicit in his critical vantage point.[11]

Strange American Funeral

Unlike Kirstein, who had the independent means to be a patron of ballet, Martin was a professional dance critic, the first on the staff of the *New York Times.* From his watchtower, his institutional position as critic of a great metropolitan newspaper, Martin willingly (perhaps haphazardly) submitted himself to a series of personal experiments. He attended modern dance concerts, allowing the images he saw there to assail his mind and senses, developing in tandem with his visual and visceral perceptions a quasi-theoretical evaluation of what was happening with respect to what *might* have happened, what *could* have happened, perhaps even what *should* have happened. For all that, he is also a witness reporting that something *did* happen, documenting the historical density of sounds and bodies in motion together with his own presence at these historical events.

Martin's lack of enthusiasm for the "spectacular" aspects of classical ballet and his constant emphasis on the emotion modern dance can transmit cause his writing to appear aligned with the left. The privileging of content over form is implicit in his repeated insistence on "direct emotional expression" as the subject matter and method of modern dance, but by underlining the modernism of a fundamentally political and emotional form, Martin placed modern dance in a high art context. Kirstein, on the other hand, despite the traditionally high art sources of classical ballet, positioned American ballet as "low" by reinforcing its permeability with popular culture. My point is to show not only how unstable were the categories of legitimate and illegitimate—high and low—in American performance culture during the Depression, but also how the ballet-versus-modern debate is, in fact, a screen for a dual critical practice of modernism.[12]

Left-wing dance critic Edna Ocko also evoked emotion as content to explain differences between formal classical and the new modern dancing: "Notice how a decaying class of society, with nothing fresh and significant to say, encourages the creation of purely *formal* art, bereft of great feelings, incapable of stirring profound emotions. . . . On the other hand, the coming of age of a new class, sensing its potential strength, interested in expressing *its* ideas, determined to organize human feelings around its purposes, creates an art work rich in *content*, overflowing with human experience and understanding."[13] Equating "human feelings" with content, as Ocko did, is a direct result of the form-versus-content debate, one of the variants of which was the ballet-versus-modern debate. One consequence of this rhetoric, however, is that content was generally associated with the particular and form with the universal. Emotion tended to be located with content and abstraction with form. Furthermore, following this logic, emotion was the enemy of form.

What must be understood further, however, is that radical performance practice used emotion as a conduit for, rather than a vessel of, content. Emotion was neither unduly subjectified nor objectified, but rather *transmitted*. It moved *between* people and thus was inappropriately anchored exclusively in either form or content. Without this interactive movement, the Left itself considered emotion indulgent and moribund, labeling it "bourgeois emotionalism," a term designating self-indulgent feelings that circulated only *inside* the individual, rather than from the individual to the social and back. In the same address, Ocko remarked, "It is this faith, that true art can organize human feelings and emotions around profound social questions, that has brought forward a new trend in modern dance today."[14] Ocko proposed that the world could be reorganized by dances that "organize human feeling and emotions." Elsewhere she called revolutionary dances "emotional crystallizations."[15] Martin might have agreed with her, except for the political context within which she placed emotion.

Martin's most sustained attack on radical modern dance occurred on the

occasion of the premiere of Anna Sokolow's *Strange American Funeral* (1935). Unable to accuse Sokolow of a lack of professionalism but clearly opposed to the choreographer's politics, Martin resorted to a theoretical argument impugning her decision to set the dance to a poem. His criticism focuses on the supposed incommensurabiltity of the poem as verbal artifact with the dance as nonverbal artifact. His argument bears examination because it sets down certain strictures about what dance can and cannot do, and raises the issue of abstraction as a fault of radical dance.

Martin's review of *Strange American Funeral* contains what is perhaps the most hard-bitten and transparent statement on the incommensurability of dance and language in the twentieth century:

> The great gulf that yawns between speech and movement is not easily bridged, for speech is essentially the means for expressing intellectualized experience, while movement is the more elemental stuff of the unintellectualized. The medium of words makes possible symbols of great economy, abstractions and generalizations; movement, being the direct externalization of emotional experience without the benefit of any rarefying processes, is extremely limited in the range of its symbolism and utterly incapable of abstraction and generalization.[16]

Strange American Funeral provides a rare occasion in which Martin's philosophical concepts on dance are actively applied in his criticism. Not only are his critical tenets all exposed, but they are applied to one of the most celebrated of left-wing choreographic works of the thirties.[17] Sokolow's choreography was set to Michael Gold's poem about an employee's death in a steel mill.[18] Jan Clepak was the victim of an industrial accident—"a worker who was caught in a flood of molten ore—whose flesh and blood turned to steel."[19] Although the choreography of *Strange American Funeral* is lost, critical accounts indicate that Sokolow eschewed realism for a montage of images concerning life and death in relation to metallization and humanity. Martin's review indicates that the choreography took a variety of standpoints in time and space. As in Gold's poem "Strange Funeral in Braddock," Clepak appears and reappears in flashbacks. Clearly Sokolow relied in this work on the poetic rather than narrative dimensions of dance composition, one important element of which was the choreographic rendering of a change from flesh and blood to steel. Muriel Rukeyser's review in *New Theatre* (July 1935) indicated that the motif of metallized bodies was a recurrent image: "The solid steel block of dancers, locked at the elbows, coming heavily downstage, fixed the meaning of the dance. Breaking and shifting to dance the steel-puddler, Jan Clepak, who is buried in his trough, and resolving again to steel, breaking to dance spring in Pennsylvania and the resolution made at Clepak's grave, and becoming steel again, they contributed to an effective and popular success."[20] Because the text was recited in performance (it had already been set to music by Elie Siegmeister), Sokolow's choreography did not meet Martin's criterion for modern dance as "the direct externalization of emotional experience." Martin accused Sokolow of confusing danced content with linguistic abstraction. In reality, his objection was to the contextualization and social situatedness of her emotion: "It was evident," Martin wrote, "that Miss Sokolow had been deeply moved by the poem. Many individual passages of her composition were superb not only in their integrity of feeling but in their boldness of imagination. But the dance

Genre
and Class
116

as a whole was inchoate and pointless."[21] Emotion and abstraction are opposed in Martin's thinking because emotion is direct and unmediated whereas abstraction is formal and symbolic.[22] Sokolow's emotion in *Strange American Funeral* was mediated by her social surroundings and thus contravened Martin's requirement that the particular in art be so by virtue of its origin in the private. Accusing Sokolow of abstraction for rendering emotion social seems terminologically perverse except for the fact that the onus of the critique was placed on the articulation of poetic language during the dance. This choice of pretext for criticism was an ideological smoke screen.

Martin wrote another essay on Sokolow and modern dance in 1939. Here, the radical choreographer is introduced in exemplary terms: "Of all the dancers who have associated themselves with the political Left, none has made clearer his intentions as an artist than Anna Sokolow."[23] In recognizing Sokolow as an exemplar of a people's dance art, however, Martin defines radical dance as the heir to nineteenth-century romanticism, which is "nothing more nor less, indeed, in its historical origins, than a people's art."[24] Martin posits three criteria of romantic art that make it also a people's art: "the movement must be vernacular movement . . . the subject matter must be free in its imaginative range . . . it must be entirely innocent of arbitrary formalism."[25] By imaginative range, Martin means "a freeing of the passions to re-experience or to enjoy synthetically high moments of feeling or excitement."[26] Martin does not ascribe these characteristics to Sokolow alone: "The entire modern dance, indeed, is perhaps the most striking example of true romanticism in our time, and Miss Sokolow's approach is only a slightly more 'class conscious' aspect of it. To look at the essential character of romance in its historic beginnings must give to the modern dance a clear notion of its own antiquity, its basic logic, and, above all, its future methods of procedure."[27] Likening a "people's art"—that is, an art for and about the proletarian masses—to romanticism is a way to evacuate the historical specificity of radical modern dance, as well as to blur distinctions between modernism and radicalism (or bourgeois and revolutionary dance). Martin gives Sokolow a leading place in the modern dance movement at the price of a theory that depoliticizes her dances. This theory has the particular advantage of reinforcing Martin's earlier position on abstraction as inimical to emotional expression: "The sole function of form in a simple and natural art of this sort is to insure that the material makes sense. Obviously this is more difficult than to build a synthetic makeshift to titillate the esthete, for it demands roots in life. . . . The spoken word, that final admission of failure, cannot illuminate movement, it can only render it unnecessary."[28]

In a 1938 essay on dance and abstraction, Martin reintegrates the necessity for an abstraction consonant with dance modernism. He gives two alternative definitions of abstraction in dance. The first "is that approach to the dance which puts aside all dramatic and literary program, and deals exclusively in terms of movement, without what is generally referred to as meaning."[29] As an example of this kind of abstraction—one totally devoid of "dramatic program," but also of "social content"—Martin cites the Rockettes: "as complete abstraction as it is possible for the human body to attain."[30] But he also speaks of the ability of dance to convey "emotional experience" as abstraction: "It [dance] is the medium for conveying those concepts which are still too deeply rooted in emotional experience to be objectified in factual [read: linguistic] terms."[31] Using music as an example, Martin asserts that "we are inclined to demand an elevated impersonality of emotion, and from the dancer we have every reason to ask the same. . . . Without this process of abstraction he is bound to be unintelligible." Through the issue of movement's intelligibility, Martin posits the necessity for abstraction in dance. If one compares the 1939 article on romanticism with the 1938 article on abstraction, one notes that their concerns converge around this concept. Of a people's art, Martin wrote: "Movement which is readily communicative to all men must be essentially that which all men employ in their own day-by-day living. If it is heightened beyond the ability of all men to perform, as it must be for purposes of art to make it more vivid, it must still remain emotionally recognizable. When it is altered beyond this point, either by deliberate manipulation or by unconscious mechanicalization, it is dead material."[32] In the article on abstraction, however, intelligibility is removed from day-by-day terms because the emotional experience of modern dance cannot be "objectified in factual terms."[33] In the context of this argument, "factual" is glossed as "literal" as well as "literary" and associated with discursive rather than movement practices. Clearly, Martin is balancing opposite conceptions of abstraction: as universalized meaning and as pure form. This tension is not resolved by recourse to a theory of the archetype. Abstraction is a theoretical escape hatch for Martin, one that brings him to the brink of paradox.

Let us return for a moment to Martin's review of Sokolow's *Strange American Funeral*. What is "elevated impersonality of emotion" if not "a symbol of great economy"? Such a symbol, however, was what Martin reproached Sokolow for essaying in *Strange American Funeral*. Rather than focus on the symbol, however, he focused on Gold's poem as purveyor of symbols in contrast to which movement was "the *direct* externalization of emotional experience."[34] The "rarefying process" Martin denied Sokolow's choreography in the review is difficult to distinguish from the universalization of the particular Martin allows modern dance in general. In a dance of social significance that makes no attempt to abstract its subject matter beyond avoiding literalism, Martin

proclaims that "dance is utterly incapable of abstraction and generalization." In a dance, that of the Rockettes, that proposes the endless circulation of capital as sex, Martin sees "complete abstraction," and for other modern dance that feigns to avoid the ideological split between capital and labor, Martin sees that "the process of abstraction" ensures intelligibility through "elevated impersonality." He defends the primacy of feeling in the 1930s, but cuts feeling off from any politics.

Figure 31: The Rockettes Chorus Line in the 1930s. (Dance Collection, New York Public Library for the Performing Arts at Lincoln Center, Astor, Lenox, and Tilden Foundations.)

Filling Station

The most successful realization of Kirstein's theory of Americanized ballet was Lew Christensen's *Filling Station* (1938).[35] The main character is ostensibly proletarian, because the ballet, according to Kirstein, was "about work, today." "It couldn't be put in a factory," he adds, "on an open road or on a farm, because

Figure 32: Ballet wrapped in transparent mass
culture. Lew Christensen as Mac in Kirstein/
Christensen's Filling Station (1938). The
worker's pose is drawn from agitprop while
the transparent costume indicates a homoerotic aesthetic. Photograph by George Platt
Lynes. (Courtesy of the photographer's estate.)

we didn't have enough dancers to suggest a mass of workers" (262). Mac, the Filling Station Attendant, was nevertheless "the type of self-reliant, agreeable and frank American working-man" (263). Mac's opening variation is virtuosic, signaling, in Kirstein's terms, his "brilliant resourcefulness" as a worker (263). His filling station is then visited by two truck drivers, Roy and Ray, who are presented as "tumblers" and "vaudeville knock-about comedians" (263). They are succeeded by a humdrum bourgeois couple: The Motorist ("a combination of Casper Milquetoast and Mut"), His Wife ("green-blond hair, summer slacks and sinister green celluloid-visor") and their little girl ("a nightmare twin of Shirley Temple or Little Orphan Annie") (263). The Child's toe-work "was indicated as the prize-number of a spoiled child's dancing-class graduation exercises" (263). They are followed by a Rich Girl and a Rich Boy who dance drunk until a gangster holds them up. *Filling Station* was populated by balletic versions of the lower, middle, and upper classes, cartoon-like figures onto all whose movement characteristics classical vocabulary was "grafted."[36] Kirstein opined that *Filling Station* combined "American social humor" with "international theatrical dancing" (265). If classical dance could be so readily grafted onto popular culture figures, many of whom were derived from the funny papers, vaudeville, and the Follies, Kirstein was positioning classical ballet alongside the entertainment industry aesthetic just as modern dance was positioned alongside the labor movement aesthetic.

Given the oppositional relationship between labor and popular culture in the 1930s, however, the labor theme Kirstein foregrounded in *Filling Station* was right wing. Publicity for the ballet shows its lack of connection to any concern for the working class. Although Mac is a worker, he is hardly a militant worker. The program note for the world premiere states that the ballet is "about an ordinary working man who does his job whatever the circumstances."[37] This worker, who could have issued from the pages of a government report on optimal employee disposition, was a *danseur noble* (Lew Christensen). Mac holds the (empty) place of a prince in a poetics of the ordinary. Publicity for the work hedges on this thematic innovation by explaining how the ballet re-exoticizes everyday life: "Some everyday happenings and objects need only be surprised out of their daily context by transformation into terms of the stage to lose their banality, suddenly to become more exotic than India and almost as strange as another planet."[38] This return of the exotic in the ordinary hardly seems to fulfill Kirstein's program of ballet modernism as "living expression of the immediate"[39] able to establish ballet "in the service of the greatest mass public."[40]

Filling Station presented a danced portrayal of the American worker's character as open, frank, and agreeable, and thus unlike foreign working-class elements in urban America. There is an implication, as well, that Mac in his simple elegance must not possess the overintellectualization characteristic of foreign and politicized elements. The denizens of Kirstein's pastoral and industrial landscape "have an unspoiled, American, rather athletic quality that is pleasant."[41] *Filling Station* allowed associations with character dance traditions to introduce class distinctions in a ballet composition (as well they might in almost any classical ballet scenario) but eliminated the ethnic positions which gave class positions meaning. Thus Mac, the worker, could be both familiar and unfamiliar—the secret of his "agreeableness." The worker was a ballet star surrounded by music hall exotics. What *Filling Station* exoticized was class itself as a social issue, submerging its edge in the familiarly humorous references of popular culture as represented in the media. Kirstein's equality of the popular with the exotic is as absurd from the point of view of his stated intentions as is Martin's equality of politically engaged art with abstraction.[42] These improbable whirligigs are moments of truth—rhetorical moments where dance modernism encounters the specter of social engagement.

Strange American Supplement

Both Kirstein and Martin engage in conceptual double binds that erect modernism at the sites of popular and mass culture, respectively. Both saw dance as the process of an abstraction of politics from movement. Both, in short, were ideologues of aesthetic modernism. Kirstein moves ostensibly from high to low, but aestheticizes low as what he considers to be the timeless technical system of ballet classicism, an enduring abstraction of human movement. Martin moves ostensibly from low to high by depersonalizing or privatizing emotion as both universal and direct, and thus acting to remove the social impetus from its manifestations in dancing bodies.

Despite their shared ideological goals, there is only one point at which the arguments of these two critics form a rhetorical tangent: when Martin attributes the qualities of abstraction proper to Kirstein's ballet dancer to the Rockette of Radio City Music Hall. It seems that here Martin confirms, perhaps unwittingly, the hidden ties between ballet and commercial theater. The Rockettes, he claims, personified "complete abstraction": "For something like ten years the Rockettes have been approaching the footlights first of the old Roxy and later of the Radio City Music Hall four or five times a day in phalanx formation performing a series of (roughly speaking) grands battements to thunderous and unquestioning applause. Dramatic program? Social content? Understandableness? Nonsense! As complete abstraction as it is possible for the human body to attain."[43] The culture war between modern dance and classical ballet represented by these two seminal figures is turned on its head by this identification of the Rockettes kickline with aesthetic abstraction. Martin's observation was made in passing and never enshrined in one of his books, but it is a slip that reveals the ballet-versus-modern wars as ideological screen, one of whose long-term effects has been to eradicate radical performance from living memory.

Since neither ballet nor modern were situated unequivocally as "high" or "low," any historically informed comparison between them raises issues of class in relation to performance. Ballet maintained its "high" status by appearing to be "low" (popular), and radical modern dance was perceived as "high" by deprecating the commodifications of popular culture in favor of the working-class audience. Each contained the supplement of the other, a supplementarity within the identity of each genre embodied by the repressed figure of the chorus girl, whose shadowy identity configures her both as ersatz or would-be ballet dancer and as proletarianized entertainment industry worker. Yet she can also be figured forth in the opposite terms. Historically implicated in American ballet, she supports the project of classical dance as popular culture; opposed to high seriousness because of her sexiness (shod feet), she exposes radical modern dance as an elitist projection while herself managing to epitomize aesthetic abstraction. In these ways, the chorus girl was the dangerous supplement of American theatrical dancing.

Chapter 6   Lives of Performers:
News, Sex, and Spectacle Theory

In Chapter 1 I argued that the opening number of *Gold Diggers of 1933*—"We're in the Money"—staged abstract commodity exchange. I turn here to the political ramifications of the film's staging of chorus girls as flesh-and-blood workers. The milieu pictured by the Hollywood film is that of New York theater. Chorus dancing was inseparable from theater (even in celluloid form), and particularly from the revue. But this form of theater had difficulty surviving the Great Depression. Nevertheless, *Pins and Needles* made the film's fantasy of a hit show on the Great Depression a paradoxical reality in 1937.[1] This chapter will proceed under the auspices of a comparison.

Pins and Needles was produced by the Labor Stage, a cultural wing of the International Ladies Garment Workers Union (ILGWU). The show began with amateur talent under the supervision of professionals, among them Harold Rome, Arthur Arent, Marc Blitzstein, Emanuel Eisenberg, Benjamin Zemach, and Gluck Sandor. Initially, no one could audition without a union card, but during the show's four-year run its cast was gradually replaced by professionals. This musical revue, built initially out of the bodies and voices of workers—garment workers rather than chorus girls—moved to a Broadway theater, toured nationally, and became a long-running box-office hit.

Both *Gold Diggers* and *Pins and Needles* employed the Broadway revue format, the first as a play within a film, the second as an actual performative event. Both the film and the show seem aligned as unmilitant views of the Great Depression. Like *Gold Diggers, Pins and Needles* humanized the chorus girls (and boys) as workers. This was done in *Pins and Needles,* however, not by romanticizing their story as workers, but by presenting actual garment workers on stage. Here we see, as in radical modern dance of the early thirties, a transferential body on stage rather than a mediating one.

From Ornament to Spectacle

In my discussion of *Gold Diggers* I shall privilege the critical concept of spectacle. The society of the spectacle, an expression denoting the loss of political agency in post–World War II consumer culture, was prefigured in the culture of the Great Depression by what Siegfried Kracauer identified in 1927 as the mass ornament. Ramsay Burt has written an excellent analysis of Kracauer's essay in the context of dance history in which he shows that Kracauer was imprecise about whether the mass ornament was a precision dancing phenomenon or one of stadium gymnastics. Curiously, in Berkeley's films—particularly *Footlight Parade* (1932)—these two practices coincide in that the patterns viewed from a distance, as in a sports stadium, are performed by the girls themselves for the camera.[2] As Kracauer explained it, the mass ornament submerged all individuality, and remained distant "from the immanent consciousness of those constituting it."[3] The tension between individuality and ornament is often expressed in Berkeley's films by a sequencing of close-ups and long shots, as if to distract us from the dehumanizing force of the pattern seen at a distance.

In backstage musical films, this dichotomy could be seen as that between spectacle and plot. *Gold Diggers of 1933,* a film about the lives of chorus girls, interspersed the ornament's spectacular linearity with cut-throughs into the performers' lives as workers, a strategy that seems suggested by Berkeley's device of the parade of faces. But what I want to examine is the role of the film's narrative in this project of individualizing women who otherwise might only be anonymous mass ornamental performers.

I preface this analysis, however, with a short foray into the place of news in radical theater, which will provide context for the critical notion of spectacle in radical theater of the 1930s. In order for the Left to position class consciousness as mass identity's cultural destination, it had to counter the spectacle of popular culture with performances that were inherently critical of the power of news as an entertainment medium. I propose two examples of this critique in *Newsboy* and *1935,* the latter an early Living Newspaper production of the

Federal Theatre Project. After a brief examination of these two theater works, we shall turn our attention to the chorus girl as depicted in *Gold Diggers of 1933* and the implicit criticism of such representations in 1936 by *Pins and Needles*.

News as Spectacle

To clarify how radical culture positioned popular culture as spectacle, I look first at theater pieces critical of journalism. *Newsboy* (1933), the agitprop play Alfred Saxe directed at the Workers Laboratory Theater, was an early example of news critique. A newsboy on the sidewalk hawking the *Daily News* and the *Mirror* is interrupted by a Voice:

> VOICE: Say, boy, how long you gonna stand there, yellin' your
> guts out under the El because somewhere—
> A MAN: In a hotel—
> A GIRL: In Frisco—
> THE CROWD (in rhythm): A follies girl—shot the brains—out of the old rip—that
> kept her.[4]

The follies girl is the quintessential popular type of tabloid journalism. Neither privileged nor everyday, she negotiates an ambiguous space between the glamorous and the lurid. The Voice contrasts the perennial items on "hold-ups—and divorces" with the unmentioned "seventeen million men and women" who are "starving in mines" and "sweating in mills." Scrambling to retrieve a dime from the ground, the newsboy encounters the smug indifference of a passerby. It becomes apparent that he is one of the seventeen million, the only personalized depiction of which occurs in the sketch of a black man threatened with lynching. The lynching sequence makes specific reference to Angelo Herndon, who is also the subject of the culminating episode in *1935,* and that play's breaking point. At the end of *Newsboy,* people in the street discover and read the *Daily Worker.* Everyone on stage has become radicalized so that what they see and experience in their lives becomes the actual subject of journalism, if the right choice of newspaper is made.

Newsboy focused on news as the commodification of life in the Great Depression by journalistic discourse, and suggested that active intervention in the dissemination of news might shift the balance of power in class struggle. Having posed the initial question to the newsboy about his complicity in the deceptive circulation of news, the Voice returns at the end to exhort him to draw the proper consequences: "Climb to the top of the Empire State Building and blare out the news—Time to revolt!" This agitational charge to the newsboy reflects the degree to which live theater assumed the responsibility not only of communicating alternative views, but also of moving spectators to action. The ethos of radical theater was founded on this belief in theater's ability to transmit to its audience a desire to effect social change rather than to contemplate the theatrical spectacle in a mesmerized state.

1935 avoided agitational address and instead developed the idea of the newspaper into a formal device governing the structure of the play itself.[5] The play characterized news as spectacle and thus prefigured facets of Guy Debord's *Society of the Spectacle.* The spectacle, for Debord, "is not a collection of images, but a social relation among people, mediated by images" (section 4). The "Great American Public" constantly keeps this relation in mind during *1935.* The public's participation as jurors in a mobile juror box suggests its passive yet concerted attention as consumers. By watching the jurors, the audience contemplates itself in a stereotypical form. *1935* portrayed the newspaper's appeal to the public and its ability to hold the public's attention as a symptom of the commodification of life in American culture. At issue here is news as the spectacle. "The real consumer," notes Guy Debord, "becomes a consumer of illusions" (section 47).

Although *1935* was not the most popular or characteristic of the Living Newspapers, it was unique for its consistently formal parody of journalism and its references to the March of Time newsreels. Unlike other Living Newspapers, *1935* steered clear of particular social problems (although like much early radical theater, it gave a large place to the criticism of racism), but for that very reason it was able to be critical of social mores and of news as a discourse that shaped society's perceptions. Production records attest that Hallie Flanagan took a particular interest in the second Living Newspaper offering. Flanagan wrote to Philip Barber and Morris Watson, "I think it is a vivid script. In fact I am surprised that with no continuous story, I am, nevertheless, interested throughout."[6] While the theme of false consciousness was difficult to treat dramatically, it nevertheless allowed for a sinister vision of American culture as laden with trivia. The trivia scenes were short vignettes in which character types were shown for the purpose of a gag. The jury itself was made up of such types: Born Leader, Yes Man, Querulous One, Helping Hand, and Lady. These characters identified themselves by short phrases that typified their point of view, a sort of verbal trivia.

1935 begins on New Year's Eve, 1934, and ends exactly one year later. Between the two celebrations a mosaic of news events is "reported" onstage. Because the Times Square crowd's performance is identical in both framing scenes, the year itself seems to resist the passage of time: the public is alienated from the present moment, which can always be exchanged for another. In this way, time stands still. The "Prop Plot" for these scenes lists "Balloons, Three Whiskey

Figure 33: The New Year's Eve scene of 1935. (National Archives and Records Administration, Washington, D.C.)

Bottles, Noise Makers." These objects of Americana on an otherwise soberly outfitted stage function as reminders of the intermittent trivia scenes encapsulating the banalization of commodity culture. Ultimately, news itself is the commodity whose hold on public attention is powerful yet tenuous. It assures the public's "unanimous indifference."[7] "It is most important," specifies a production note in the script, "that this [New Year's Eve] scene be directed in a stylized manner, stressing the automatic gestures, the absence of realistic emotion and color of the crowd."[8] As the New Year is rung in, the Voice of the Living Newspaper exhorts the numb and passive Times Square crowd: "1935 is here. Well, what are you waiting for? Get going! Make news! (Music) Make news. Bite a dog. Invent a new mousetrap. Win the sweepstakes. Marry an heiress. Divorce a count. Write a crazy song. Catch a big fish. Fight a champion. Swim the channel. Explore the Arctic. Corner the market. Have sextuplets. Make News! Make News!"[9] The

Figure 34: The jury at a ball-game from 1935. (National Archives and Records Administration, Washington, D.C.)

phrase "Make News!" was the ironic inversion of *Newsboy*'s "Time to revolt!" Although exhorted to "make news," the Crowd can only consume it; however, this participation in consumption masquerades as thoughtful reflection and action. "Lived reality," wrote Debord, "is materially invaded by the contemplation of the spectacle while simultaneously absorbing the spectacular order, giving it positive cohesiveness" (section 8). The Great American Public is reduced to contemplation of the life surrounding it as a spectacle. It was doubtless difficult to represent the newspaper's inducement of machine-like indifference in its passive spectators because, in order to make the point in theatrical terms, the potential for energy had to be shown. Flanagan and Morris's run-through notes recommended "more excitement under the stylized gestures." They added: "Think the scene should work toward a greater climax. Like the words of the announcer, 'Make News, etc.'"[10]

The only scene in which this public/jury does show animation is the "Jury Interlude" in which the jurors watch a baseball game. Here, the jurors' roles as spectators are overtly assumed rather than inferred by their general passivity: they participate with abandon in that which appears devoid of social consequence. Watson wrote to Flanagan that "From a director's standpoint, [this scene] is very experimental, for it is necessary that the audience get the illusion of a baseball game being played."[11] Here, in other words, the jurors create the spectacle in a literal theatrical sense, and thus impart some of their human, creative potential.

What Debord says of "the spectacle" could be said here as well of *1935*'s vision of print journalism: "The spectacle presents itself simultaneously as all of society [the entire year 1935], as part of society [the newspaper] and as *instrument of unification* [of the Great American Public that consumes news without interiorizing its consequences]" (section 3).

The Times Square celebrants—the Great American Public—occupy a jury box in other scenes as well, beginning with the trial of Bruno Richard Hauptmann for the kidnapping and murder of the Lindbergh baby. This scene focuses on the trial as a media event ("There's nothing like *justice* for a show!") with its celebrities and media bribes.[12] Everything the public is called upon to ponder and judge is thus presented as already packaged for its consumption. The jury is maneuvered into finding Hauptmann guilty by the media. As the Voice says in the "First Jury Scene": "Only a mere handful will make the news of the day. But the others, the millions who make up this nation, will become the Great American Public of 1935. . . . They read the news. . . . They react to it. . . . We are interested in their opinion."[13] The status of the public as consumer demonstrates how journalism can dissuade from meaningful social participation. Neil Larsen's recent characterization of news is relevant here: "One reads journalistic prose not only to find out 'what really happens,'" writes Larsen, "but more fundamentally to confirm that what happens does not in any way alter what already is."[14] News, in other words, renders class static by reducing it to a popular phenomenon in which the working public spectates a celebrity upper class. The function of news as spectacle is to immobilize the politics of class, to forestall class consciousness. *1935* was a "living" newspaper not only because it acted out the news, but also because it questioned the power of news to "make" anything other than itself.

The Angelo Herndon scene was an exception to this rule in that the issue of racism permitted a content-oriented presentation of injustice. Herndon, a communist organizer, was threatened with a sentence of eighteen years on a Georgia chain gang. In *1935*, the Prosecutor announces that Herndon's trial is "the trial of Lenin, Karl Marx, and Kerensky" as well.[15] Indeed, although Herndon's sentence is specific to American race prejudice, Herndon himself is represented as a worker. He responds to the Prosecutor: "You may succeed in killing one, two, even a score of working class organizers . . . but you cannot kill the working class!"[16] A Negro Prisoner's harrowing description of life on the chain gang recounted against a silhouetted background projection of the chain gang itself brings home the unmitigated cruelty of racism. This scene functions as the climax of *1935*. The other face of banality is social injustice and inhumanity.

After the Herndon scene, the Voice of the Living Newspaper wonders "what the public is thinking." When one jury
member answers "Say, I got an idea," the Voice censures him:
"No ideas, please. Ideas disturb people and make them dis-
satisfied. We don't want to be here all night. You just sit still in silent judgment
while we go ahead and finish off the year. Come on, now, let's go. News! News!
News! . . . the News is made . . . we will now take you to Times Square where
the Great American Public has dropped its cares and forgotten the past as a
New Year approaches. . . . Let's make *Whoopee!*"[17] The jury then "scrambles
out of its jury box and rushes downstage" to reproduce another New Year's Eve
scene. The society of the spectacle requires that time stop, that all events are
reduced to a level of common abstraction. This principle of indifferentiation
guarantees their "unanimous indifference," the fact that as individualists, they
resemble each other.

VOICE OF THE LIVING NEWSPAPER: Why do you have to act like an individualist?
THE LISTLESS ONE: Because I am an *Individualist.*

*Figure 35: The Angelo Herndon scene
from 1935. (National Archives and
Records Administration, Washington,
D.C.)*

Lives of
Performers
131

VOICE OF THE LIVING NEWSPAPER: I thought so. . . . That makes you just like everybody else.[18]

The confusion between individualism and indifferentiation or indifference is epitomized most of all in *1935* by trivia: images of popular, but not mass, culture. Flanagan was enthusiastic about the trivia scenes, noting in her letter to Watson that "The trivia is so amusing that I think it should be built up with many more episodes, such as the grocery boy calling up Jean Harlow, included."[19] The final words of *1935* are those of a Vendor over a loudspeaker: "Peanuts and popcorn!" News, in other words, is an instance of the cheapest commodity fetishism: popular culture both created and distributed by the media.

Simulacrums of Radicalism

Although Living Newspapers challenged news media by offering spectators news while making them critically aware of their positions as theater spectators, they did not explain the fascination of the commodity itself, its power to render the public passive spectators rather than active participants in their own lives. Whether conveyed by print or on film, news might exemplify what Debord called "the pseudo-use of life" (section 49), but its critiques failed to explain the convergence of commodity with spectacle that characterized its particular efficacy. For the power of the image in spectacle we must look instead to the thirties chorus girl of the post-Ziegfeld era, of Radio City Music Hall and Busby Berkeley films. The chorus girl lived the condensation of experience in the image—"life in one stiff jolt," as a character in the film *Ziegfeld Girl* put it, "life running instead of walking. Life at a mile a minute." As a tawdry and glamorous subject of tabloid journalism, she embodies the attractions of news as capital's advertisement, but she also stands for the power of dissemination proper to mass media.

Gold Diggers tells the story of a Broadway musical's folding and then being reinvented. We glimpse the dying show in the first scene as the rehearsal of the large production number "We're in the Money," which is interrupted by the sheriff's office for nonpayment of debts. The police enter and confiscate the dancers' costumes, practically ripping them off their backs. "They close before they open," remarks Trixie (Aline MacMahon), and Fay (Ginger Rogers) responds, "The Depression, dearie." After this aborted dress rehearsal, the show's producer, Barney Hopkins (Ned Sparks) gets the idea for a Depression Follies. The indigent but spirited girls between jobs share a tenement apartment where Hopkins develops his idea with the help of neighboring composer Brad (Dick Powell), who is found composing at his piano across the airshaft.

Hopkins envisions a musical in which the unemployed march as a lachrymose army suggesting a sadly regimented version of Michael Gold's "romance of millions of men and women in the world today": "That's what this show's about—The Depression. . . . Men marching in the rain—jobs—jobs—marching—marching—marching in the rain——and in the background will be Carol—spirit of the Depression—a blue song—no, not a blue song—but a wailing—a wailing—and this woman—this gorgeous woman—singing this number that tears your heart out—the big parade—the big parade of tears—."[20] The big parade materializes in the film's final number as "The Forgotten Man," the title of the show within the film.

Rubin's discussion of the film treats the opening number and closing production numbers and thus focuses exclusively on Berkeley's use of mass ornament. He sums up by saying, "'Remember My Forgotten Man' is one of Hollywood's most hard-hitting political statements of the 1930s."[21] While Rubin's claims about the impact of unemployment on male identity and heterosexual performance are well founded, something is left out of the political reality of the thirties that is required of political resistance: a position on class. But to determine how the film addresses class, we must look beyond the spectacular production numbers to the plot along which they are strung. Only in this way can we ask what "The Forgotten Man" promises to say about the Great Depression, and what it actually delivers.

In the very scene where the idea for the new musical is formulated, its new-found composer, Brad, who supplied the "Forgotten Man" theme on the piano, volunteers money to finance the show, leading to speculation among the cast that he may be a fugitive from justice. Despite the cast's suspicions, Brad becomes increasingly essential to the show's success. When pressed to replace an injured leading man, Brad mysteriously refuses, but then relents and leads the show to success as a performer as well as a composer. This very public performance, however, exposes his true class status as a Boston blue blood. His family, represented by his brother Lawrence (Warren William) and the trustee of his estate, Peabody (Guy Kibbee), embark upon a mission to save Brad from the theater, and from his nascent romance with a chorus girl, Polly. The creation of a new musical on the ruins of the old, a musical in tune with the Great Depression, becomes subsumed to an elaborate subplot that all but displaces this project. Many of the production numbers are justified as rehearsals for the new show. But only the frame scenes of the film—"We're in the Money" and "The Forgotten Man"—actually represent these two performances as events marking an epistemological shift brought about by the Great Depression itself.

Brad's brother Lawrence decides to seduce the chorus girl Polly away from his composer brother in order to abort their marriage. In a case of mistaken identity, however, he woos the wrong chorus girl, Carol (Joan Blondell), and Peabody becomes enamored of Trixie. These two women pick up the role of the chorus in the opening number and expand it in narrative terms. They circulate as capital in three ways: on the stage, in the millionaires' bedrooms, and ultimately in the bargain necessary to make funds flow between wealthy capitalists and Broadway producers. As Patricia Mellencamp notes, "they do not have access, except through sexual wiles, to the 'conditions of production,' particularly financing."[22] The chorus girls exploit the wealthy men for the good of the show.

The plot intricacies of this deception and its romantic entanglements occupy most of the film, and terminate in marriage for all three couples, announced in the wings of the theater just prior to the "Forgotten Man" number. The film is thus about class warfare—blue bloods versus chorus girls—reconfigured as a battle of the sexes, but as Lise Vogel points out, insistence on sexual difference confines women to "a theoretical limbo outside the class structure."[23] The narrative works against the ideals of the show the narrative is designed to support. Perhaps this is inevitable when the "Spirit of the Depression" must be "gorgeous." We shall see that, as Mellencamp also shows, "the film equates marriage and the couple—the happy ending—with capitalism."[24]

The film presents not only an equation of economics with sex but of sex with class struggle, and in this way it also provides a solution. The film thus mirrors the strategy of the new show in that the relation of sex to money and/ or the economy is not displaced, but merely transformed into a bathetic register. Marriage requires that the wealthy capitalists no longer frequent gold diggers for thrills, but actually fall in love with them. The film progresses from selling sex viscerally to selling sex emotionally. The girls become absorbed into capital through marriage.

Two further points with respect to the plot concern the positioning of class in the film. In a restaurant scene in which all three couples are present, Brad's brother Lawrence has a moment alone with Polly in which he locates her in his own class sphere: "I've been watching you. You are so obviously a girl of breeding. . . . You're the sort of girl who is not cheap, not vulgar, not at all like people of the theater. You're the girl my brother should be interested in." This dialogue, overheard by the others, serves to situate the union of Polly and Brad in a sanctified zone whose only other expression is the musical number "Pettin' in the Park." This scene counterbalances "The Forgotten Man" in that it shows upper-class heterosexual relationships at the center of the movie.

At the end of the film, just prior to "The Forgotten Man," Lawrence and Peabody threaten to stop the show. They bring a police officer backstage to annul the marriage between Polly and Brad. This is a duplication of the disruption of "We're in the Money" by the police. But this second disruption fails:

producer Hopkins unmasks the officer as a "ham actor," and the show goes on. This subterfuge on the part of the blue bloods undoes class distinctions, placing the Bradford clan all squarely in show business. Similar to the way such identity reversal can work in baroque theater-within-the-theater, its rollback effect here retroactively disseminates artificiality through all the preceding social relations. It is not by accident that at this moment, the "Forgotten Man" number begins.

The film's story expands the logic of "We're in the Money" into narrative terms. Recall that in that number, chorus girls were walking advertisements for capital, their legs kicking up from under the curved circumference of the giant coins they wear. The song's pig-latin refrain, sung by Rogers's lips in close-up, signals the substitution of capital's actual scarcity with sexual currency. "We're in the Money" all too clearly means not "we have come into money," but rather "we stand in for money." This punning displacement is reinforced by the pseudosecret of a transparently coded language: Rogers sings the song in pig latin, in which the word "oneyme" sounds almost like (it's) "only me." That is, she sounds out capital's relocation in Eros as a purely syntactical and thus quasi-natural reordering: "we're in the money" should be understood, not as the fantasy of sudden riches (the chorus girl's fantasy par excellence), but rather more literally and also more theoretically to mean "we constitute money or physically incorporate money in our own bodies." We are to be found in money and as money, and, if need be, we can become it. Class struggle is actually not a form of division within democracy, but a figure of unity. This amounts to a denial of class.

The capitalists join the chorus girls in the classless netherworld of the theater. Erasing the problem of class, the film signals its own amnesia around the "forgotten man" who is unable to enter the game of sex and money, because he is deprived of power, even theatrical power. Once this happy marriage of labor and capital is forged in the wings, the "Forgotten Man" number can begin. At this point, Joan Blondell appears as a torch-song singer amidst tenement buildings, at whose windows appear solitary women marked by age and ethnicity. Blondell sings:

> Ever since the world began
> A woman's got to have a man.
> Forgetting him you see
> Means you're forgetting me
> Like my forgotten man.

Blondell's sexualized relation to the forgotten man abstracts her from working-class identity. The eroticizing potential of "We're in the Money" is supplanted by the sentimentalizing potential of "Remember My Forgotten Man." *Gold Diggers* focuses on the theme of the Great Depression, but does so to the detriment of a critical consciousness of class. Only when all the film's protagonists have become "performers" and thus have become feminized can the film address the Great Depression through the hit "show." This is the show's condition of possibility and the reason for the necessity of such an intricate narrative to qualify it. *Gold Diggers* is about class distinctions, but everyone in the film only plays at them. When class collapses into love and marriage, the social outside presupposed as reality in the Great Depression evanesces: the world becomes a stage. What must disappear prior to the "social statement" of "Remember My Forgotten Man" is the presence of class as social fact.

From Labor Union to Broadway Revue

After *Gold Diggers* narrated its version of progress from entertainment to socially conscious theater, *Pins and Needles* turned radical theater into entertainment by appropriating the revue format to political satire. The show was made up of a series of sketches that changed over time. "Originally," writes Harry Merton Goldman, "the bulk of material in the sketches was satire about the union officers, the struggles between labor and management, and management and government."[25] Later, it transformed into a topical revue, and was in need of "constant revision." The players of *Pins and Needles* were real-life garment workers (with some professionals in their ranks under false pretenses) whose performance in a successful Broadway musical brought them celebrity. Consequently, the chorus boys and girls of *Pins and Needles* became what the chorus girls of Berkeley's plot pretended not to be in the film but were in real life—stars. Notwithstanding their success, however, the union performers continued to labor as garment workers during the show's run. They performed unglamorous class on the stage primarily through the signs of their Jewish ethnicity until the show's growing financial success induced the producer to anglicize the cast.[26]

In spite of its politics and its initial ethnicity, *Pins and Needles* garnered widespread approbation, including a performance at the White House "where President and Mrs. Roosevelt applauded the players and laughed heartily at the most undiplomatic lines."[27] As one editorial cartoon indicated, a strike scene met with bemused approval, rather than inducing police and journalistic hysteria. Countless newspaper articles described this phenomenon: "Found: something on which capital and labor can agree. It's *Pins and Needles,* the garment workers' revue, which has turned out to be one of the surprise hits of the season. At *Pins and Needles* you find Park Avenue mixing with the Bronx and Flatbush. Wearers

Figure 36 (top): A people's chorus line: Pins and
Needles *choristers dancing before a photo-mural of
historical union leaders (1938).*

Figure 37 (bottom): An editorial cartoon on Pins and
Needles. *The caption reads, "Labor Stage provides
amusement for one of New York City's finest." (*Pins and
Needles *clippings file, Billy Rose Theatre Collection,
New York Public Library for the Performing Arts at
Lincoln Center, Astor, Lenox, and Tilden Foundations.)*

of ermine and tophats mingle with theatregoers who sport the latest creations from the bargain basements. A worker may find his own boss in the seat next to him."[28]

Pins and Needles demonstrated that working-class women could be chorus girls and still remain workers. Hollywood chorus girls were scripted as "gold diggers" resorting to baiting wealthy men, whereas the cast of *Pins and Needles* were "plain, simple, common, ordinary, everyday men and women who work for a living." Garment workers were scripted to "bubble over with energy and good spirits," thanks largely to their union representation.[29] In fact, they could become stars who would never go to Hollywood. These were not, however, the "unspoiled" and "athletic" bodies of young American ballet dancers Denby had seen in *Filling Station,* but Jewish immigrants from Eastern Europe and Italians from southern Italy. When Katherine Dunham worked on the show's choreography, a number of her company members (all professional dancers) performed in it: Talley Beatty, Dorothy Harrison, Alice Sands, and Archie Savage.

One consequence of workers going professional, however, was to compromise the social critique of earlier radical theater. Yet the conciliatory tone of the revue must also be related to the labor policies of its producing organization, the ILGWU. Formed in 1900, the union gained government recognition early in its existence by signing a Protocol of Peace, which stripped its members of the right to strike between 1910 and 1916.[30] The discouragement of militancy is one of the show's effects. The weapons of radical theater have become the tools of the trade: pins and needles.

But *Pins and Needles* presented social awareness as a sexy and humorous alternative to, rather than as an advertisement for, capital. Its showstopper song—"Sing Us a Song with Social Significance"—suggested the possibility of a substitution of values:

> We're tired of moon songs
> Of star and of June songs
> They simply make us nap
> And ditties romantic
> Drive us nearly frantic
> We think they're all full of pap
> Nations are quaking, history's making
> Why sing of stars above?
> While we are waiting, father time is creating
> New things to be singing of.
> Sing us a song with social significance
> All other things are taboo.
> We want a ditty with heat in it

Appealing with feeling and meat in it
Sing us a song with social significance
There's nothing else that will do
It must be packed with social fact
Or we won't love you.[31]

As the show developed and changed with its growing popularity, this song was transferred from a neutral and open space to a set depicting men's and women's washrooms. With its more elaborate production values, "Sing Us a Song" called for a change in precedence between social and sexual relations, framed as a romantic yearning for social relation as a ground of personal interactions including, but not limited to, sexual ones. "Social significance" thus carried a visual promise of heterosexual division and attraction rather than a gender-neutral image of political solidarity. Men and women no longer mingled, but were separated in men's and women's washrooms, where they sang while washing their hands—the hands that labored. The decor suggested an interim space, a divide between work and other physical pursuits that required sexual differentiation as well. Thus the romanticism of "social significance" in a love song marked a soft-

Figure 38: "Sing Us a Song with Social Significance" in the early days of Pins and Needles. *(Billy Rose Theatre Collection, New York Public Library for the Performing Arts at Lincoln Center, Astor, Lenox, and Tilden Foundations.)*

"Standard"

Figure 39: A more elaborately produced version of "Sing Us a Song with Social Significance." (Billy Rose Theatre Collection, New York Public Library for the Performing Arts at Lincoln Center, Astor, Lenox, and Tilden Foundations.)

ening of the urgency of social change. Social significance was somewhere between the workplace and bourgeois romanticism. Yet as the song's lyrics also indicated, love and romance were contingent on "social fact," not diluted by it.

Despite this creation of a worker's universe for all to enjoy, certain scenes of *Pins and Needles* gestured more pointedly to social critique. In "Vassar Girl Finds a Job," for example, the class indeterminacy of chorus girls is evoked by creating a parallel indeterminacy for Daisy, a Vassar graduate obliged to earn her living selling corsets in Macy's department store. When cast member Ruth Rubenstein frames her own head above the body of a mannequin sporting ladies' undergarments, she implicitly parodies the chorus girl's sexual commodification as well as the glamour system linking her to fashion. She appeared to be stripping but was in fact only undressing the store mannequin.[32]

Rubenstein's critique in this scene has three aspects. It reifies the parable of the commodified body as prostituted because women's undergarments are ap-

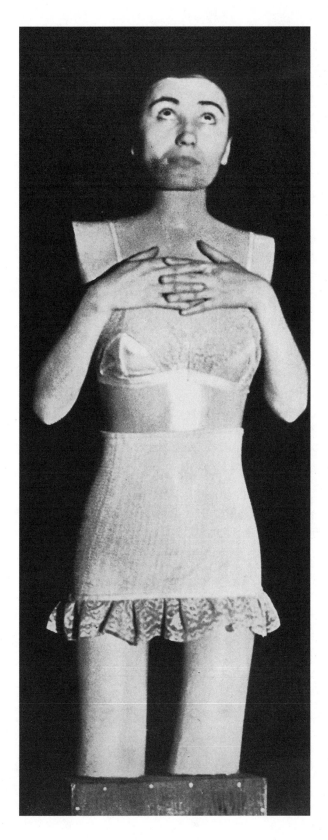

Figure 40: Ruth Ruben-stein playing a salesgirl at Macy's in Pins and Needles.

pended to a lifeless and shapeless mannequin separate from her own body. It reverses the commodification of woman's work as sexual performance by performing work as the display of feminine paraphernalia without sexual content. It counters the elimination of women from working-class status by performing the two preceding aspects as integral to "work." Given that Daisy's work is to sell undergarments and Rubenstein's work outside the theater is to fabricate them, the Rubenstein/Daisy parody of a chorus girl's performance as a sexual/theatrical worker is revealed as labor. A bona fide worker, one who actually produces brassieres in the garment industry but who also plays the role of salesgirl on stage, performs this labor. In fact, her role in a Broadway play becomes another level of work arising from the contradiction of a body interceding at every level of production and distribution. Rubenstein is a parody of the female body whose movement is the equivalent of abstract exchange; rather than embodying sex, money, and the commodity, she embodies the social condition of work underlying the possibility of exchange. Further, the rags-to-riches scenario of the chorus girl conventionally began with a department store job: this was the case in the Ziegfeld film *Glorifying the American Girl.* In other terms, the salesgirl conveys a parody of the chorus girl as performed by a garment worker who is a performer. From garment-worker sewing-machine girl to salesgirl to anti–chorus girl, Rubenstein's number made visible the complex relationship of work to performance underlying the historical specificity of her presence on stage.

Exploring workers' feelings, politics, and ethnicity without being confrontational, *Pins and Needles* placed professionalism at risk. Its erasure of the amateur-versus-professional distinction also erased any sharp demarcation between performative and social acts. Yet this lack of distinction was itself commodified by the revue format in which the amateurism and ethnicity of the performers received a polish and timing that made it salable. The Labor Stage and the Federal Theatre Project were two instances during the Great Depression in which the relationship of workers to capital was particularly fluid, allowing the performance of critique to appear, in its own right, spectacular— or at least highly entertaining.

Life magazine ran an article on Ruth Rubenstein highlighting the apparent indifference of the actress and garment worker to the show's success. Two captioned photographs comment on Rubenstein's "double life"—on stage as a "chain-store daisy" and at work in the garment industry fabricating brassieres. The second photo caption reads, "Sewing-machine girl is what the 'chain-store daisy' is off stage. Her name is Ruth Rubenstein, she is 20 years old, and she lives with her family in Brooklyn. At a New York brassiere factory she earns $23 a week, of which she pays .40 in dues to her union local, No. 32. For starring in

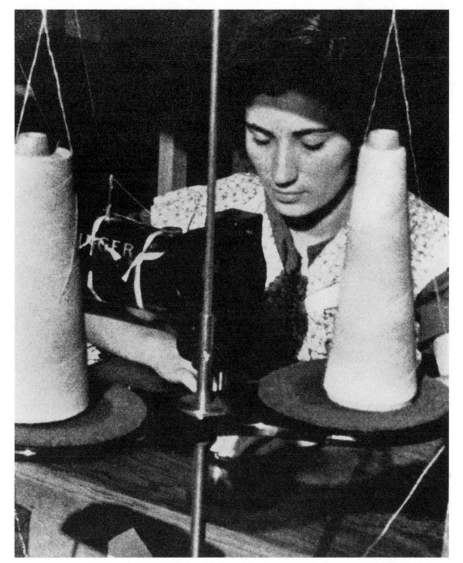

Pins and Needles, Ruth gets .50 for supper money on the night of each performance. She expects no other salary for the exceptional comedy talent she contributes to the cause of trade unionism."[33] Rubenstein's seeming indifference to the possibilities of social and economic transformation implicit in her theatrical success indicates how the performance of radical aesthetic values could undermine mainstream assumptions about cultural capital and therefore also about "professionalism."

Rubenstein's status as a noted Broadway performer in a commercially successful show only served to highlight the fact that in actuality she was a worker. This meaning of work played on the ambiguities of self-display while reaffirming the ethnic identity of the nonglamorous garment worker: trade union ethics offset show business opportunism. The fact that she maintained her commercially successful performance at a level of underclass consciousness was anomalous to the mass media. Rubenstein's refusal to commodify her performative work aesthetically, economically, or socially as "professional" was profoundly nettling to mainstream journalism.

Similar issues of the value of performative work had been debated just prior to *Pins and Needles* in the context of the Federal Theatre and Dance Projects. By looking at the production of human values in place of "professional" ones in a context where labor actions were possible, we see an extension of the radical modern dance aesthetic as an ethic. This is the subject of chapter 7.

Chapter 7 **Strikes, Revues, and the Organized Dancer**

Any treatment of the relation of dance to labor surely must take concrete issues of employment into consideration. Aside from culture industry dancers who intermittently gained employment in commercial venues and ballet dancers who either shared these venues or worked in privately funded companies, the modern dancer confronted the prospect of regular employment only once during the decade, with the institution of the Federal Dance Project. Part of the Works Progress Administration (or WPA), the project was a federally subsidized dance theater. The quickly ensuing controversies that swirled about the project reveal a massive historical resistance to bringing dance and labor into parity as salaried activities. This is the situation examined in this chapter.

Ideology was conventionally defined in the 1930s in the context of class struggle, and therefore the gendered ideologies subtending production and reproduction in social life are frequently assumed to have gone unrecognized or ignored during this decade. The brief history of the Federal Dance Project presents evidence to counter this assumption. Not only did predominantly female bodies perform labor and capital in modern dance up until the project, but a social conflict between modern dancer and chorus girl during the project broached the issue of (theatrical) work itself as productivity. Thus, dance contributed to the redefinition of woman's place in depression-era society while also engaging in the work of representing it. This chapter sets out the terms of ideological conflict between performance genres—modern dance and chorus dance—opposed not only in their aesthetics, but also in their ideologies, of work.

In the history of American performance, the FDP is a usually unrecognized precursor to the National Endowment for the Arts, although the FDP was actually far more ambitious than the endowment, being not merely a granting agency, but a national producing organization. It was in the business of not only supporting artists but also actually employing them. Nowhere did opposition about the acceptable relation of dance to labor become more polarized than in the creation and subsequent dismantling of the FDP within its brief period of existence between 1936 and 1937. The internal conflict was played out between project choreographer Helen Tamiris and the managing producer, choreographer Don Oscar Becque. My analysis will not dwell on internal conflicts as much as on the issues raised about dancers by the organizational events surrounding the project's inception and demise. These issues are fundamentally political in that they concern the relationship of dance to labor.

When dancers became federal employees, the relation of dance to labor could no longer be limited to staged performance. These artists evolved, in other words, from dancers representing workers into workers who perform, that is, into workers whose work is that of performance. The Right maintained that radical modern dancers confused politics with art. The Left burdened show and classical dance with false consciousness for its vapid naïveté or complicity with the entertainment market. Modern dancers in the Federal Dance Project demonstrated that a woman dancing is a woman performing the work of dance. Thus in 1937, women's history, labor history, and dance history converged.

The relationship of dancers to labor must be reconstructed before the backdrop of a professionalization debate that engaged modern dancers and chorus girls from the formation of the FDP in 1936 to its strikes in 1937. I shall also consider Fanny Brice's 1936 Ziegfeld Follies parody of radical dance, and critiques of the radical dancer on both the left and right.

Transvaluating Value

Before turning to the formation and demise of the Federal Dance Project itself, some discussion of Hallie Flanagan's goals for the Federal Theatre Project will be useful in developing the full ramifications of this debate. In her inaugural address as national director of the FTP, Flanagan narrated the partnership of

theater and government as an encounter between a working-class woman and a male intellectual: "An intellectual, walking alone, philosophizing about art, is confronted by a woman who emerges from a motionless crowd of workers in the background. The worker woman says: 'Is this the appointed hour? Is this the time and place where we should meet?' The intellectual, removing his hat, remarks cautiously. 'I do not think we have met before.' To which the woman worker replies, 'I've walked the world for six years. I've noticed you. I knew that some day you would notice me.'"[1] Flanagan adds, "Is it too much to think that, for two great forces, mutually in need of each other, the federal theater project of 1935 may be the appointed time and place?"[2] Notable in her sketch is the performer's working-class female body presented as a "mass body" emerging from a "motionless crowd of workers." Elsewhere Flanagan asserted that the FTP "is a theatre of, for, and by the professional worker."[3] Here theater's "professional worker" is gendered feminine. The female body on stage must have conveyed a double significance for Flanagan: as theatrical workers actresses played working-class women; but, in a more abstract and pervasive sense, their bodies signified labor power. This second aspect of the female body's significance on stage—the embodiment of power—was realized, however, with more evident force in modern dance.[4]

The male figure sketched by Flanagan—happened upon "philosophizing about art"—does not represent worker identity. He recalls instead experimental directors and theorists active in workers' theater of the late twenties in New York, such as John Bonn or Alfred Saxe, who had learned from Meyerhold and Piscator in Russia and Germany. In Flanagan's sketch, the director's intellectual strengths palliate labor power's potential for artistic frailty. Because the FTP was "a relief project, for the unemployed in the theatre profession," *Theatre Arts Monthly* noted that "in dealing with the weakest people in the theatre—it [the FTP] has begun irremediably at the wrong end."[5] But until the project was brought under the congressional scrutiny of the Dies Commission, Flanagan remained undaunted by such liabilities: "If we have 6,000 theatre people on relief we all know that probably 4,000 of them are not of the calibre to experiment. However, we must keep steadily in mind that we do not work with the 6,000 alone. We also work with 600 whom we may choose to work with them ... Let us not, therefore, overemphasize the weakness of the material with which we work."[6] The FTP returned theater workers to socially and economically productive livelihoods because their work was deemed necessary to the nation's cultural health. This principle, however, quickly turned controversial, and the dancing body became a site at which conflicts over the productivity or nonproductivity of theatrical work were played out.

What was the basis of this controversy? The Federal Theatre Project relied upon the synonymy of the terms *professional* and *worker* to justify its mission but also saw a wedge driven between these terms by adversaries. A double criterion emerged whereby *professional* connoted a critical and commercial evaluation of skill whereas *worker*—understood as the unemployed—connoted an egalitarian standard. *Professional* and *worker* stood for skilled and unskilled labor, respectively. Also at stake in the "professionalism" debate was the theater worker's expression of his or her politics in performance. Right-wing opinion considered this unprofessional. "The Theatre Project," responded Flanagan, "is not primarily an art form, but a life force. It is born, not of some vague theorizing about art, but of economic necessity. In that fact lies its strength. Do you think that the FTP is less potent because there is remembrance of hunger in the pit of its stomach?"[7] Remembered hunger, Flanagan maintains, does more than characterize unskilled labor: it generates theatrical power. Thus, without identifying her political position, Flanagan vindicated the political nature of performance as a necessary by-product of its desired physical and emotional power. By recognizing the power of performance to inhere in experience as much as in training, her statements turned professionalism on its head. We find here, as in earlier agitprop performance and workers' dance, the transferential working-class body as a theatrical vehicle devoid of skills but demonstrating something perhaps as important as skills.

Flanagan's gendered scenario contrasts with the situation of radical modern dancers and choreographers, women who since the early thirties had performed both their own labor power and their own intellectual and artistic direction. The female modern dancer raised the question, how and when is a woman (just) a (theatrical) worker? As an intellectual, she was not usually wholly worker identified. Where was her worker identity grounded when she danced labor without being, strictly speaking, a dance-worker, or an actual employee, let alone a recognizable "professional"? Despite considerable movement skills, she had to be considered "amateur," having had for the most part no entertainment industry employment. Moreover, modern dance was in its early phases of development and was still to define its own professional standards.

Dance manager Frances Hawkins acknowledged the modern dancer's ambiguous social and economic status at the First National Dance Congress. "The concert dancer," she observed, "occupies the anomalous position of being both employer and employee."[8] When less obviously skilled than other dancers, the modern dancer was more likely to be perceived as a true wage earner, but a non–wage-earning dancer. Hawkins also noted that "while the mere working on garments makes one a garment worker; studying, or even practicing the dance in public, does not make one a dancer: much less a professional dancer."[9] Social events surrounding the Federal Dance Project were to spectacularize the vexed connection between dance and work and, by extension, the controversy over the professional versus the amateur theatrical worker. But even prior to the FDP, the self-employed modern dancer was poised to embody the thorny issues of professionalization with respect to labor and dance.

Organization of a Field

At the Federal Dance Project's inception in 1936, the dance community was called upon to organize itself. John Caldwell, the vice president of the City

Projects Council, cautioned a gathering of one hundred dancers at New York City's Port Authority Building: "The administration cares not a whoop in Hades whether you're dancers or not; it is interested in employing *professionals*."[10] This statement is hardly understandable unless one realizes that the word *dancer* was practically synonymous at this time with *worker*. He expected dancers, a newspaper article further specified, to "forget esthetic scruples and work together toward a governmental subsidy of their own."[11] Caldwell wished that no aesthetic issue would obstruct the identification of fundable excellence defined as professionalism. This leveling of the playing field, however, was both unrealistic and naive. The call for the stylistically and politically diverse field of theatrical dance to organize itself into a homogeneous block of professionals had the effect of accelerating already existing polarities between modern dancers and chorus girls. Resistance to the setting aside of "aesthetic scruples" revealed how rooted stylistic distinctions had already become in ideological positions.

The high quality of some Federal Theatre Project productions rendered politically oriented art (especially Living Newspapers) financially competitive with private investment art. When FTP work was recognized as "a salable commodity," its aesthetic and economic values quickly became a political issue.[12] Should the government launch a theater (indeed, a potentially national theater) that destabilized the political economy of theater? Should a radical or progressive political message garner box office profits as well as connect with its audience?[13] A rivalry developed between the market value of most successful theatrical commodities and FTP workers' "flaming" words in "brilliantly bare" spaces.

Flanagan's most radical rhetoric differentiated between the ethical and economic meanings of the term "value": "The main point to keep in mind in dealing with labor on the Federal Theatre is that we are not employers in the usual sense of the word because our jobs came into being only because workers were in need of work. *We have no real value* to the Works Progress Administration."[14] Flanagan meant that no abstract exchange occurred in which use could be suspended. Statements such as these acknowledged a will to reorganize the market for theatrical value on a noncommercial standard—one that operated outside the political economy financially, aesthetically, and philosophically. Here, use value is placed in a relation with aesthetics without commodification: "The artistic values can be no greater and no more lasting than the human values we achieve. However, the reverse is also true: that the human job we are doing can be no better than the artistic standards we are developing."[15] In this conflation of the human and the aesthetic, we perceive the exact inversion of the chorus girl's value as class value underwritten by racial and national attributes. Flanagan envisioned FTP theater as the happy (momentary and theatrical) embodiment of use value. She defined value outside the system of exchange. This is to propose a performative economy in which values are implicit not in the product but in the process, not in work done but in labor itself. In theater, value depended on energy expended, not on productivity. Her vision of a value-sustaining and nevertheless wage-earning theatrical working underclass contradicted the market, a contradiction that was only underlined by her allegory of the female theatrical worker.[16] And, as we shall see, it collapsed over the heads and around the bodies of modern dancers on the Federal Dance Project.

The Professionalization Debate

The radical-conservative split between modern dancers and chorus girls crystallized as an issue of amateurism versus professionalism. This began in organizations such as the National Dance League, which charged that WPA funds were used "only by a small group of amateurs interested only in so-called modern dancing of the gymnastic, revolutionary type."[17] The league's investigation reported that "stenographers, clerks, sales girls and a variety of other workers who showed an interest in modern dancing now man the project . . . while ballet dancers, ballroom dancers, chorus girls and other professionals are refused employment on this project." This accusation was not limited to dance. Flanagan quoted a congressman's allegation: "They have not employed actors, but . . . have put on garment workers, fish peddlers, and so forth."[18]

These controversies held the limelight in 1937 during the project's gradual demise in the wake of cutbacks. Dancers' sit-down strikes were organized and characterized in the press as "undignified and highly unprofessional and unethical . . . in reality instigated by radical and political organizations."[19] Behind these accusations lurked the question of performers' class identity and loyalties. The performing laborer already existed symbolically on the left-wing stage when women and men danced and acted the roles of workers. Inasmuch as modern dancers depicted workers, or actually were workers (and thus skilled "amateur" dancers playing themselves for a public of their peers) they were accused of usurping the legitimate identity of performative workers. Modern dancers frequently accused of amateurism—of being workers who dabble in dance, rather than legitimate performers—were pitted against professionals: ballet dancers and more especially chorus girls, who comprised a category within which ballet dancers readily fit themselves since the Ziegfeld Follies of the 1920s. The charge of unprofessionalism thinly veiled the graver charge of political radicalism. The politics of skill, on the other hand, guaranteed political neutrality.

Our present culture inherits from these debates an ambivalence about defining dance as work and a habit of idealizing dance outside the social but also depressing it within the social. Political radicalism was associated with theatrical amateurism in order to preserve the integrity of a commercial brand of performance wherein the chorus girl occupied the lowliest working-class status possible in popular imagination. The chorus girl was the most highly specialized professionalized performer, but the least specialized of workers. She was the most skilled of unskilled workers. The modern dancer of the most radical sort, on the other hand, was a worker specialized in class consciousness but, by the same token, a rank amateur whose familiarity with performances was limited to the physical techniques required mostly for strikes.

During his tenure as head of the Federal Dance Project, Don Oscar Becque accused radical dancers of lacking the artistic abilities necessary for the theatrical expression of their political convictions. He accused them of being indistinguishable from those whom they wished to represent, and thus of lacking the necessary distance to perform worker identity. The true performer's work was, for Becque, to represent what she was not—the surest way of identifying her professionalism, and also her true market value. "Less attention must be paid," wrote Becque, "to over-earnest young ladies who shakily stare into amber spots on Sunday evenings and effectively carry sandwich signs in picket lines during the week, denouncing everything except bad dancers."[20] Becque defined theatrical work as mimicry. His rhetoric implied that the physical control required to command a stage is incommensurable with the stamina needed to protest in the street. Representing worker consciousness was not equivalent to working because theatrical representation and social identity were necessarily asymmetrical. Radical dancers represented the proletariat in their dances, whereas chorus girls were the show business proletariat in the flesh, albeit veiled as a "girl" proletariat. The latter could mimic, but the former could not. Beyond that distinction, a "whoop in Hades" was not given "whether you're a dancer or not." Theatrical work must at all cost be severed from politics.

This position pretended to ignore ideological differences between modern dancers and chorus girls. The chorus girl's politics as evinced in her performance were to vivify capital's values by embodying its desirability in the playful stimulation of surplus value. This value could be and was rhetorically conveyed as "the free and joyous candid expression of the happier human emotions."[21] We recognize in these words the well-adjusted cheerfulness of the Taylorized worker, but also that sex appeal naturalizes skill. Sex is the sign of skill. Chorus girls could easily admit to working-class origins without chagrin because stardom, for which all might hope, entailed the mythic upgrading of their social class. An advertisement for a "new serial story," *Blondie of the Follies,* in the *New York Journal American* (25 July 1932), announced the fictional

Blondie's "amazing career, from tenement obscurity to the dazzling heights of Broadway fame." Hollywood musicals about the lives of performers depicted chorus girls as penniless but always luxuriously outfitted and well groomed. Scarce means of subsistence were still connoted as plentiful. Chorus girls were shown to inhabit a declassed and de-ethnicized social sphere—the vestibule to their dreams of success—where they starved with bravado, wit, and panache. The drama of being between jobs was staged as a state of being between classes. Thus their very social precariousness veiled an embeddedness in a specific labor situation, denying their working-class status by purveying a mystique of performance as personal, social, and sexual success. All this was behind the idea of professionalization in hard, social terms. The professional dancer was not only to be apolitical; professionalization itself was represented as declassification. Dance professionalization was a classic instance of ideology as the inversion of an actual state of affairs into its illusory opposite.

If the chorus girl's performative identity was ostensibly classless, the modern dancer's class identity was publicly averred with the first New York left-wing solo dance concerts in 1934 and 1935. Edna Ocko probably organized this concert, for she had noted elsewhere that "soloists . . . have not as yet been encouraged," although solos were at the heart of historical modern dance.[22] Revolutionary dance was not as readily associated with the solo genre. It had stressed instead mass movement for untrained or only recently and partially trained groups. But Ocko underlined the originality, indeed the almost contradictory import, of "revolutionary dance solos."[23] What called for evaluation in the radical soloist's work was skill and artistry, criteria that set off a new phase of debate since the soloist's necessarily singular personality and commanding presence became vulnerable through the solo to identity critiques. The radical soloist would destabilize such critique with satire. Sokolow's *Histrionics* (1934) is the only radical solo to my knowledge that took the chorus girl as a target, cutting "to the heart of both the pathos and rottenness in the Broadway dance arena."[24]

Emanuel Eisenberg, occasional dance critic and press representative for the Group Theater, attacked the radical soloists as "bourgeois ladies." "She [the soloist] is essentially presenting a character dance; she is someone pretending to be somebody else through mood assumption and soul-state, for, by the cultural conditioning of a training and style, she is still and unmistakably the Lady of bourgeois ideals."[25]

Eisenberg indicts the "training and style" radical soloists obtained from their "bourgeois" teachers, and consequently the choreographic language they used to portray the working class. By insisting that performers and roles should be indistinguishable, he imports an earlier agitprop aesthetic into the solos. Any evidence of technique leading to the fashioning of working-class identity is suspect. He accuses dancers, in short, of *imitating* rather than *being* those whom they dance. This is exactly the reverse of Becque's critique. Behind Eisenberg's noticeably misogynist viewpoint is an issue of identification and technique. He doesn't claim that radical dancers are bourgeois-identified, but that their technique condemns them to appear so. The dancer appears bourgeois "by cultural conditioning of a training and style" derived from teachers, modernist choreographers such as Graham and Wigman (through the latter's disciple in New York, Hanya Holm).

Although debates over technique were internal to left-wing thought on dance, they raised the issue not only of what social class dancers could represent on stage, but also of where they belonged as public figures in the broader economic and social spectrum.[26] Technique was a class issue. Were dancers misrepresented by their techniques, their ways of moving, and should they not therefore invent new ways of moving to better represent who they were and whom they identified with? How politically adaptable were styles? Whereas chorus girls bolstered bourgeois ideology while appearing to titillate, modern dancers sought a performative identity whose style was perhaps not yet transparently transferable to their social intent. By rejecting sexual allure as the naturalization of skill, the strength required of their technique was also the given effect. However impressive that strength was, it appeared as unskilled labor. Like emotion, it seemed directly transferred from offstage.

Eisenberg's claim that, as "ladies," radical modern dancers could not depict other than bourgeois class status resists the evidence that shortly after the advent of the New Deal in 1933, dancers became identified as workers and their performances with a kind of work. This occurred despite attempts by chorus girls, ballet dancers, and ballroom dancers to cultivate a white-collar image. With the "upgrading" of dancers to workers, chorus girls were paradoxically demoted in popular imagination to a *Lumpenproletariat.* "When the New Deal set out to come to the aid of all parties," noted an anonymous journalist in "A Brief History of Federal Theatre in the South," "it included the artist as well as the ditch-digger, the chorus girl as well as the contractor." This rhetorical inversion encapsulates two imaginary economic continuums: from artist to chorus girl, and from contractor to ditchdigger. With it and despite the democratic equality of New Deal thinking, the journalist positions chorus girls as the ditchdiggers of artist-workers. Evidently, he or she did not suspect that modern dancers also qualified for federal relief.

Public Spotlights

Popular press discourse permits us to track a new awareness of the dancer-worker unstably positioned between culture industry and movement culture.

As modern dancers achieved a complex social as well as aesthetic relation to labor, political conservatives argued more vehemently to disqualify dance as work. A newspaper report on a 1936 Federal Dance Project audition grappled with issues of female bodies laboring as dancers. The journalist observed the dancers moving in a way that "baffles the non-professional."[27] The dancers are said in the article's subtitle to "nearly bend themselves double." His difficulty with their movement is not only due to unfamiliarity with the modern aesthetic, although this is clearly the case, but betokens a reluctance to associate modern dance with wage labor (the dancers' salary is given in the headline). The dancer, like a laborer, responds to instruction or command, but what she accomplishes is not legible as productive to this observer: "'Take some jumps,' cried one of the judges, before she really had time to get back her breath; 'take any kind of jumps.' Miss Morris chose to stand facing the judges, hop up into the air, spread her legs as far apart as possible, and flap them back together again before she hit the planks."[28] As in the title, "It's Scientific, It's Rhythmic, and It's Worth $23.86 per Week," which acknowledges skill but represents it as a grotesque distortion of physical ability, the awkward, nonspecialist precision of his description highlights the journalist's focus on movement's lack of value: what can these movements be exchanged with, economically or semantically? he seems to ask. H. Allen Smith is baffled that $23.86 per week will be paid for modernist physical exertion in the theatrical marketplace. He therefore predictably begins to as-

Figure 43: A Federal Dance Project audition in 1936. (Hallie Flanagan Papers, Billy Rose Theatre Collection, New York Public Library for the Performing Arts at Lincoln Center, Astor, Lenox, and Tilden Foundations)

sess the dancers as chorus-girl commodities, the only physical commodities that obey market standards rather than value-fixing by the federal government: "Miss Remos was easily the most beautiful of the lot. This incontrovertible fact was mentioned to one of the dance devotees who attended, and he scoffed. Scoffed with his face. He said that looks made no difference. A dancer is a dancer, and it doesn't matter what she looks like. One doesn't consider looks."[29] The journalist's train of thought seems to be the following: If dancers can earn wages, then dance must be labor. If dance is labor, it must produce sex appeal.

"Modernistic" focus on movements whose technicality ("scientificity") promotes no sexual images is thus "baffling" to the journalist. His assumption that a modern dancer's criterion of excellence is her personal beauty betrays a train of thought that links feminine labors to arts of display. Yet this conclusion is simultaneously disturbed by the knowledge that the audition is conducted by a federal work project. Government sponsorship abstracts modern dance from the demands of the market, making the New Deal state a purveyor of this incomprehensible aesthetic, one which abjures its own participation in the market by ambiguating its meanings. The journalist feigns—at least for the benefit of his readers—not to understand a movement aesthetic replacing entertainment with scientificity, market values with government sponsorship, and sex appeal with salaried "body flexibility."

The modern dancer's work upsets the social continuities of capital as image in that it rewards the "scientific" in place of the spectacular. The term scientific poses the conundrum of feminine, expressive culture occupying the realm of instrumental rationality, which is traditionally male. Thus a significant contribution of the Federal Dance Project to labor history was to showcase women as wage-earning performers within the realm of labor, but outside the work of amusement and burlesque. In this regard, the FDP undermined what Joan Wallach Scott has called "the contradiction woman/worker."[30] Even more significantly, once dance is allowed to thrive outside of market structures, it is enabled to construct an oppositional ideology of the value and significance of human movement in social patterns.

Satiric Interlude

"My feet are full of splinters
There's water on my knee
A broken-down, expressionistic dancer—that's me"
Ziegfeld Follies, 1936

When Berkeley's first *Gold Diggers* film glorified the American chorus girl, albeit ambivalently as a gold digger, the Ziegfeld Follies were in crisis. Florenz Ziegfeld had died in 1932. Columnist Mark Hellinger said, "The depression killed the master showman. The doctors can blame it on his heart or whatever they choose, but they cannot tell me what I already know. For more than a year now money worries have troubled him greatly. And bit by bit, as the months rolled on, these worries became greater and greater."[31] The Follies themselves survived the Great Depression because the Shubert organization bought the rights to produce them. Throughout the twenties and up until 1934, "Glorifying the American Girl" had been the theme-format of the Ziegfeld productions. The first Shubert-produced Ziegfeld Follies, *Time Marches On* (1936), evidenced a self-conscious departure from the chorus girl format and a preference for the stand-up comic. A male chorus introduced the show:

> Gone is the day of the showgirl
> Whose charms captivate the Don Juan
> This year we cater to no girl
> Time marches on.[32]

Although chorus girls were still present in the 1936 Follies, influential radical discourse obliged *Time Marches On* to wield humor as a weapon against the class struggle. In the same opening number Bob Hope sang:

MAN: Ladies and Gentlemen, just because you don't see me surrounded by a bevy of beautiful squaws please don't get the impression this isn't the Ziegfeld Follies because it's the Follies alright but on a basis entirely new. We feel that the day of the girlie-girlie show is definitely through. In fact we even have a song about it.

BOYS: Beauty is fleeting and flimsy
Though she have the neck of a swan.

MAN: This year we're featuring whimsy

BOYS: Time marches on.[33]

Another number, "The Economic Situation," offers an explanation for the decline of the chorus girl on the New York stage. Eve Arden appeared at the head of a chorus of "Economists" who complain about the intrusion of topical, intellectual matters in boy-girl relationships. Arden laments:

> You're sitting with a man on a moonlit verandah
> You've got stars and music and other propaganda
> And what happens? Does he make love? No!
> You have a discussion
> About the effect of the dynamo on the Russian.[34]

Figure 44: Eve Arden and the Twelve Economists in Time Marches On *(1936). (Shubert Archive, New York City.)*

The Twelve Economists concur: "It used to be all you'd ever have to say / Was 'Aren't you wonderful' / But the economic situation has changed all that."[35] It was no longer culturally feasible to "glorify" the American girl on the margins of economic crisis: she had to be glorified within that crisis. Humor promoted the relocation of crisis in the sexual sphere.

Satiric humor was also turned against radical modern dance. Fanny Brice, best known for her comic personification of Baby Snooks, performed a burlesque rendition of radical modern dance in *Time Marches On*. Although it was thought to be a parody of Martha Graham's 1929 solo *Revolt*, Brice apparently said "revolt" during the act with a pronounced Yiddish accent. Fanya Geltman remembers that Brice also said "My name was Fanny and I changed it to Fanya," indicating that the source of the parody may have been Geltman's solo of the same name.[36] The aim taken at a confluence of art and politics along with the emphasis on Jewishness does indicate that left-wing modern dance was the target.[37]

Like the displaced chorus-girl economists who interacted with Eve Arden in the same show, Brice's radical dancer complains about "Modernistic Moe" (short for mo-dern) who "seduced" her into the modern dance field:

I used to work in a night club
For sixty bucks a week

Figure 45: Fanny Brice in the "Modernistic Moe" number of the Ziegfeld Follies. Photo: Murray Korman. (Billy Rose Theatre Collection, New York Public Library for the Performing Arts at Lincoln Center, Astor, Lenox, and Tilden Foundations.)

To please the chumps
I did the bumps
And turned the other cheek.
It wasn't as artistic
but at least it used to pay;
When I was truckin'
There's no use talkin'
I ate three times a day.

. . . .

Since Modernistic Moe
Made me leave the show
I'm interpreting the rhythm of the masses.
I crawl around the stage
Interpreting the age
But the masses, they won't even come on passes.
I got the harmony of the body
And the melody of the feet
I got coordination
But I ain't got to eat.
Staccato and dynamic
The movement that revolts
A future panoramic
Of nuts, and screws, and bolts.
The movement of the masses
On the economic scene
Every movement has a meaning
But what the hell does it mean?[38]

In Brice's burlesque, the female soloist has been exploited by a male left-wing intellectual, Moe, who set her up to represent the masses but in actuality converted her into one of the suffering unemployed. Pretending to be a worker, Brice unwittingly becomes one.

Her new movement aesthetic that would ostensibly infuse original actions with new meanings is actually one whose economics make no sense. The attribution of significant meaning to movements created and performed outside the commercial theater market—meanings whose untoward significance might actually suggest a different model of exchange—are exposed as false in two related ways. Although social significance imbues new movements with new meanings, the overall meaning of the performance remains ambiguous ("Every movement has a meaning / But what the hell does it mean?"). Further, its message is erroneous and misleading: The immediate social effect of radical performance is to visit injuries and hunger upon its performers; this, in turn, removes their marketability and embroils them in the worst social and economic ills. Modern dance is the inverse of labor efficiency in that it produces fatigue and waste. Thus, for Brice, radical dance simulates deprivation in the performer's body by causing her to move in ways that actually induce physical pain and injury ("My feet are full of splinters / There's water on my knee") as an "aesthetic" requisite. Brice's number constitutes a reverse parody of surplus value. Chorus girls produce consumable sex for others; modern dancers produce pain for themselves. "The movement that revolts," at which Brice's mod-

Figure 46: Fanny Brice: "But what the hell does it mean?" (Shubert Archive, New York City.)

ern dancer becomes adept, is also characterized as mechanizing; its "staccato and dynamic" qualities are dehumanizing and desexualizing. By lumping radical dance with aesthetic modernism, further ill effects are derived. The text confuses the social outlook of radical performance with "a future panoramic / of nuts, and screws, and bolts"—that is, with the aesthetic fascination of machine culture—whose modernist aspirations threaten sexual divisions of labor. As men become swallowed up in labor, they have neither the time nor the means to treat women as luxury objects. As machines invade the workplace, gender distinctions fade.

Rather than re-envision women according to the dictates of a New World economic order, the Follies—and contemporaneous Hollywood musicals about the trials and tribulations of chorus girls—opt for a chorus girl who rejuvenates capitalism by reinventing the market in her own image. The model for capital's circulation in performative terms is entertainment.

Performing the Strike

Eisenberg accused radical dancers of appearing bourgeois, Brice accused them of foolishly proletarianizing themselves, and Becque insisted they were too proletarian to be representable by their own dances. Clearly the radical modern dancer was between a rock and hard place. Despite these negative views of the signifying potential of radical dancers, the Federal Dance Project contextualized them in an entirely different way: as federal wage earners—civil servants first, proletarian or culture industrial second. The ability and willingness of dancers to strike on their own behalf further enhanced this new identity. What Flanagan's gendered allegory of theater workers had prefigured in 1935 was realized in the performances of the 1937 strikes.

The strike of May 20, 1937 at the Nora Bayes Theatre on Forty-fourth Street in Broadway's theater district utilized two stages. One was the street, where pickets paraded before the theater, and the other the auditorium, where performer and audience concluded the second scheduled performance of the evening by occupying the theater:

The curtain came down after the second production at 11:05 P.M. Before the audience could stir, Charles Weidman, star of the cast, came before the curtain and made a brief speech ending with the request that the audience join the sit-down. There was a general cheer from the capacity audience of 700, but a small percentage got up and hustled out. . . . At the lusty approbation from the audience some one rang up the curtain, and the cast, still in costume, came out and squatted on the apron of the stage. Some one started to sing "Hail! hail! the gang's all here" and everyone joined in, including the band. Other songs followed and at intervals there was a steady chant of "W.P.A. must go on."[39]

A photo of the crowd outside the theater published in the *New York American* provided this legend: "Pickets from the supporting cast in Broadway's newest innovation—a sit-in strike in the Nora Bayes Theatre. . . . The strike threw the entertainment district into turmoil as after-theatre crowds rushed to view the spectacle." Police moved in to close Forty-fourth Street: "In a few moments the street was a mass of struggling people . . . Confusion spread into Times Square and the surrounding theatrical district. Fights broke out . . . an air of impend-

ing battle pervaded the area."[40] Police attempted to pre-
vent those who wanted to leave the theater from doing so.

Inside the theater, the *Daily Worker* reported the
seamless passage from performance to strike for which
Waiting for Lefty had been a rehearsal: "The most exciting
moment occurred when the audience kept their seats and
became actors in the drama, and for the first time in the-

*Figure 47: "W.P.A Cast Joined by Audi-
ence for All-Night Theater Sit-Down," in
Herald Tribune (May 20, 1937). (Hallie
Flanagan Papers, Billy Rose Theatre
Collection, New York Public Library for
the Performing Arts at Lincoln Center,
Astor, Lenox, and Tilden Foundations.)*

atre history, the line of the footlights was crashed and audience and performers joined in the common fight."[41] Sit-downs were symptomatic of mass action
without top-down union leadership and control. The inherent radicalness of
this kind of action engendered alarming speculation: "The latest thing in
strikes is the 'sit-down.' It is also called the 'sit-in,' 'stay-in,' the 'folded arm,' or
the 'occupation' strike. Instead of walking out of their factory, store or office,
the strikers simply remain at their machines, benches or desks, but stop work.

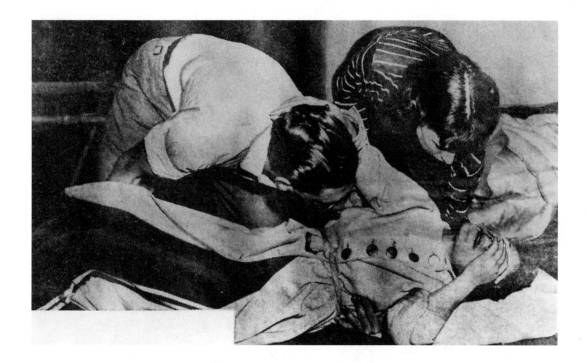

Figure 48: A collapsed WPA hunger striker (1937). (Hallie Flanagan Papers, Billy Rose Theatre Collection, New York Public Library for the Performing Arts at Lincoln Center, Astor, Lenox, and Tilden Foundations.)

It may last a day or a night, if it is spontaneous, or a longer period if it is well organized. . . . Its illegality in the seizure of property and its revolutionary implications if extended to a logical conclusion are obvious."[42] Photos of reclining strikers illustrated the sit-down and the lie-down. Some strikers were photographed collapsing from fatigue and hunger. Others were shown reclining, exhausted, in public places. These images imply that dance workers naturally engaged in idleness.

The unemployed dancer was a tautology. Moreover, when people who strike in the workplace also dance to pass the time—or "caper at the scene," as one journalist put it—dance is positioned as a consequence of the strike's unproductive actions. The flip side of modern dances about work was the intrusion of social dance into the workplace and time. This provided another opportunity to link strikes and dancing as related forms of unproductive labor. Evaluating a dancer's strike by presumably aesthetic standards inferred that dance itself was a labor action whose tendency toward inactivity in the sit-down was a metaphor for its movement and an indicator of its unprofessionalism. The further inference was that the federal government should cease funding dance. Political engagement was prima facie evidence of unprofessionalism.

Radical modern dance provided an opportunity to contemplate women in public as workers, and the vigorous opposition to it was as much based on this

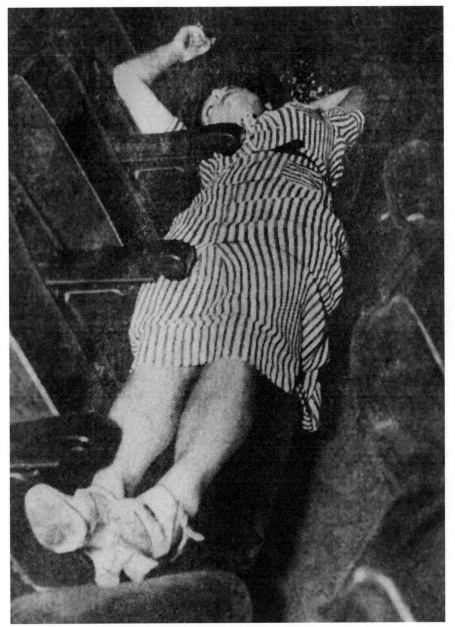

Strikes, Revues, and the Organized Dancer

165

fact as on the politics of its subject matter. Not only did women play active and determining roles in the struggle to recognize dance as work—a struggle that has hardly begun—but labor itself acquired a gender through the particular ability of modern dance to transmit and disseminate workers' emotions. Radical modern dance provided an image not just of women working, but of women's work as labor's representation.

Modern dancers labored. In so doing, they contributed to the reproduc-

Figure 50: Strikers social dance during their occupation of the Norma Bayes Theatre. (Hallie Flanagan Papers, Billy Rose Theatre Collection, New York Public Library for the Performing Arts at Lincoln Center, Astor, Lenox, and Tilden Foundations.)

tion of labor culture in performance or, more precisely, in its repeated rehearsal. Rehearsal is a phenomenon that, without assuring existing relations, unveils new potentials. The understanding of dance as labor in the thirties hinges on a dual premise: (1) labor as the reception of wages for energy expended, (2) labor as the investment of emotional capital as cultural rehearsal. This is the terrain across which dance and work continue to stage unsatisfying and furtive encounters.

The Performative Economy

This book has outlined the engagement of dance with emotion and form, genre and class. I abstain from an account of what came after. Despite the inherent historical interest of sequels, they can tend to generate a false sense of closure. The point, here and now, lies elsewhere. History shows that workers were not to be dancers, and that dancers were not workers. What, then, is and was the work of dance?

Radical modern dance was founded on a rejection of the rationalization of labor practices under industrial capitalism. It proposed alternative physical techniques productive of personality and emotion. Increasingly, its burden was to embody class. Based on the above analyses, I invite the reader to entertain the following paradox: the work of dance—its product—was ideology, but metakinetic "exchange"—the transfer of expression and interpellation to its audience—was its labor.[43] In the performative economy of the thirties, what is exchanged (identity) is not produced, and what is produced (ideology) is not exchanged. This alone—if nothing else—assures that the energy expended by dancing be political.

But dance is also political because of the way its models proliferated throughout the social world. While accomplishing acts of interpellation, choreography also provided the corporeal rationale for labor organizational systems to "perform." Neither of these functions—whether focused on the individual or the collective—supports a reflective idea of dance in relation to culture. Together, they posit the performative economy as the field within which dance becomes (a) modern movement.

Notes

Introduction

1. See Ellen Graff, *Stepping Left: Dance and Politics in New York City, 1928–1942* (Durham, N.C.: Duke University Press, 1997). Graff's study is the first comprehensive treatment of North American left-wing dance in the thirties. I am much indebted to her work although I take differing positions on some points.

2. A renewed interest in these problems from a very different perspective is evident in Rudolf Laban and F. C. Lawrence, *Effort* (London: Macdonald and Evans, 1947).

3. I refer to these terms as they are used in the English language.

4. Hannah Arendt, *The Human Condition* (Chicago: University of Chicago Press, 1958), 80.

5. Angelo Herndon, *Let Me Live* (New York: Random House, 1937), 129.

6. Terry Eagleton, *Ideology: An Introduction* (London: Routledge, 1991), 101. See also Janet Wolff, *Aesthetics and the Sociology of Art* (Ann Arbor: University of Michigan Press, 1996).

7. Sam H. Friedman, interview by Debra Bernhardt, unaudited transcript, 19 February 1986, Tamiment Institute Library, New York University. Friedman was the executive director of Rebel Arts, which had three dance groups. Friedman continues: "I have to explain to people—especially to anti-socialists and anti-communists— I said, you know, this was not terrible—these people didn't say, 'Lo, I'm going to join

a movement which is totalitarian, and which is a slavocracy, which is Stalinist.' They became communist for the same reason that we [prior to the thirties] became socialists—see? And their hearts were in the right place until, in the case of some of them, until they became part of the apparatus, and then it was too late."

8. Edith Segal was the most politically explicit of left-wing choreographers. See Graff, *Stepping Left,* 29–32.

9. Fanya Geltman del Bourgo, interview by Karen Wickre, Works Progress Administration Oral Histories, Research Center for the Federal Theatre Project, George Mason University, 16 December 1977. Geltman's testimony demonstrates how modern dance helped to counteract "the weakening of the proletarian basis of the [Communist] Party, the weakening of the contacts of the Party with the workers." Green, "Some Questions of the Work of the CPUSA," in *The Communist International in America: Documents, 1925–1933* [New York: Bolshevik League, n.d.], 77. Geltman's depiction of workers leaving their machines refers to the perceived weakness in the relation between street cells and factory labor.

10. Anna Sokolow has cited Yiddish theater as one of the sources of expressive power in the thirties, which spread to politically active choreographers. Anna Sokolow, interview by author, New York, 13 September 1996.

11. This connection is being increasingly emphasized in recent scholarship on the cultural performances of radicalism. See, for example, Colette A. Hyman, *Staging Strikes: Workers' Theatre and the American Labor Movement* (Philadelphia: Temple University Press, 1997) and Kirk W. Fuoss, *Striking Performances/Performing Strikes* (Jackson: University Press of Mississippi, 1997).

12. Tillie Olsen, *Yonnondio: From the Thirties* (New York: Delta/Seymour Lawrence, 1974), 37 (emphasis added).

13. For an account of modernism's obsessions with the real thing, see Miles Orvell, *The Real Thing: Imitation and Authenticity in American Culture, 1889–1940* (Chapel Hill: University of North Carolina Press, 1989).

14. On the distinction between working-class social emotion and middle-class psychological depth, see Joel Pfister, *Staging Depth: Eugene O'Neill and the Politics of Psychological Discourse* (Chapel Hill: University of North Carolina Press, 1995), especially chapter 3.

15. Graff writes that American radicals were spiritual, an appropriate term because it connotes deep belief. But the term also obscures bodiliness unless the connection is specifically explicated, as Stefan Brecht does in a different context: "The immanentist spiritualism of humanist communism views spirit as the form of human bodies insofar as they relate to one another." Stefan Brecht, "On Grotowski," *Drama Review* 14, no. 2 [1970]: 188.

16. I borrow this term from Glen A. Mazis, *Emotion and Embodiment: Fragile Ontology* (New York: Peter Lang, 1993). To avoid electronic associations, I prefer *e/motion* to Mazis's *e-motion.*

17. Max Horkheimer and Theodor W. Adorno, *Dialectic of Enlightenment,* trans. John Cumming (New York: Continuum, 1999), 67.

18. This cartoon was published in *Vogue* in 1936, and reproduced in *The Thirties in Vogue,* ed. Carolyn Hall (New York: Harmony Books, 1985), 77.

19. Louis Althusser, "Is It Simple to Be a Marxist in Philosophy?" in *Essays in Self-Criticism,* trans. Grahame Lock (London: New Left Books, 1976), 189.

20. "A Satire on Periodicals," *Los Angeles California Evening News* 15 January 1937.

21. Dance scholars have recently begun to exhume this history. See Graff, *Stepping Left;* Stacey Prickett, "Marxism, Modernism, and Realism: Politics and Aesthetics in the Rise of the American Modern Dance" (Ph.D. diss., Laban Centre for Movement and Dance, 1992); Julia Lawrence Foulkes, *Modern Bodies: Dance and American Modernism from Martha Graham to Alvin Ailey* (Chapel Hill: University of North Carolina Press, 2002). Prickett's account highlights the contradictions between modernism and realism, and thus mirrors Graff's emphasis on the tensions between modern art and social process. Foulkes's account highlights the body and national identity, although my concern here is to focus on the body and emotion in relation to cultural politics and aesthetic ideologies. Prickett has also published a series of articles on the early stages of radical dance. See her "Dance and the Workers' Struggle," *Dance Research* 7, no. 1 (1990): 47–61, and "From Workers' Dance to New Dance," *Dance Research* 7, no. 1 (1989): 47–64. Another relevant collection of essays is Lynn Garafola, ed., *Of, by and for the People: Dancing on the Left in the 1930s,* Studies in Dance History vol. 5, no. 1 (Madison, Wis.: Society of Dance History Scholars, 1994). On the triumph of formalism in the 1950s, see Gay Morris, "Post-War American Dance: A Sociological Study of the Avant-Garde" (Ph.D. diss., Goldsmiths College, University of London, 2001).

22. Vsevolod Meyerhold, "Biomechanics," in *Meyerhold on Theater,* trans. and ed. Edward Braun (New York: Hill and Wang, 1969), 198.

23. Its necessity provides some cultural explanation for the rapid Americanization of Stanislavski's method in radical New York theater of the 1930s and the corresponding rejection of Brecht's acting and production aesthetics outside of the Living Newspaper Unit of the Federal Theatre Project.

24. Graff, *Stepping Left,* 132–152.

25. Mark Franko, *Dancing Modernism/Performing Politics* (Bloomington: Indiana University Press, 1995), 33. See the essay "Bodies of Radical Will" (pages 25–37), which is preliminary to this book.

26. In no way do I link emotional movement with a voluntaristic appeal to the irrational or the antirational that characterizes fascism. See Zeev Sternhell, *The Birth of Fascist Ideology: From Cultural Rebellion to Political Revolution,* trans. David Maisel (Princeton: Princeton University Press, 1994).

27. Gilles Deleuze, *Cinema I: The Movement-Image,* trans. Hugh Tomlinson and Barbara Habberjan (Minneapolis: University of Minnesota Press, 1986), 98. I cite Deleuze because he defines *affect* in the way I do here. Elsewhere, however, his theory of art provides no alternatives to affect. See Gilles Deleuze and Felix Guattari, *What Is Philosophy?* trans. Hugh Tomlinson and Graham Burchell (New York: Columbia University Press, 1994).

28. Mazis, *Emotion and Embodiment*, xii.

29. I avoid Jacques Rivière's *expression* and *emotion* as used in his 1913 essay on Vaslav Nijinsky's *Rite of Spring*. See "Le Sacre du Printemps," in *What Is Dance?* ed. Roger Copeland and Marshall Cohen (New York: Oxford University Press, 1983), 115–123. Although I adopted Rivière's terminology in my earlier book, I prefer *affect* to *expression* here because the latter denotes the entire field of the theatrical transmission of feeling. *Affect* and *emotion* are moreover key terms in the contemporary writing of Mary Austin and Edna Ocko (see chapter 3).

30. For an analysis of Graham's politics in the thirties, see my *Dancing Modernism/ Performing Politics*, 38–72.

31. Dudley, interview by the author, New York, 17 July 1996. Dudley was born in 1912 and grew up in Westchester County, New York, where she studied dance with her mother. In 1928 she met filmmaker Leo Hurwitz, whom she later married. She helped found the New Dance Group in 1932 with Miriam Blecher, Edna Ocko, and Fanya Geltman, whom she met at the Wigman School in New York. Dudley performed with Martha Graham before dedicating herself to her own work in collaboration with Sophie Maslow and Bill Bales.

32. Stanley Burnshaw, "Finale to a Brilliant Season," *New Masses* 16, no. 1 (2 July 1935): 43.

33. "[T]he more deeply embodied bodies [are] the female body, the racialized body, [and] the working body." Mark Seltzer, *Bodies and Machines* (London: Routledge, 1992), 64.

34. Dudley, interview, 17 July 1996.

35. For an account of the relation of dance to class in the Progressive era, see Linda Tomko, *Dancing Class: Gender, Ethnicity and Social Divides in American Dance, 1890–1920* (Bloomington: Indiana University Press, 1999).

36. See Lila Abu-Lughod and Catherine A. Lutz, "Introduction: Emotion, Discourse, and the Politics of Everyday Life," in *Language and the Politics of Emotion,* ed. Lila Abu-Lughod and Catherine A. Lutz (Cambridge: Cambridge University Press, 1991), 7. The contributions to this anthology establish the anthropology of emotion as manifested in language. The view of emotion as a social operator is central to my concerns, although I see its linguistic manifestation here as supplementary to its kinetic transmission.

37. The intellectual formation of Dance Studies, which came about in the 1980s, can be said to locate its historical condition of possibility in the thirties. Lynne Conner cites the simultaneous development of "two American cultural forces: journalism and modern dance." See her *Spreading the Gospel of the Modern Dance: Newspaper Dance Criticism in the United States, 1850–1934* (Pittsburgh: University of Pittsburgh Press, 1997), 1.

38. Si-Lan Chen, *Footnote to History,* ed. Sally Banes (New York: Dance Horizons, 1989), 239.

39. Slavoj Žižek, "The Spectre of Ideology," in *Mapping Ideology,* ed. Slavoj Žižek (London and New York: Verso, 1994), 1.

40. Corey Ford, "Impossible Interview: Sally Rand vs. Martha Graham," *Vanity Fair,* December 1934, 40.

41. Geltman del Bourgo, interview, 120.

42. See Carol Martin, *Dance Marathons: Performing American Culture in the 1920s and 1930s* (Jackson: University of Mississippi Press, 1994).

43. Martha Graham, *Blood Memory* (New York: Doubleday, 1991), 93.

44. For a discussion of the development of the idea of high art in American theater and music since the nineteenth century, see Lawrence W. Levine, *Highbrow/Lowbrow: The Emergence of Cultural Hierarchy in America* (Cambridge, Mass.: Harvard University Press, 1988).

45. Marion Sellers, "The Dance Project—W.P.A. Stepchild," *New Theatre* (August 1936): 24.

46. On the hearings themselves, see Hallie Flanagan's 1938 testimony in Eric Bentley, ed., *Thirty Years of Treason: Excerpts from Hearings Before the House Committee on Un-American Activities, 1938–1968* (New York: Viking Press, 1971), 3–47.

Chapter 1   Organization and Performative Economies of Work

1. Recent research that explores the investments of ideologies in mass physical tropes includes Jeffrey T. Schnapp, *Staging Fascism: 18BL and the Theater of Masses for Masses* (Stanford: Stanford University Press, 1996); Peter Jelavich, *Berlin Cabaret* (Cambridge, Mass.: Harvard University Press, 1993); and Nicoletta Misler, "Designing Gestures in the Laboratory of Dance," in *Theatre in Revolution: Russian Avant-Garde Stage Design, 1913- 1935,* ed. Nancy van Norman Baer (San Francisco: Fine Arts Museum of San Francisco, 1991), 156–175.

2. For a discussion of these terms, see chapter 2.

3. This aspect of the problem will be dealt with in Part II.

4. Publicity material for *America Sings,* Hallie Flanagan Papers, Billy Rose Theatre Collection, New York Public Library for the Performing Arts at Lincoln Center. Hallie Flanagan was the director of the Federal Theatre Project.

5. John McGee to Hallie Flanagan, 30 April 1936, Flanagan Papers. McGee was an assistant to Flanagan.

6. Ibid.

7. Publicity material for *America Sings,* Flanagan Papers.

8. Ibid.

9. Ibid.

10. Ibid.

11. Albert Prentis, "Basic Principles," *Worker's Theatre* (May 1931): 1–2 (emphasis added). For a fuller discussion of agitprop see Douglas McDermott, "The Theatre Nobody Knows: Workers' Theatre in America, 1926–1942," *Theatre Survey* 6, no. 1 (1965): 65–82, and Stuart Cosgrove, "Prolet-Buehne: Agit-prop in America," in *Performance and Politics in Popular Drama: Aspects of Popular Entertainment in Theatre, Film and Television, 1800–1976,* ed. David Bradby, Louis James, and

Bernard Sharratt (Cambridge: Cambridge University Press, 1980), 201–212. Cosgrove stresses that American agitprop performance brought race into class politics and integrated theatrical production: "New York agit-prop groups were the first to make a concerted effort to introduce black actors and writers into a theatre tradition which was entrenched in white taste" (pages 203–204).

12. Prentis, "Basic Principles," 1–2.

13. Jane Dudley, "The Mass Dance," in *Dancing Modernism/Performing Politics,* ed. Mark Franko (Bloomington: Indiana University Press, 1995), 119–122.

14. "Workers Dance League," *New Theatre* (January 1934): 16. The New Dance Group was characterized in 1934 as "a mass organization with the purpose of (1) performing before workers, students, and the regular dance concert audience; (2) performing for the purpose of educating and stimulating the audience to significant aspects of the class struggle; (3) training performing troupes to undertake this task; (4) training the individuals who are to make up these performing troupes; (5) themselves becoming a part of the class struggle through practical and theoretical education." "The Dance: The New Dance Group, an Analysis," *New Theatre* (March 1934): 17.

15. Dudley, "Mass Dance," 119.

16. Ibid., 120.

17. Edith Segal, "Directing the New Dance," *New Theatre* (May 1935): 23.

18. Ruth Allerhand, "The Lay Dance" [reprint of a 1935 article], in *Dancing Modernism/Performing Politics,* ed. Mark Franko (Bloomington: Indiana University Press, 1995), 135–137.

19. Allerhand, "Lay Dance," 136.

20. Dudley, "Mass Dance," 120.

21. Allerhand, "Lay Dance," 137.

22. *Program and Constitution of the Communist Party of America. Adopted at the Joint Unity Convention of the United Communist and Communist Parties* (n.p.: Central Executive Committee of the Communist Party of America, May 1921), section 5, 43.

23. Ibid., 43.

24. Ibid.

25. Ibid., 19.

26. Ibid.

27. Dudley, "Mass Dance," 120.

28. Ibid.

29. Ibid. The antiballet rhetoric usually relied upon historical critiques of ballet.

30. *Program and Constitution,* 53.

31. Dudley, "Mass Dance," 120.

32. Segal, "Directing the New Dance."

33. Ibid.

34. *Program and Constitution,* 19.

35. Segal, "Directing the New Dance."

36. See Vivian Gornick, *The Romance of American Communism* (New York: Basic Books, 1977), 248.

37. "Des symptômes maladifs indiquant un refoulement de certains instincts fondamentaux qui demandent à être à tout prix satisfaits." André Philip, *Le problème ouvrier aux Etats-Unis* (Paris: Librairie Félix Alcan, 1927), 160 (my translation).

38. "Il sera possible de transférer l'instinct créateur du travailleur d'une oeuvre individuelle à oeuvre collective; si l'on donne à l'ouvrier une information complète sur la production de l'usine et son rôle dans la vie économique de la nation, si on lui explique en détail quelle est sa fonction dans la création de l'oeuvre totale, on aura sans doute pas détruit le caractère répulsif ou monotone de son travail, mais on lui aura donné le sentiment de collaborer à une oeuvre utile." Ibid., 162 (my translation).

39. "Before 1900 there was very little organized research in American industry, but by 1930 industrial research had become a major economic activity," according to David F. Noble, *America by Design: Science, Technology, and the Rise of Corporate Capitalism* (New York: Alfred A. Knopf, 1977), 111.

40. Rexford B. Hersey, *Workers' Emotions in Shop and Home: A Study of Individual Workers From the Psychological and Physiological Standpoint* (Philadelphia: University of Pennsylvania Press, 1932), 29.

41. Ibid., 30.

42. Ibid., 36.

43. Edward Thomas, *Industry, Emotion and Unrest* (New York: Harcourt, Brace and Howe, 1920), 223.

44. See Flanders Dunbar, *Emotions and Bodily Changes: A Survey of Literature on Psychosomatic Interrelationships, 1910–1945* (New York: Columbia University Press, 1946); the first two editions of this book were published in 1935 and 1938.

45. Henry Ford, *My Life and Work* (Garden City, N.J.: Doubleday, Page, 1922), 104.

46. Antonio Gramsci, "Americanism and Fordism," in *Selections from the Prison Notebooks of Antonio Gramsci* (New York: International Publishers, 1971), 300.

47. Ibid., 309.

48. Ibid. "American industrialists," adds Gramsci, "have understood all too well this dialectic."

49. Walter Benjamin discussed the issue of distraction in relation to film spectatorship in the thirties, in his "The Work of Art in the Age of Mechanical Reproduction," in *Illuminations,* ed. Hannah Arendt (New York: Shocken Books, 1969), 217–252.

50. Graff, *Stepping Left: Dance and Politics in New York City, 1928–1942* (Durham, N.C.: Duke University Press, 1997), 35.

51. The Rockettes' first strike took place on 15 September 1967.

52. Siegfried Kracauer, "Girls and Crisis (1931)," in *The Weimar Republic Source Book,* ed. Anton Kaes, Martin Jay, and Edward Dimendberg (Berkeley: University of California Press, 1994), 565.

53. Alfred Sohn-Rethel, *Intellectual and Manual Labour: A Critique of Epistemology,* trans. Martin Sohn-Rethel (London: Macmillan, 1978), 57.

54. See Siegfried Kracauer, "The Mass Ornament," in *The Mass Ornament: Weimar Essays,* ed. Thomas Y. Levin (Cambridge, Mass.: Harvard University Press, 1995), 75–88.

55. Linda Mizejewski, *Ziegfeld Girl: Image and Icon in Culture and Cinema* (Durham, N.C.: Duke University Press, 1999).

56. Kracauer, "Girls and Crisis," 565.

57. Wayburn cited in Barbara Stratyner, *Ned Wayburn and the Dance Routine: From Vaudeville to the Ziegfeld Follies,* Studies in Dance History no. 13 (Madison, Wis.: Society of Dance History Scholars, 1996), 90.

58. Kracauer, "Girls and Crisis," 565.

59. Stratyner, *Ned Wayburn,* 53–57.

60. Frederick Winslow Taylor, *Principles of Scientific Management* (1911; reprint, New York: Norton Library, 1967). See also Frank B. Gilbreth and Lillian M. Gilbreth, *Fatigue Study* (New York: Sturgis and Walton, 1916). Unlike Russian constructivist performance, radical American performance critiqued Taylorization in the thirties. See Harry Braverman, *Labor and Monopoly Capital: The Degradation of Work in the Twentieth Century* (New York: Monthly Review Press, 1974), 12.

61. Sohn-Rethel, *Intellectual and Manual Labor,* 155.

62. Kracauer, "Girls and Crisis," 565.

63. Sohn-Rethel, *Intellectual and Manual Labor,* 6–7.

64. Ibid., 18.

65. The identification of 1933 as the severest year of the Great Depression is Roosevelt's: "In the midst of the greatest and most disastrous of these depressions, the very foundation of individual life was crumbling in the spring of 1933, because of the appalling increase in suffering and destitution due to the fact of unemployment." Franklin Delano Roosevelt, "Address at San Diego Exposition, October 2, 1935," in *The Public Papers and Addresses,* vol. 4 (New York: Random House, 1938), 408.

66. See Martin Rubin, *Showstoppers: Busby Berkeley and the Tradition of Spectacle* (New York: Columbia University Press, 1993), 102.

67. Patricia Mellencamp, "The Sexual Economics of *Gold Diggers of 1933*," in *Close Viewings: An Anthology of New Film Criticism,* ed. Peter Leman (Tallahassee: Florida State University Press, 1990), 177–199.

68. Guy Debord, *Society of the Spectacle* (Detroit: Black and Red, 1983), section 49. Further references will appear in the text by section number.

69. Sohn-Rethel, *Intellectual and Manual Labour,* 24.

70. Ibid., 25.

71. Lucy Fischer, "The Image of Woman as Image: The Optical Politics of *Dames*," in *Sexual Stratagems: The World of Women in Film,* ed. Patricia Erens (New York: Horizon Press, 1979), 41–61.

72. Rubin, *Showstoppers,* 36–37.

73. Lucy Fischer, "The Image of Woman," 42.

74. Sohn-Rethel, *Intellectual and Manual Labour,* 52. Pamela Robertson says that

"Berkeley effaces the myth of live entertainment, denying both the labor and the appeal of song and dance." Pamela Robertson, "What Trixie and God Know: Feminist Camp in *Gold Diggers of 1933*," in *Guilty Pleasures: Feminist Camp from Mae West to Madonna* (Durham, N.C.: Duke University Press, 1996), 64.

75. Georg Lukàcs, *History and Class Consciousness,* 90, cited in Rosin McDonough, "Ideology as False Consciousness: Lukàcs," in *On Ideology* (London: Hutchinson, 1997), 42.

76. Lukàcs, *History and Class Consciousness,* cited in McDonough, "Ideology as False Consciousness," 42.

77. Sohn-Rethel, *Intellectual and Manual Labor,* 53.

78. Kracauer concluded his "Girls and Crisis (1931)" essay with this remark: "One market crash after the other has rocked the economy, and the crisis has long since given the lie to one's faith in never-ending prosperity" (565).

Chapter 2   Essentialized Affect and E/motion

1. Michael Gold, "John Reed and the Real Thing," in *The Mike Gold Reader* (New York: International Publishers, 1954), 28. "Proletarian avant-garde" is the term used by Michael Denning to characterize the work of American artists after the modernist generation of the 1920s. Michael Denning, *The Cultural Front: The Laboring of American Culture in the Twentieth Century* (London: Verso, 1996), 64–66.

2. Joseph Freeman cited in James D. Bloom, *Left Letters: The Culture Wars of Mike Gold and Joseph Freeman* (New York: Columbia University Press, 1992), 94. Freeman and Gold were the two most prominent male literary voices of left-wing New York culture in the early thirties.

3. Jane Dudley, interview by author, New York, 14 July 1996.

4. "Creative practice took precedence over literary criticism and theory in the Marxist cultural critique of the 1930s–50s era." Alan M. Wald, *Writing from the Left: New Essays on Radical Culture and Politics* (London: Verso, 1994), 2.

5. Documentary films of the period were not, however, limited by this conception. See William Alexander, *Film on the Left: American Documentary Film from 1931 to 1942* (Princeton: Princeton University Press, 1981). I offer thanks to Bill Nichols for calling my attention to this book.

6. James Agee and Walker Evans, *Let Us Now Praise Famous Men* (Boston: Houghton Mifflin, 1939), 4.

7. On the postmodern relinquishing of a depth model, see Fredric Jameson, *Postmodernism, or the Cultural Logic of Late Capitalism* (Durham, N.C.: Duke University Press, 1991), 10–16.

8. See Raymond Williams, "Structures of Feeling," in *Marxism and Literature* (Oxford: Oxford University Press, 1977), 128–135. As Williams demonstrates, the prejudice against "structures of feeling" and the preference for institutional history entail an ideological divide between the social and the personal.

9. American communist obedience to the foreign party line is thus weighted as official evidence against the more personal, "native" experience of radicalism. See Theodore Draper, "The Life of the Party," *New York Review of Books,* 13 January 1994, 45–51, and "The Old Left: An Exchange," *New York Review of Books,* 23 June 1994, 62–63.

10. Williams, "Structures of Feeling," 133. See also Annette T. Rubenstein, "The Cultural World of the Communist Party: An Historical Overview," in *New Studies in the Politics and Culture of U.S. Communism,* ed. Michael E. Brown, Randy Martin, Frank Rosengarten, and George Snedeker (New York: Monthly Review Press, 1993), 239–260. "For me," writes Rubenstein, "this climate was best epitomized in the radical theater—not so much the plays as the actual theater experience" (248).

11. Williams first introduced this term in the context of his study of modern drama: "What I am seeking to describe is the continuity of experience from a particular work, through its particular form, to its recognition as a general form, and then the relation of this general form to a period." See Raymond Williams, *Drama from Ibsen to Brecht* (New York: Oxford University Press, 1969), 17.

12. *Blackwell Dictionary of Twentieth-Century Social Thought,* ed. William Outhwaite and Tom Bottomore, s.v. "radicalism" (Oxford: Blackwell, 1993).

13. On the relation of emotion to embodiment, as the reversible sensory dimensions of tactility, moving, and being moved, see Mazis, *Emotion and Embodiment.*

14. A discussion of interpellation follows in chapter 3.

15. Williams, *Drama from Ibsen to Brecht,* 18.

16. Rena Fraden, *Blueprints for a Black Federal Theatre, 1935–1939* (Cambridge: Cambridge University Press, 1996), 16.

17. Jane Dudley, interview, 14 July 1996.

18. Richard Wright, *Black Boy (American Hunger)* (1945; reprint, New York: Harper Collins, 1993), 452.

19. Ibid., 296.

20. Ibid., 330.

21. Ralph Ellison, *Invisible Man* (1947; reprint, New York: Vintage, 1980), 116.

22. Wright, *Black Boy,* 439.

23. Mark Naison, *Communists in Harlem During the Depression* (New York: Grove Press, 1983), xv.

24. Wright, *Black Boy,* 439.

25. The layering of theology, radical politics, and the representation of New York tenement life has been frequently noted, particularly with reference to the writing of Michael Gold and Henry Roth. See Morris Dickstein, "The Tenement and the World: Visions of Immigrant Life," in *The Future of American Modernism: Ethnic Writing between the Wars,* ed. Silliam Boelhower (Amsterdam: VU University Press, 1990), 62–93.

26. Michael Gold, *Jews without Money* (1930; reprint, New York: Carroll and Graf, 1958), 158.

27. Ibid., 309.

28. Ibid.

29. In an early essay, "Toward Proletarian Art (1921)," Gold used the metaphor of upward movement: "The method of erecting this proletarian culture must be the revolutionary method—from the deepest depths upward." *Mike Gold: A Literary Anthology* (New York: International Publishers, 1972), 69.

30. See Melissa Dabakis, *Visualizing Labor in American Sculpture: Monuments, Manliness, and the Work Ethic, 1880–1935* (Cambridge: Cambridge University Press, 1999).

31. Stacey Prickett, "'The People': Issues of Identity within the Revolutionary Dance," in *Of, by and for the People: Dancing on the Left in the 1930s,* Studies in Dance History vol. 5, no. 1 (Madison, Wis.: Society of Dance History Scholars, 1994), 65–103.

32. I discuss *Filling Station* in chapter 5.

33. *Labor Symphony* premiered 4 October 1934 at Storrs Hawley Armory in Connecticut.

34. George Chauncey, *Gay New York: Gender, Urban Culture, and the Making of the Gay Male World, 1890–1940* (New York: Basic Books, 1994), 331–354.

35. Paula Rabinowitz, *Labor and Desire: Women's Revolutionary Fiction in Depression America.* Chapel Hill: University of North Carolina Press, 1991), 40–41.

36. Michael Gold, "The Loves of Isadora," *New Masses* 4 (March 1929): 21.

37. Larry Warren, *Anna Sokolow: The Rebellious Spirit* (Princeton: Princeton University Press, 1991), 37.

38. I refer again to Rabinowitz: "Women's revolutionary fiction can be read as a genre within a genre, as a 'secondary zone' of literary radicalism whose boundaries contain and exceed the narrative of class struggle that animated proletarian realism." For Rabinowitz, "the suppression of the female voice in both history and narrative" came about "because literary radicals portrayed themselves in extremely masculine terms in order to combat their marginalization within both leftist and American culture by metaphorically identifying themselves with the masculine proletariat." *Labor and Desire,* 64, 37.

39. Nevertheless, many of the dances they created employed words.

40. Dudley, interview, 14 July 1996.

41. As Eric Lott has pointed out of nineteenth-century American sentimentalist fiction, "the sentimentalist strategies for representing white women and blacks were often identical, each image lending the other emotional and political force." Eric Lott, *Love and Theft: Blackface Minstrelsy and the American Working Class* (New York: Oxford University Press, 1993), 32.

42. Catherine A. Lutz, "Engendered Emotion: Gender, Power, and the Rhetoric of Emotional Control in American Discourse," in *Language and the Politics of Emotion,* ed. Lila Abu-Lughod and Catherine A. Lutz (Cambridge: Cambridge University Press, 1991), 70.

43. See Barbara Melosh, "Manly Work," in *Engendering Culture: Manhood and Wom-*

anhood in New Deal Public Art and Theater (Washington, D.C.: Smithsonian Institution Press, 1991), 84–97.

44. "'Racial characteristics,' whether psychological or somatic, are always metaphors for the difference between the sexes." Etienne Balibar, "Racism and Nationalism," in Etienne Balibar and Immanuel Wallerstein, *Race, Nation, Class: Ambiguous Identities* (London: Verso, 1991), 56.

45. See Robert L. Snyder, *Pare Lorentz and the Documentary Film* (Reno: University of Nevada Press, 1994).

46. This film fits within a problematic of New Deal documentarism, as discussed by John Tagg in "The Currency of the Photograph: New Deal Reformism and Documentary Rhetoric," in *The Burden of Representation: Essays on Photographs and Histories* (Minneapolis: University of Minnesota Press, 1988), 153–183.

47. Pare Lorentz, *FDR's Movie Maker: Memoirs and Scripts* (Reno: University of Nevada Press, 1992), 166.

48. "I liked him," remarks Clurman of Clifford Odets, the author of *Waiting for Lefty,* "for being so physical a person. He reacted to everything, not with words or articulate knowledge, but with his body." See Harold Clurman, *The Fervent Years: The Story of the Group Theater and the Thirties* (New York: Hill and Wang, 1957), 111.

49. See the useful distinctions made by Adela Pinch, *Strange Fits of Passion: Epistemologies of Emotion, Hume to Austen* (Stanford: Stanford University Press, 1996). Pinch locates this distinction in the several ways Hume understands feeling: "Hume's Treatise tells two different stories about the status of feelings. On the one hand, it asserts that feelings are individual, and that philosophy itself as well as social and aesthetic experience depends on individuals who can rely on the individual authenticity of their emotional responsiveness. On the other hand, it also contends that feelings are transsubjective entities that pass between persons; that our feelings are always really someone else's, that it is passion that allows us to be persons, rather than the other way around" (19).

50. Martha Graham, *Blood Memory* (New York: Doubleday, 1991), 5. The term *abstraction* may be a trifle misleading here, and should perhaps be limited to aspects of gestural design. Rather than abstracting the subject, impersonality renders her more present as a psychological mystery. This is how visual abstraction and psychological depth join forces.

51. This split could be further contextualized by Edward Gordon Craig's diatribe against personality and emotion in the theater. See his "The Actor and the Ubermarionette" in *Gordon Craig on Movement and Dance,* ed. Arnold Rood (New York: Dance Horizons, 1977), 37–87. Craig's essay is a fundamental text of theatrical modernism in the sense that impersonality represents a modernist position.

52. Mignon Verne, "Tamiris and Group in Revolutionary Dance Recital," *Daily Worker,* 16 January 1935, 5.

53. For further analysis of this piece and its context in the larger work *Southern Landscape,* see my "Aesthetic Agency in Flux: Talley Beatty, Maya Deren, and the Modern Dance Tradition in *Study in Choreography for Camera,*" in *Maya Deren*

and the American Avant-Garde, ed. Bill Nichols (Berkeley: University of California Press, 2001), 118–131.

54. Alfred Sohn-Rethel, *Intellectual and Manual Labour: A Critique of Epistemology,* trans. Martin Sohn-Rethel (London: Macmillan, 1978), 17.

55. Barbara Morgan, "Dialogue with Photographs," *Massachusetts Review* 24, no. 1 (spring 1983), 74. Barbara Morgan (1900–1992) was the preeminent modern dance photographer between 1935 and 1948. Her documentation of Graham's dances during this period has been influential in the dissemination of the choreographer's vision. See her *Martha Graham: Sixteen Dances in Photographs* (Dobbs Ferry, N.Y.: Morgan and Morgan, 1980).

56. Cited in Susan Manning, *Ecstasy and the Demon: Feminism and Nationalism in the Dances of Mary Wigman* (Berkeley: University of California Press, 1993), 16.

57. Fredric Jameson, *The Political Unconscious: Narrative as Socially Symbolic Act* (Ithaca: Cornell University Press, 1981), 20. Catherine A. Lutz has written that "one of the most critical boundaries that is constituted in Western psychological discourse is that between the inside and the outside of persons; individualism as ideology is fundamentally based on the magnification of that particular boundary." "Engendered Emotion," 73. Graff notes that "the dance is about Graham's valiant effort, the glory of the individual spirit *against* the group." Ellen Graff, *Stepping Left: Dance and Politics in New York City, 1928–1942* (Durham, N.C.: Duke University Press, 1997), 107.

58. Edna Ocko, "Dance Reviews," *New Theatre* (April 1936): 37 (emphasis added). Ocko refers to *Horizons* (1936). Although Ocko was consistently critical of Graham, it is noteworthy that in this review she attributes no politics to Graham's assumed avoidance of emotional qualities. Edna Ocko (Meyers) was the leading left-wing dance critic of the thirties and forties. She served as dance editor of *New Theatre* and published her own dance reviews, frequently under pseudonyms, for many other publications. She became a psychologist in the late 1960s, using her married name, Edna Meyers. See "Reviewing on the Left: The Dance Criticism of Edna Ocko," selected and introduced by Stacey Prickett, in *Of, by and for the People: Dancing on the Left in the 1930s,* ed. Lynn Garafola, Studies in Dance History vol. 5, no. 1 (Madison, Wis.: Society of Dance History Scholars, 1994), 65–103.

59. Janet Mansfield Soares, *Louis Horst: Musician in a Dancer's World* (Durham, N.C.: Duke University Press, 1992), 67. In 1934 Horst founded a pro-Graham dance journal, the *Dance Observer,* which combated the growing influence of left-wing dance criticism in the concert dance scene.

60. Sophie Maslow, interview by author, New York, 27 August 1996.

61. Graff, *Stepping Left,* 60.

62. "Young dancers involved with the worker's dance had been trained in diverse styles of dance, ranging from classical ballet and ethnic styles to 'Duncanesque' expressionism and the emergent modern dance of Graham." Stacey Prickett, "Marxism, Modernism, and Realism: Politics and Aesthetics in the Rise of the

American Modern Dance" (Ph.D. diss., Laban Centre for Movement and Dance, 1992) 85. Many were also trained in German modern dance.

63. Graff, *Stepping Left*, 51.

64. Referring to the earliest experiments in Germany with the "re-theatricalization" of movement, Eugenia Casini-Ropa posits instead a kinship between dance that explored the bases of individual expression and dance that sought the communicational bases of social and political movement. See her *La danza e l'agitprop: I teatri-non-teatrali nella cultura tedesca del primo Novecento* (Bologna: Il Mulino, 1988), 17.

65. Henry Gilfond, "Workers' Dance League," *Dance Observer* 1, no. 8 (1934): 89–90.

66. Prickett, "Marxism, Modernism, and Realism," 277. Chilkovsky would respond on anthropological grounds, as she did to me in a recent phone conversation: "Dance and music are normal cultural patterns of any society. The Duncan school recognized that dancers are people first. Human beings like to bunch together in social groups. Everything they do is partly societal behavior." Chilkovsky also accused formalist critics of "a narrow-minded view of what society *is.*" Nadia Chilkovsky, telephone conversation with author, 15 September 2001.

67. Jack Chen to Si-Lan Chen, 3 May 1937, Leyda Papers, Tamiment Institute Library, New York University, Jack Chen, 1931–1978, series 1, box 1, folder 2.

68. Dudley, interview, 14 July 1996.

69. Graff, *Stepping Left*, 75.

70. Little information has emerged on the choreography of Lily Mehlman, another member of Graham's company. Among non-Graham dancers, full-length studies of Miriam Blecher and Nadia Chilkovsky are sorely needed. Full-length critical studies of Dudley and Maslow are, for that matter, still lacking.

71. Dudley joined the Graham company in 1935. Sokolow was studying at the Neighborhood Playhouse when Graham and Louis Horst joined the faculty in 1928.

72. Dudley, interview, 17 July 1996.

73. This situation is set forth in Franko, *Dancing Modernism/Performing Politics* (Bloomington: Indiana University Press, 1995), 38–74. The critical texts in the debate over Graham's politics are reproduced in the appendix to that volume.

74. "The pressure on Martha to join the Communist movement was extravagant." Agnes de Mille, *Martha* (New York: Random House, 1991), 193.

75. Sokolow, interview.

Chapter 3 Metakinetic Interpellations

1. Terry Eagleton, *Ideology: An Introduction* (London: Routledge, 1991), 222.

2. "*All ideology hails or interpellates concrete individuals as concrete subjects,* by the functioning of the category of the subject." Louis Althusser, "Ideology and Ideological State Apparatuses (Notes toward an Investigation)," in *Lenin and Philosophy and Other Essays,* trans. Ben Brewster (New York: Monthly Review Press, 1971), 173.

3. Ibid., 174.

4. Winfield first presented *Negro* on a program of works by himself and Edna Guy entitled "First Negro Dance Recital" by the New Negro Art Theatre on 29 April 1931 at the Theatre in the Clouds in New York City. The description quoted is probably the choreographer's synopsis. Joe Nash Collection, Hemsley Winfield folder, Schomburg Center for Research in Black Culture, New York Public Library.

5. Judith Butler asks: "Are there other ways of being addressed and constituted by the law, ways of being occupied and occupying the law, that disarticulate the power of punishment from the power of recognition?" See her "Gender is Burning: Questions of Appropriation and Subversion," in *Bodies That Matter: On the Discursive Limits of "Sex"* (New York: Routledge, 1993), 122.

6. See Jacques Rancière, *Le Partage du sensible: Esthétique et politique* (Paris: La Fabrique, 2000).

7. "Pan-Africa means intellectual understanding and co-operation among all groups of Negro descent in order to bring about at the earliest possible time the industrial and spiritual emancipation of the Negro peoples." W. E. B. Du Bois, "Pan-Africa and New Racial Philosophy," *Crisis* 40, no. 11 (1933): 247.

8. John Martin, "The Modern Dance 4: Its Technical Basis," *American Dancer* 10, no. 5 (1937): 15.

9. John Martin, "The Modern Dance 1: Its Place in the Field," *American Dancer* 10, no. 2 (1936): 15.

10. "Ballet Experts Explain Dance Art," *Herald Examiner*, 20 January 1938. Transcribed in the Federal Theatre Project book for *Ballet Fedre* (Chicago). Production Records of the Federal Theatre Project, Library of Congress, Washington, D.C..

11. John Martin, "The Modern Dance 3: How It Functions," *American Dancer* 10, no. 4 (1937): 47.

12. Ibid., 15 (emphasis added).

13. Paul Love, "The Dance in America," *Theatre Guild Magazine* 7, no. 8 (1931): 42.

14. Love's remarks also suggest how nativist modernism could be engendered. See Walter Benn Michaels, *Our America: Nativism, Modernism, Pluralism* (Durham, N.C.: Duke University Press, 1995). It is precisely this sort of irrationality that should be distinguished from the interpersonal flux of e/motion. Ocko critiqued Martin's assumption of irrationality in metakinetic perception in her 1937 review of the critic's book *America Dancing:* "If we checked our intellects with our hats, our plight at a modern dance recital would be sorry indeed! Pity the poor beheaded spectator when confronted with a forty minute suite, with seriously written program notes, with costumes—yes, even with musical themes and tonalities introduced and repeated according to the plans conceived by the dancer. His sensitive musculature will be painfully overtaxed by the dancer who willfully, consciously, creates an organic choreographic whole, designed to *mean* something to an audience." Edna Ocko, "The Modern Dance in America," *New Theatre and Film* (April 1937): 34.

15. Blanche Evan, "From a Dancer's Notebook," *New Theatre* (April 1936): 31.

16. Graham, "Affirmations: 1926–1937," in *Martha Graham,* ed. Merle Armitage (New York: Dance Horizons, 1966), 100.

17. "The Modern Dance: An Interview with Martha Graham," transcribed from a broadcast over KGW, the National Broadcasting Company, and reproduced in the souvenir booklet *Martha Graham and Dance Group.* Si-Lan Chen Collection, Tamiment Institute Library, New York University.

18. John Martin, "The Dance: Miss Graham," *New York Times,* 8 February 1931.

19. A similar if more problematic exchange between Graham's choreography and Martin's critical principles occurred in 1946 at the premiere of her *Dark Meadow.* See my "History/Theory—Criticism/Practice," in *Corporealities: Dancing Knowledge, Culture and Power,* ed. Susan L. Foster (London: Routledge, 1995), 25–52.

20. In an article entitled "The Emphasis on Modernism" (*New York Times,* 18 October 1929), Martin wrote: "In the sense that modern painting and modern music represent a fundamental change of viewpoint from the romanticism that preceded them this viewpoint externalizing itself in radical forms, there is no modern dance." One can assume that *Primitive Mysteries* caused Martin to see modern dance as integral to aesthetic modernism, but the argument against the presence of formalism in modern dance remains consistent in Martin's thought and undergirds the theory of "metakinesis"—a sign of the abiding romanticism of modern dance. Martin sounds this theme throughout the thirties.

21. Graham, "Affirmations," 100.

22. Katherine Dunham, "Notes on the Dance: With Special Reference to the Island of Haiti," in *7 Arts 2,* ed. Fernando Puma (New York: Doubleday, 1954), 72.

23. John Martin, "The Dance: New England," *New York Times,* 15 August 1937. The review was of a performance in Bennington, Vermont.

24. Mary Austin, *The American Rhythm* (New York: Harcourt, Brace, 1923), 3. This work was reprinted in 1930; page numbers given are to the original edition. Austin's subject was not music but the meter of Native American poetry as "the basic motor impulses which underlie the English gesture" (11). Subsequent references will be included parenthetically in the text.

25. For further treatment of this relationship, see Jacqueline Shea-Murphy, *The People Have Never Stopped Dancing: Contemporary Native American Stage Dance and Modern Dance History* (forthcoming).

26. "The rhythmic forms to which the environment gives rise," wrote Austin, "seem to pass through the autonomic system, into and out of the subconscious without our having once become intellectually aware of them" (4). This anti-intellectualism is equally part of indigenous American identity for Austin: "life presented itself on the Western continent, in terms of things lived through rather than observed or studied" (10).

27. Evan, "From a Dancer's Notebook," 31.

28. Graham, "Affirmations," 99. I am indebted here to Amy Koritz's analysis of Graham's terms in her "Re/Moving Boundaries: From Dance History to Cultural

Studies," in *Moving Words: Re-Writing Dance,* ed. Gay Morris (London: Routledge, 1996), 92–98.

29. Graham, "Affirmations," 100. The accent here is on "culture" rather than on "new." As Van Wyck Brooks wrote: "The acquisitive life has lost the sanction of necessity which the age of pioneering gave it. A new age has begun, an age of intensive cultivation, and it is the creative life that the nation calls for now." "Young America," in *Three Essays on America* (New York: Dutton, 1934), 148.

30. *Program for the First National Dance Congress and Festival,* 25 May 1936, 5–7.

31. A photo of Graham by Barbara Morgan at the Dance Collection of the Lincoln Center Library for the Performing Arts, New York, is notated, probably in Morgan's hand, as "running."

32. Julien Bryan and Jules Bucher shot the film of *Frontier* between 1936 and 1939 without a soundtrack. Sound was added in 1987, when the film was produced with the subtitle "American Perspective"; the dance's original subtitle was "American Perspective of the Plains." Graham does not dance "full-out," but is still careful to indicate or "mark" her performance.

33. Graham, "Graham 1937," in *Martha Graham,* ed. Merle Armitage (New York: Dance Horizons, 1966), 87.

34. The following analysis was enabled by Dudley's 1993 reconstruction and reinvention with Tom Warfield in the solo role. As with all of Dudley's work, this must be viewed through a complex lens in terms of the relationship between the past and the present. Dudley herself originally performed the solo. See the video of the *New Dance Group Retrospective Concert* (1993) available from the American Dance Guild, New York.

35. The full text of Sol Funaroff's *Time Is Money* is reprinted in *Of, by and for the People: Dancing on the Left in the 1930s,* Studies in Dance History vol. 5, no. 1, ed. Lynn Garafola (Madison, Wis.: Society of Dance History Scholars, 1994), 43.

36. Dudley, interview, 14 July 1996.

37. Karl Marx, *Economic and Philosophic Manuscripts of 1844* (Moscow: Foreign Language Publishing House, 1961), 67.

38. Ibid., 72.

39. Ibid., 71.

40. Dudley, interview, 14 July 1996.

41. Marx, *Manuscripts of 1844,* 107.

42. Ibid., 112.

43. Paul Ricoeur, *Lectures on Ideology and Utopia,* ed. George H. Taylor (New York: Columbia University Press, 1986), 39.

44. Ibid., 30–31.

45. Joseph Freeman, Introduction to *Proletarian Literature in the United States: An Anthology* (New York: International Publishers, 1935), 13.

46. Agnes Heller, "The Historical Dynamics of the Bourgeois World of Feeling," in *A Theory of Feelings* (Assen, The Netherlands: Van Gorcum, 1979), 185.

47. On the panhumanist versus the pancontinental interpretation, see Segun Gbade-

gesin, "Kinship of the Dispossessed: Du Bois, Nkrumah, and the Foundations of Pan-Africanism," in *W. E. B. Du Bois: On Race and Culture,* ed. Bernard W. Bell, Emily R. Grosholz, and James B. Stewart (London: Routledge, 1996), 219–242.

48. Lynne Fauley Emery, *Black Dance from 1619 to Today* (Princeton: Dance Horizons, 1972), 250.

49. Thomas de Frantz, "Simmering Passivity: The Black Male Body in Concert Dance," in *Moving Words, Re-Writing Dance,* ed. Gay Morris (London: Routledge, 1996), 111.

50. George Hutchinson, *The Harlem Renaissance in Black and White* (Cambridge, Mass.: Harvard University Press, 1995), 184.

51. Alain Locke, as quoted in *Theatre Arts Monthly* 26, no. 8 (August 1942): 538. In this sense, *Kykunkor* answered Locke's call for a return to authentic African culture in the name not of a primitivism but of a formalism. See Alain Locke, "The Legacy of the Ancestral Arts," in *The New Negro* (1925; reprint, New York: Atheneum, 1970), 254–267.

52. Leonore Cox, "On a Few Aspects of Negro Dancing," in *Proceedings of the First National Dance Congress and Festival* (New York: 66 Fifth Ave., 1936), 52–55. The *Kykunkor* program booklet attributes to Dafora a dislike of jazz and a disapproval of the distortion of spirituals: "It is only when they are kept true, when they express the sorrow and longing of the slaves, that they are good."

53. Edwin Denby, "In Brightest Africa," Asadata Dafora Papers, Schomburg Center Research in Black Culture, New York Public Library.

54. Notably the dancer Frances Atkins who is listed in the program as Musu Esami and who danced opposite Dafora. She also had appeared in the work of Hemsley Winfield.

55. A synopsis from the program of the 13 August 1934 performance at the International House Auditorium on Riverside Drive in upper Manhattan clarifies that the exchange of spirits between the bridegroom and the witch woman was a matter of life and death.

56. W. J. Henderson, "Native African Opera Moves," *New York Sun,* 21 June 1934.

57. Gilbert Seldes, Review of performance of *Kykunkor, or Witch Woman,* by Shologa Oloba, New York, *Esquire* (August 1934).

58. John Martin, "The Dance: African Lore," *New York Times,* 13 May 1934.

59. "African Opera Presents Different Picture of the Jungle: *Kykunkor* Gives the Lie to Fantastic White Beliefs," *New York Amsterdam News,* 23 June 1934, 9. When *Kykunkor* was adapted for a Federal Theatre Project production at the Lafayette Theater in 1936, an expository framing scene of missionary dialogue was inserted to clarify the plot.

60. Leonore Cox, "Scanning the Dance Highway," *Opportunity* 12, no. 8 (1934): 246.

61. Ibid.

62. Houston A. Baker Jr., *Modernism and the Harlem Renaissance* (Chicago: University of Chicago Press, 1987), 53.

63. Martin, "African Lore."

64. Margaret Lloyd, "Interview," *Christian Science Monitor,* 26 May 1945, 5.

65. For the classic expressions of this failed relationship, see Wright, *Black Boy,* and Ellison, *Invisible Man.* For a reassessment of African American involvement in the Communist Party, see Mark Naison, *Communists in Harlem During the Depression* (New York: Grove Press, 1983).

66. On the Left's preoccupation with this audience, see the appendix of left-wing dance criticism in my *Dancing Modernism,* 109–144. In 1933, the Workers Dance League sponsored a forum entitled, "What shall the Negro dance about?" See "Colored Artists Play Big Part in Workers Dance in New York," *Washington Tribune,* 12 October 1933.

67. Owen Burke, "Dance Review," *New Masses,* 22 December 1936.

68. Julian Seaman, Review of performance of *Kykunkor, or Witch Woman,* by Shologa Oloba, New York, *Daily Mirror,* 19 May 1934.

69. Hallie Flanagan, "Radio Dinner in New York City," transcript (15 March 1937), Flanagan Papers. On Flanagan's goals for the Federal Theatre Project, see Loren Kruger, "A People's Theatre," in *The National Stage: Theatre and Cultural Legitimation in England, France, and America* (Chicago: University of Chicago Press, 1992), 133–187. Nevertheless, a comparative study of *Kykunkor* with its sequel, *Bassa Moona,* would show how the FTP remake distorted the meaning of the original.

Chapter 4 Cultural Cross-Dressing as Class Construction

1. Of these works, only the last continues to be performed.

2. I adopt the term *cultural cross-dressing* from Alan M. Wald, *Writing from the Left: New Essays on Radical Culture and Politics* (London: Verso, 1994), 152–161.

3. Si-Lan Chen was born in Trinidad on 9 March 1909. She met Jay Leyda, one of Sergei Eisenstein's film students, in Moscow in 1933. They were married in 1934, but were not able to return to the United States until 1937. Chen wrote a letter to the Workers Dance League in 1934 asking if it would sponsor a U.S. tour. The league expressed interest but noted that if Chen were to come as a representative of Soviet Art or as an individual who had lived in Moscow, she would need to get permission from Moscow. Jeanya Marling to Sylvia Chen, National Secretary of the Workers Dance League, 13 March 1934, Leyda Papers, Tamiment Institute Library, New York University.

4. Chen worked extensively with Russian choreographer Kasian Goleizovsky. See her autobiography, *Footnote to History,* ed. Sally Barnes (New York: Dance Horizons, 1989).

5. Milly Mitchell, "Silvia Chen Dances: Shows Rare Miming Ability" (Moscow, 17 January 1932). Leyda Papers, Scrapbook, series 3, box 2, folder 11.

6. John Martin, "Dances Given Here in Aid of Chinese," *New York Times,* 6 March 1939.

7. The only dancer in New York working from a classical Chinese base in the thirties

was Sophia Delza. Delza taught t'ai chi ch'uan, "an ancient Chinese exercise art," and performed "authentic Chinese dances" on the concert stage. Publicity pamphlet, Tamiment Institute Library, New York University.

8. Silvia Chen, "Trend of the Modern Dance," unidentified newspaper clipping, Leyda Papers.

9. "Chinese Girl to Fight Japs with Dance of Propaganda," *New York Post,* 25 January 1938. Scrapbook, Leyda Papers.

10. Martha Baxter, "Dances of Modern China: American Debut of Sylvia Chen, Chinese and Soviet Dancer, to Aid Anti-Japanese Fight," *Daily Worker,* 28 January 1938.

11. "A Soviet Utopia for Women: Mr. Eugene Chen's Daughter Paints Bright Picture," unidentified clipping, Shanghai, 1935, Leyda Papers.

12. Scrapbook, Leyda Papers. Si-Lan Chen's brother, Jack Chen, probably wrote this press copy.

13. Si-Lan Chen, typescript on folk art, box 7, folder 20, Leyda Papers.

14. Si-Lan Chen, "Impressions of Georgia and Turkestan," *Daily Chronicle* (Georgetown, British Guiana, no date).

15. Si-Lan Chen, "Dancers in the War," *Dance Observer,* 9, no. 7 (1942): 1, 96.

16. Si-Lan Chen, manuscript essay entitled "The Art of the Dance," Leyda Papers (emphasis added).

17. Si-Lan Chen, typescript on folk art (see note 13).

18. Helen Becker was born on 23 April 1902. See Pauline Tish, "Helen Tamiris (1902–1966)," in *Jewish Women in America: An Historical Encyclopedia,* vol. 2, ed. Paula Hyman and Deborah Dash Moore (London: Routledge, 1997), 9–12.

19. Susan Manning, "Black Voices, White Bodies: The Performance of Race and Gender in *How Long Brethren,*" *American Quarterly* 50, no. 1 (1998): 24–46.

20. Hallie Flanagan, "Shotgun Wedding," a talk given at the Federal Arts Conference in Washington, D.C., on 12 May 1937. Typescript, Flanagan Papers. The "shotgun wedding" referred to in the talk was that of performance and government.

21. Ellen Graff, *Stepping Left: Dance and Politics in New York City, 1928–1942* (Durham, N.C.: Duke University Press, 1997), 96.

22. Manning, "Black Voices, White Bodies," 27.

23. See Landon R. Y. Storrs, *Civilizing Capitalism: The National Consumer's League, Women's Activism, and Labor Standards in the New Deal Era* (Chapel Hill: University of North Carolina Press, 2000).

24. Manning, "Black Voices, White Bodies," 33.

25. Ibid., 40.

26. John Latouche and Earl Robinson, "Ballad for Americans," Victrola America Historical Recordings, recorded 1 February 1940.

27. Graff, *Stepping Left,* 21.

28. Michael Denning, *The Cultural Front: The Laboring of American Culture in the Twentieth Century* (London: Verso, 1996), 132.

29. Wald, *Writing from the Left,* 1.

30. Philip S. Foner and Herbert Shapiro, *American Communism and Black Americans: A Documentary History, 1930–1934* (Philadelphia: Temple University Press, 1991).

31. See Fraden, *Blueprints*, 97. In defense of Flanagan, however, Fraden points out that "the importance of creating separate racial units, of insisting that racial equality would be achieved only through autonomous, separated units, was key to Flanagan's thinking as well as to someone like Rose McClendon."

32. Hallie Flanagan, *Arena* (New York: Duell, Sloan, and Pearce, 1940), 51.

33. Naison, *Communists in Harlem*, xviii.

34. Jane Dudley, interview by Richard Wormser, 1981. Oral History of the American Left, Tamiment Institute Library, New York University.

35. Fanya Geltman del Bourgo, interview by Karen Wickre, Works Progress Administration Oral Histories, Research Center for the Federal Theatre Project, George Mason University, 16 December 1977.

36. Manning, "Black Voices, White Bodies," 35.

37. Ibid., 37.

38. Michael Rogin, "'Democracy and Burnt Cork': The End of Blackface, the Beginning of Civil Rights," *Representations* 46 (spring 1994): 1–34.

39. One of the only such crossover figures of the period was Group Theatre actress Frances Farmer. Interestingly, Farmer succumbed to a nervous breakdown in the 1940s, described in the press as due to emotional excess.

40. Michael Rogin, *Blackface, White Noise: Jewish Immigrants in the Hollywood Melting Pot* (Berkeley: University of California Press, 1998), 38, 62.

41. Ibid., 68.

42. Rogin, "Democracy and Burnt Cork," 9.

43. Ramsay Burt, *Alien Bodies: Representations of Modernity, "Race," and Nation in Early Modern Dance* (London: Routledge, 1998), 189.

44. Jane Dudley, "Breaking Down *Harmonica Breakdown*," interview by David Sears, *Ballet Review* 58 (winter 1984): 60.

45. Ibid., 61.

46. John Martin cited in Dudley, "Breaking Down," 66.

47. Lois Balcom, "Reviews," *Dance Observer* 8, no. 6 (June–July 1941): 82.

48. Dudley, "Breaking Down," 67.

49. Dudley, interview, 17 July 1996.

50. Dudley, "Breaking Down," 61.

51. Ibid.

52. Ibid.

Chapter 5 The Ballet-versus-Modern Wars as Ideology

1. Consider Graham company dancer Bonnie Bird's account of her attendance at a Broadway audition, conducted by another modern dancer, Charles Weidman. "Glaring at me with exasperation, he shook his head as he sternly reprimanded, 'Look around you! What do you see? Don't EVER go to another Broadway audi-

tion wearing a modern dance leotard and BARE FEET!'" What is at stake here besides a breach of etiquette? Bonnie Bird and Joyce Greenberg, "A Bird's-Eye View of *Hooray for What!*" *The Passing Show: Newsletter of the Shubert Archive* 18, no. 1 (1995): 6.

2. Kirstein published two articles in the left-wing *New Theatre* to defend the contemporary relevance of classical ballet technique to the masses. See Lincoln Kirstein, "Revolutionary Ballet Forms," *New Theatre* (October 1934): 12–14, and "The Dance as Theatre," *New Theatre* (May 1935): 20–22.

3. Kirstein was not entirely traditional because he looked to the Diaghilev era for inspiration, and particularly to the modernist choreography of Vaslav Nijinsky.

4. Lincoln Kirstein, "Blast at Ballet (1937)," in *Ballet: Bias and Belief. Three Pamphlets Collected and Other Dance Writings of Lincoln Kirstein* (New York: Dance Horizons, 1963), 246. Further references to this pamphlet will be given by page numbers in the text.

5. Camille Hardy, "Ballet Girls and Broilers: The Development of the American Chorus Girl, 1895–1910," *Ballet Review* 8, no. 1 (1980): 119. "From the term 'ballet girl,'" writes Hardy, "came the slightly disreputable aura that attached itself to the chorus girl as her identity emerged" (102).

6. See Dawn Lille Horwitz, "Fokine and the American Musical," *Ballet Review* 13, no. 2 (summer 1985): 57–72.

7. Charles Francisco, *The Radio City Music Hall: An Affectionate History* (New York: Dutton, 1979), 84.

8. *Serenade* was "the first work Balanchine choreographed for American dancers." See Eakins Press Foundation, *Choreography by George Balanchine: A Catalogue of Works* (New York: Eakins Press Foundation, 1983), 117.

9. Kirstein, "Blast at Ballet," 257. He neglected to note that European classical dancing developed from the roots of character dance. Study of the Renaissance dancing manuals he so often referred to could have revealed to him that classical dance vocabulary was itself adapted from popular vernaculars, the original *materia choreographica* he so often touted. What Kirstein proposed, however, was to append the already historically developed classical technique to contemporary entertainment and thus to display further adaptations of which classical technique was capable.

10. For further analysis of Martin's position, see Mark Franko, "History/Theory." For an account of Martin's institutional identity as dance critic, see Lynne Conner, *Spreading the Gospel of the Modern Dance: Newspaper Dance Criticism in the United States, 1850–1934* (Pittsburgh: University of Pittsburgh Press, 1997).

11. For a detailed discussion of this view see John J. MacAloon, "Olympic Games and the Theory of Spectacle in Modern Societies," in *Rite, Drama, Festival, Spectacle: Rehearsals toward a Theory of Cultural Performance*, ed. John J. MacAloon (Philadelphia: Institute for the Study of Human Issues, 1984), 241–280. On communitas, see Victor Turner, *The Ritual Process: Structure and Anti-Structure* (New York: Walter de Gruyter, 1995).

12. This formulation is indebted to Susan Manning's understanding of ballet and modern dance as dual practices of modernism. The genealogy of dance modernism, Manning argues, has been disputed by critics along generic rather than philosophical lines. See Susan Manning, *Ecstasy and the Demon: Feminism and Nationalism in the Dances of Mary Wigman* (Berkeley: University of California Press, 1993).

13. Edna Ocko, "Dance in the Changing World: A New Trend," in *Proceedings of the First National Dance Congress and Festival* (New York: 66 Fifth Ave., 1936), 26.

14. Ibid.

15. Edna Ocko, "The Revolutionary Dance Movement," *New Theatre* (June 1934), 27–28.

16. John Martin, "The Dance: With Words. Anna Sokolow Ventures a Choreographic Setting for a Poem," *New York Times,* 30 June 1935, 4.

17. *Strange American Funeral* premiered 9 June 1935 at the Park Circle Theater in New York as part of the New Dance League June Dance Festival. See Larry Warren, *Anna Sokolow: The Rebellious Spirit* (Princeton: Princeton University Press, 1991), 302.

18. Michael Gold, "Strange Funeral in Braddock," in *Mike Gold: A Literary Anthology,* ed. Michael Folsom (New York: International Publishers, 1972), 126–128.

19. Program from the dance recital of Anna Sokolow's Dance Unit, 28 February 1937. Anna Sokolow program file, Dance Collection, New York Public Library for the Performing Arts in New York City.

20. Muriel Rukeyser, "The Dance Festival," *New Theatre* (June 1935): 33. Since Sokolow also choreographed works on Italian fascism during the 1930s—particularly *Excerpts from a War Poem (F. T. Marinetti)*—it is possible that fascism and capitalism came in for parallel critiques in *Strange American Funeral*. On metallization in fascist performance, see Schnapp, *Staging Fascism*.

21. Martin, "The Dance: With Words."

22. It is tempting to read Martin's review as a critical quid pro quo for left-wing critiques of Graham as cold, passionless, and abstract. Martin turns these same accusations against Sokolow, the most accomplished of the politically radical choreographers. On the debate over Graham's relation to emotion and coldness, see my "Emotivist Movement and Histories of Modernism: The Case of Martha Graham," in *Dancing Modernism/Performing Politics* (Bloomington: Indiana University Press, 1995), 38–74.

23. John Martin, "The Dance: Romanticism. A Venerable Tradition with Light to Shed on Modern Trends," *New York Times,* 5 March 1939, 8.

24. Ibid.

25. Ibid.

26. Ibid.

27. Ibid.

28. Ibid.

29. John Martin, "The Dance: Abstraction. Staring a Hobgoblin Out of Countenance," *New York Times,* 11 December 1938.

30. Ibid. Martin was not the first to make such a judgment. See Siegfried Kracauer, "The Mass Ornament," in *The Mass Ornament: Weimar Essays,* ed. Thomas Y. Levin (Cambridge, Mass.: Harvard University Press, 1995). In Kracauer, the kickline's abstraction is the aesthetic equivalent of instrumental rationality. This layering of aesthetic and ideological analysis is absent from Martin's writing. For further analysis in the spirit of Kracauer, see Peter Jelavich, *Berlin Cabaret* (Cambridge, Mass.: Harvard University Press, 1993), 180–186.

31. Martin, "The Dance: Abstraction."

32. Martin, "The Dance: With Words."

33. Martin, "The Dance: Abstraction."

34. Martin, "The Dance: With Words," 4 (emphasis added).

35. *Filling Station,* which Kirstein commissioned and authored, was premiered by Ballet Caravan at Avery Memorial Auditorium, Hartford, Connecticut, on 6 January 1938, on a program of "all-American ballets." It was revived in 1951 by the San Francisco ballet where Christensen eventually settled. It is being revived again by the same company in the year of this writing.

36. "The traditional classic dance was grafted on American character-dancing." Kirstein, "Blast at Ballet," 264.

37. *Filling Station* program, Christensen-Caccialanza Collection, San Francisco Performing Arts Library and Museum.

38. Ballet Caravan publicity sheet, Christensen-Caccialanza Collection, San Francisco Performing Arts Library and Museum.

39. Kirstein, "The Dance as Theatre," 22.

40. Ibid., 20.

41. Edwin Denby, *Dance Writings,* ed. Robert Cornfield and William Mackay (New York: Knopf, 1986), 48.

42. Although the influence of Jean Cocteau's ideas on the poetics of the ordinary is clearly present here, these ideas also clash with the sociocultural context of depression-era America.

43. Martin, "The Dance: Abstraction."

Chapter 6   Lives of Performers: News, Sex, and Spectacle Theory

1. *Pins and Needles* opened at the Labor Stage in New York City on 27 November 1937.

2. See Ramsay Burt, "The Chorus Line and the Efficiency Engineers," in *Alien Bodies: Representations of Modernity, "Race," and Nation in Early Modern Dance* (London: Routledge, 1998), 84–100.

3. Siegfried Kracauer, "The Mass Ornament," in *The Mass Ornament: Weimar Essays,* ed. Thomas Y. Levin (Cambridge, Mass.: Harvard University Press, 1995), 77.

4. *Newsboy,* reprinted in Jay Williams, *Stage Left* (New York: Charles Scribner's Sons, 1974), 90.

5. *Highlights of 1935* or *Front Page Highlights of 1935* (both draft titles for the show

that was ultimately called *1935*) was produced by the WPA Living Newspaper Unit, directed by Joseph Losey under the supervision of Morris Watson. It premiered at the Biltmore Theater in New York City on 12 May 1936 and ran for seventy-five performances. The radicalism of this production was not lost on some reviewers. Robert Garland said *1935* was "backed by the government and applauded by an audience that quite obviously had none too much in common with the backer." Robert Garland, "1935 Story Is Vividly Told on Stage," *World Telegram* 13 May 1936.

6. Hallie Flanagan to Philip Barber and Morris Watson, 22 April 1936. Unbound Federal Theatre Project Production Bulletins, 1936–1939, box 487, National Archives, Washington, D.C.

7. Lorraine Brown, ed. *1935*, in *Liberty Deferred and Other Living Newspapers of the 1930s Federal Theatre Project* (Fairfax, Va.: George Mason University Press, 1989), 45.

8. Ibid.,10.

9. Ibid., 11.

10. Hallie Flanagan to Philip Barber and Morris Watson, 22 April 1936. Watson agreed, and wrote back to Flanagan that further work and the addition of music were building this scene to a climax.

11. Morris Watson, Interdepartmental Memo to Hallie Flanagan on the run-through of *1935* (4–24–36), 27 April 1936, Unbound Federal Theatre Project Bulletins, National Archives, Washington, D.C.

12. Brown, *1935*, 21.

13. Ibid.

14. Neil Larsen, *Modernism and Hegemony: A Materialist Critique of Aesthetic Agencies* (Minneapolis: University of Minnesota Press, 1990), 21.

15. Brown, *1935*, 55.

16. Ibid., 56. The text was taken directly from Herndon's own documentation of the trial transcribed in his autobiography, *Let Me Live* (New York: Random House, 1937).

17. Ibid., 59.

18. Ibid., 12.

19. Hallie Flanagan to Philip Barber and Morris Watson, 22 April 1936. Unbound Federal Theatre Project Production Bulletins, 1936–1939, box 487, National Archives, Washington, D.C.

20. Arthur Hove, ed., *Gold Diggers of 1933* (Madison: University of Wisconsin Press, 1980), 72. Because the published script does not correspond entirely to the finished film, further quotes will be transcribed from the soundtrack.

21. Martin Rubin, "The Crowd, the Collective, and the Chorus: Busby Berkeley and the New Deal," in *Movies and Mass Culture*, ed. John Belton (New Brunswick: Rutgers University Press, 1996), 74.

22. Patricia Mellencamp, "The Sexual Economics of *Gold Diggers of 1933*," in *Close Viewings: An Anthology of New Film Criticism*, ed. Peter Leman (Tallahassee: Florida State University Press, 1990), 180.

23. Lise Vogel, *Marxism and the Oppression of Women: Toward a Unitary Theory.* New Brunswick, N.J.: Rutgers University Press, 1983), 159.

24. Mellencamp, "Sexual Economics," 180.

25. Harry Merton Goldman, "*Pins and Needles:* An Oral History" (Ph.D. diss., New York University, 1977), 246.

26. Ibid., 106–108.

27. *Pins and Needles* clippings file, Billy Rose Theatre Collection, Lincoln Center Library for the Performing Arts, New York.

28. "Capital and Labor Meet at the Theatre," *Pins and Needles* clippings file, Billy Rose Theater Collection, Lincoln Center Library for the Performing Arts, New York.

29. "Who's Who in the Cast," *Pins and Needles* clippings file.

30. "Much of the power that could have been used against the employers towards the end of achieving substantial changes in employer-worker relations, was instead used to undermine and discourage rank-and-file militancy." Robert Laurentz, "Racial/Ethnic Conflict in the New York City Garment Industry, 1933–1980" (Ph.D. diss., State University of New York at Binghamton, 1980), 119.

31. *Pins and Needles* souvenir program, *Pins and Needles* clippings file.

32. Goldman, "*Pins and Needles,*" 139.

33. "A Labor Union Goes into the Show Business with a Sparkling Musical Revue," *Life,* 27 December 1937, 53.

Chapter 7   Strikes, Revues, and the Organized Dancer

1. Hallie Flanagan, "Is This the Time and Place?" address to the Federal Theatre Regional Directors in Washington, D.C., 8 October 1935, typescript, box 24, p. 1. Flanagan Papers. The scene derives, according to Flanagan, from a student-written play, *My Country Right or Left,* probably performed at the Vassar Experimental Theater where Flanagan taught.

2. Ibid., 7.

3. Hallie Flanagan, "A Tree from Thirst," typescript, box 24, p. 6, Flanagan Papers.

4. As Barbara Melosh has pointed out in her book *Engendering Culture,* most dramatic roles for women were restricted to those of wife, mother, or domestic laborer so familiar in drama of the period. Flanagan favored an experimental theater for some, if not all, FTP productions: "Our designers, like our writers and our directors, need to study montage, speed, line, light, and acrobatics." Flanagan, "A Tree from Thirst."

5. Edith J. R. Issacs, "Setting Sail: Broadway in Prospect," *Theatre Arts Monthly* 20, no. 10 (October 1936): 767.

6. Flanagan, "Is This the Time and the Place?" 3.

7. Hallie Flanagan, "January 3rd statement on Federal Theater Project," typescript, volume 1 (1935–1936), Flanagan Papers.

8. Frances Hawkins, "Economic Status of the Dancer," in *Proceedings of the First Na-*

tional Dance Congress and Festival (New York: 66 Fifth Ave., 1936), 78. The festival program of the First Congress attempted to bridge the generic tensions described in this chapter. It included a "Ballet Program," a "Folk Dance Program," a "Modern Program," and a "Variety and Theatre Program" (97–104).

9. Ibid., 77–78. Hawkins initially defines the professional dancer as a "dancer whose concert appearances contribute substantially to her income" (77). The garment worker metaphor for unskilled labor is not fortuitous. Many nonprofessionals, notably the entire cast of *Pins and Needles,* were drawn from the ranks of garment workers.

10. "Dancers Will Seek Own WPA Project," *New York Times,* 7 January 1936 (emphasis added).

11. Ibid.

12. Flanagan, "Is This the Time and Place?" 1. "The W.P.A. Federal Theatre announces itself as in the field for consideration this season on the same terms as the regular professional theater. This brave gesture is in line with the uncompromising attitude the director, Hallie Flanagan, has taken from the beginning." Issacs, "Setting Sail," 766.

13. Flanagan noted of the WPA that "relief" had several meanings: "All over America artists, relieved temporarily at least from unemployment and at the same time from the constant pressure to make more money or gain more prestige than the next person, are playing, acting, dancing, painting as they have never done before." Hallie Flanagan, "A Theatre for People," typescript, c. 1936, Flanagan Papers.

14. Hallie Flanagan, "Public Works, Ancient and Modern," 11–13 August 1936, Policy Board Conference, typescript, p. 8 (emphasis added).

15. Ibid.

16. Loren Kruger has discussed the dilemma of the FTP from the perspective of its implied audience: "At stake in the conflicting claims of art theatre, government relief, commercial success, and social critique was thus not merely the legitimacy of a popular audience, but the agency of that audience in the public sphere of America." Kruger, "A People's Theatre," in *The National Stage: Theatre and Cultural Legitimation in England, France, and America* (Chicago: University of Chicago Press, 1992), 139.

17. T. P. Headen, "WPA Dancing Out of Step: Amateur Group Accused of Monopolizing Floor," *New York Sun,* 25 May 1936.

18. Hallie Flanagan, "Somebody Must Be Wrong," *Survey Graphic* (December 1939): 778.

19. "Decry Radicalism in Dance Project: Dance Teachers Condemn Sit-Downs and Propaganda as Unprofessional," WPA clippings file, Dance Collection, New York Public Library for the Performing Arts at Lincoln Center.

20. Don Oscar Becque, "Dance at the Crossroads," *Dance Magazine* 1, no. 3 (1936): 8, 28.

21. In the terms of Donald Grant, vice president of the Dancing Teachers Business Association, who was cited in "Decry Radicalism."

22. See Edna Ocko, "The Revolutionary Dance Movement," *New Theatre* (June 1934). A review of this concert by Steve Foster, "The Revolutionary Solo Dance," *New Theatre* (January 1935): 23, gives a fuller picture of these works. The 25 November 1934 program at the Civic Repertory included Jane Dudley's *The Dream Ends, Time Is Money*, and *In the Life of a Worker;* Miriam Blecher's *Awake, The Woman*, and *Three Negro Poems;* Nadia Chilkovsky's *Parasite, Homeless Girl, Song of the Machine*, and *March;* Edith Segal's *Tom Mooney*, Sophie Maslow's *Themes from a Slavic People*, Anna Sokolow's *Histrionics* and *Romantic Dances,* and Lilly Mehlman's *Defiance*, as well as two collaborative trios by Maslow, Mehlman, and Sokolow: *Challenge* and *Death of a Tradition*. None of these dances have survived the thirties other than Dudley's *Time Is Money*.

23. Edna Ocko, "The Dance," *New Masses* 13, no. 10 (1934): 30. The concert, she wrote, "presented for the first time in the history of the American theatre seven artists in revolutionary dance solos."

24. "The Solo Recital," *New Dance* (January 1935): 5.

25. Emanuel Eisenberg, "Ladies of the Revolutionary Dance," *New Theatre* (February 1935): 10–11. Although Eisenberg is not specific about the event, it seems likely that his essay responds to the November 1934 concert. Eisenberg was the press representative of the Group Theater and a contributor to the book *Pins and Needles*.

26. Jeanne Lunin Heymann noted in her early article on the Dance Project that "for nearly three decades American dancers had struggled for recognition of their fledgling art; their protest signaled the beginning of a fight to win recognition for their rights and privileges as workers in a time of economic adversity." "Dance in the Depression: The WPA Project," *Dance Scope* 9, no. 2 (1975): 30.

27. H. Allen Smith, "It's Scientific, It's Rhythmic, and It's Worth $23.86 per Week," *New York World-Telegram*, 20 August 1936.

28. Ibid.

29. Ibid. Born in 1913, Susanne Remos had accumulated eclectic credits by 1937 that included the Ziegfeld Follies of 1933 and the Theatre Guild's *Parade* in 1935. "Biographies of 'Young Choreographers Laboratory,' June 12, 1936." Federal Dance Project Clippings File, Dance Collection, Lincoln Center Library for the Performing Arts.

30. Joan Wallach Scott, *Gender and the Politics of History* (New York: Columbia University Press, 1988), 155. I am indebted to Scott's exploration of work in relation to the feminine body.

31. Mark Hellinger, "All in a Day," *Daily Mirror*, 25 July 1932.

32. *Time Marches On*, typescript at the Shubert Archive, Shubert Foundation, New York. The male chorus was Ben Yost's California Varsity Eight.

33. Ibid.

34. Ibid.

35. Ibid.

36. "I did my first solo called *Revolt*, which Fanny Brice then took into the Ziegfeld Follies." Fanya Geltman del Bourgo, interview by Karen Wickre, Works Progress

Administration Oral Histories, Research Center for the Federal Theatre Project, George Mason University, 16 December 1977.

37. I thank Sophie Maslow for calling my attention to Brice's number. According to Maslow, Brice quoted the "runs in place" from Graham's *Revolt,* suggesting the solo was a composite of different sources.

38. "Modernistic Moe," in *Time Marches On* (1936), Shubert Archive script, pp. 56–57. The lyrics for "Modernistic Moe" were written by Ira Gershwin and Billy Rose.

39. "W.P.A. Cast Joined by Audience for All-Night Theater Sit-Down," *Herald Tribune,* 20 May 1937. According to reports, the strike lasted until 5 A.M. or 5:20 A.M.

40. "U.S. Theatre Is Seized by W.P.A. Strikers," *Daily Mirror,* 20 May 1937.

41. Louise Mitchell, "Note to Mr. Hopkins: 'Dancers Don't Think with Their Feet,'" *Daily Worker,* 21 May 1937. Because the 1934 taxi strike on which Odet's play was based had been resolved by the time of production, critic Gerald Weales accused *Waiting for Lefty* of offering "a moment of community that substitutes for direct action and makes it unnecessary." Gerald Weales, "Waiting for Lefty," in *Critical Essays on Clifford Odets,* ed. Gabriel Miller (Boston: Hall, 1991), 147.

42. Russell B. Porter, "'Walk Out' Becomes 'Sit-Down.' Form of Protest Learned from the French Is Tried Out in Industry and in Relief Corps," *New York Times,* 13 December 1936. The sit-down originated in the rubber and auto industries: "Organization from above was rejected and mass action stressed." See P. K. Edwards, *Strikes in the United States, 1881–1974* (New York: St. Martin's, 1981), 156–157.

43. A similar splintering of interpellation into symbolic and imaginary registers is theorized by Rastko Močnik in "Ideology and Fantasy," in *The Althusserian Legacy,* ed. Ann E. Kaplan and Michael Sprinker (London: Verso, 1993), 139–140.

Bibliography

Abu-Lughod, Lila, and Catherine A. Lutz. "Introduction: Emotion, Discourse, and the Politics of Everyday Life." In *Language and the Politics of Emotion,* edited by Lila Abu-Lughod and Catherine A. Lutz, 1–23. Cambridge: Cambridge University Press, 1991.

Agee, James, and Walker Evans. *Let Us Now Praise Famous Men.* Boston: Houghton Mifflin, 1939.

Alexander, William. *Film on the Left: American Documentary Film from 1931 to 1942.* Princeton: Princeton University Press, 1981.

Allerhand, Ruth. "The Lay Dance." [Reprint of a 1935 article.] In Mark Franko, *Dancing Modernism/Performing Politics,* 135–137. Bloomington: Indiana University Press, 1995.

Althusser, Louis. "Ideology and Ideological State Apparatuses (Notes toward an Investigation)." In *Lenin and Philosophy and Other Essays,* translated by Ben Brewster. New York: Monthly Review Press, 1971.

———. "Is It Simple to Be a Marxist in Philosophy?" In *Essays in Self-Criticism,* translated by Grahame Lock. London: New Left Books, 1976.

Arendt, Hannah. *The Human Condition.* Chicago: University of Chicago Press, 1958.

Austin, Mary. *The American Rhythm.* New York: Harcourt, Brace, 1923.

Baker, Houston A. Jr. *Modernism and the Harlem Renaissance.* Chicago: University of Chicago Press, 1987.

Balcom, Louis. "Reviews." *Dance Observer* 8, no. 6 (June–July 1941): 82.

Balibar, Etienne. "Racism and Nationalism." In *Race, Nation, Class: Ambiguous Identities,* ed. Etienne Balibar and Immanuel Wallerstein, 37–67. London: Verso, 1991.

Becque, Don Oscar. "Dance at the Crossroads." *Dance Magazine* 1, no. 3 (1936): 8, 28.

Benjamin, Walter. "The Work of Art in the Age of Mechanical Reproduction." In *Illuminations,* edited by Hannah Arendt. New York: Schocken Books, 1969.

Bentley, Eric, ed. *Thirty Years of Treason: Excerpts from Hearings before the House Committee on Un-American Activities, 1938–1968.* New York: Viking Press, 1971.

Biernacki, Richard. *The Fabrication of Labor: Germany and Britain, 1640–1914.* Berkeley: University of California Press, 1995.

Bird, Bonnie, and Joyce Greenberg. "A Bird's-Eye View of *Hooray for What!*" *The Passing Show: Newsletter of the Shubert Archive* 18, no. 1 (1995): 6–14.

Bloom, James D. *Left Letters: The Culture Wars of Mike Gold and Joseph Freeman.* New York: Columbia University Press, 1992.

Braverman, Harry. *Labor and Monopoly Capital: The Degradation of Work in the Twentieth Century.* New York: Monthly Review Press, 1974.

Brecht, Stefan. "On Grotowski," *Drama Review* 14, no. 2 (1970): 178–192.

Brooks, Van Wyck. "Young America." In *Three Essays on America.* New York: Dutton, 1934.

Brown, Lorraine, ed. *Liberty Deferred and Other Living Newspapers of the 1930s Federal Theatre Project.* Fairfax, Va.: George Mason University Press, 1989.

Burke, Owen. "Dance Review." *New Masses* (22 December 1936).

Burnshaw, Stanley. "Finale to a Brilliant Season." *New Masses* 16, no. 1 (2 July 1935): 43.

Burt, Ramsay. *Alien Bodies: Representations of Modernity, "Race," and Nation in Early Modern Dance.* London: Routledge, 1998.

Butler, Judith. "Gender Is Burning: Questions of Appropriation and Subversion." In *Bodies That Matter: On the Discursive Limits of "Sex."* New York: Routledge, 1993.

Casini-Ropa, Eugenia. *La Danza e l'agitprop: I theatri-non-teatrali nella cultura tedesca del primo Novecento.* Bologna: Il Mulino, 1988.

Chauncey, George. *Gay New York: Gender, Urban Culture, and the Making of the Gay Male World, 1890–1940.* New York: Basic Books, 1994.

Chen, Si-Lan [Sylvia]. *Footnote to History.* Edited by Sally Banes. New York: Dance Horizons, 1989.

———. "Dancers in the War." *Dance Observer* 9, no. 7 (1942): 1, 96.

Christensen-Caccialanza Collection, San Francisco Performing Arts Library and Museum.

Clurman, Harold. *The Fervent Years: The Story of the Group Theater and the Thirties.* New York: Hill and Wang, 1957.

Conner, Lynne. *Spreading the Gospel of Modern Dance: Newspaper Dance Criticism in the United States, 1850–1934.* Pittsburgh: University of Pittsburgh Press, 1997.

Cosgrove, Stuart. "Prolet-Buehne: Agit-prop in America." In *Performance and Politics in Popular Drama: Aspects of Popular Entertainment in Theatre, Film and Television, 1800–1976,* edited by David Bradby, Louis James, and Bernard Sharratt, 201–212. Cambridge: Cambridge University Press.

Cox, Leonore. "On a Few Aspects of Negro Dancing." *Proceedings of the First National Dance Congress and Festival,* 52–55. New York: 66 Fifth Ave., 1936.

———. "Scanning the Dance Highway." *Opportunity* 12, no. 8 (1934): 246.

Craig, Edward Gordon. "The Actor and the Ubermarionette." In *Gordon Craig on Movement and Dance,* edited by Arnold Rood, 37–87. New York: Dance Horizons, 1977.

Dabakis, Melissa. *Visualizing Labor in American Sculpture: Monuments, Manliness, and the Work Ethic, 1880–1935.* Cambridge: Cambridge University Press, 1999.

"The Dance: The New Dance Group, an Analysis." *New Theatre* (March 1934): 17.

Debord, Guy. *Society of the Spectacle.* Detroit: Black and Red, 1983.

de Frantz, Thomas. "Simmering Passivity: The Black Male Body in Concert Dance." In *Moving Words, Re-Writing Dance,* edited by Gay Morris, 107–120. London: Routledge, 1996.

Deleuze, Gilles. *Cinema I: The Movement-Image.* Translated by Hugh Tomlinson and Barbara Habberjan. Minneapolis: University of Minnesota Press, 1986.

Deleuze, Gilles, and Felix Guattari. *What Is Philosophy?* Translated by Hugh Tomlinson and Graham Burchell. New York: Columbia University Press, 1994.

de Mille, Agnes. *Martha.* New York: Random House, 1991.

Denby, Edwin. "In Brightest Africa." Asadata Dafora Papers, Schomburg Center for Research in Black Culture, New York Public Library.

———. *Dance Writings.* Edited by Robert Cornfield and William Mackay. New York: Knopf, 1986.

Denning, Michael. *The Cultural Front: The Laboring of American Culture in the Twentieth Century.* London: Verso, 1996.

Dickstein, Morris. "The Tenement and the World: Visions of Immigrant Life." In *The Future of American Modernism: Ethnic Writing between the Wars,* edited by Silliam Boelhower, 62–93. Amsterdam: VU University Press, 1990.

Draper, Theodore. "The Life of the Party." *New York Review of Books,* 13 January 1994, 45–51.

DuBois, W. E. B. "Pan-Africa and New Racial Philosophy." *Crisis* 40, no. 11 (1933).

Dudley, Jane. "The Mass Dance." In Mark Franko, *Dancing Modernism/Performing Politics,* 119–122. Bloomington: Indiana University Press, 1995. First published in *New Theatre* (December 1934): 17–18.

Dunbar, Flanders. *Emotions and Bodily Changes: A Survey of Literature on Psychosomatic Interrelationships, 1910–1945.* 3rd ed., New York: Columbia University Press, 1946.

Dunham, Katherine. "Notes on the Dance: With Special Reference to the Island of Haiti." In *7 Arts 2,* edited by Fernando Puma, 69–76. New York: Doubleday, 1954.

Eagleton, Terry. *Ideology: An Introduction.* London: Routledge, 1991.

Eakins Press Foundation. *Choreography by George Balanchine: A Catalogue of Works.* New York: Eakins Press Foundation, 1983.

Edwards, P. K. *Strikes in the United States, 1881–1974.* New York: St. Martin's, 1981.

Eisenberg, Emanuel. "Ladies of the Revolutionary Dance." In Mark Franko, *Dancing Modernism/Performing Politics,* 129–133. (Bloomington: Indiana University Press, 1995). First published in *New Theatre* (February 1935): 10–11.

Ellison, Ralph. *Invisible Man.* 1947. Reprint, New York: Vintage, 1980.

Emery, Lynne Fauley. *Black Dance from 1619 to Today.* Princeton: Dance Horizons, 1972.

Evan, Blanche. "From a Dancer's Notebook." *New Theatre* (April 1936): 31, 44–45.

Fischer, Lucy. "The Image of Woman as Image: The Optical Politics of *Dames.*" In *Sexual Stratagems: The World of Women in Film,* edited by Patricia Erens, 41–61. New York: Horizon Press, 1979.

Flanagan, Hallie. *Arena.* New York: Duell, Sloan, and Pearce, 1940.

———. Hallie Flanagan Papers, Billy Rose Theatre Collection, New York Public Library for the Performing Arts at Lincoln Center.

———. "Somebody Must Be Wrong." *Survey Graphic* (December 1939): 776–781.

Foner, Philip S., and Herbert Shapiro. *American Communism and Black Americans: A Documentary History, 1930–1934.* Philadelphia: Temple University Press, 1991.

Ford, Corey. "Impossible Interview: Sally Rand vs. Martha Graham." *Vanity Fair,* December 1934, 40.

Ford, Henry. *My Life and Work.* Garden City, N.J.: Doubleday, Page, and Company, 1922.

Foster, Steve. "The Revolutionary Solo Dance." *New Theatre* (January 1935), 23.

Foulkes, Julia Lawrence. *Modern Bodies: Dance and American Modernism from Martha Graham to Alvin Ailey.* Chapel Hill: University of North Carolina Press, 2002.

Fraden, Rena. *Blueprints for a Black Federal Theatre, 1935–1939.* Cambridge: Cambridge University Press, 1996.

Francisco, Charles. *The Radio City Music Hall: An Affectionate History.* New York: Dutton, 1979.

Franko, Mark. "Abstraction Has Many Faces: the Ballet/Modern Wars of Lincoln Kirstein and John Martin." *Performance Research* 3, no. 2 (1998): 88–101.

———. "Aesthetic Agency in Flux: Talley Beatty, Maya Deren, and the Modern Dance Tradition in *Study in Choreography for Camera,*" in *Maya Deren and the American Avant-Garde,* edited by Bill Nichols, 118–131. Berkeley: University of California Press, 2001.

———. "Emotivist Movement and Histories of Modernism: The Case of Martha Graham." In *Dancing Modernism/Performing Politics.* Bloomington: Indiana University Press, 1995.

———. "History/Theory—Criticism/Practice." In *Corporealities: Dancing Knowledge, Culture and Power,* edited by Susan L. Foster, 25–52. London: Routledge, 1995.

———. "Strikes, Revues, and the Work of Dance in the 1930s." *Annals of Scholarship* 13, nos. 1–2 (1999): 1–19.

Freeman, Joseph. Introduction to *Proletarian Literature in the United States: An Anthology.* New York: International Publishers, 1935.

Fuoss, Kirk W. *Striking Performances/Performing Strikes.* Jackson: University Press of Mississippi, 1997.

Garafola, Lynn, ed. *Of, by and for the People: Dancing on the Left in the 1930s.* Studies in Dance History 5, no. 1. Madison, Wis.: Society of Dance History Scholars, 1994.

Gbadegesin, Segun. "Kinship of the Dispossessed: DuBois, Nkrumah, and the Foundations of Pan-Africanism." In *W. E. B. DuBois: On Race and Culture,* edited by Bernard W. Bell, Emily R. Groshola, and James B. Stewart, 219–242. London: Routledge, 1996.

Gilbreth, Frank B., and Lillian M. Gilbreth. *Fatigue Study.* New York: Sturgis and Walton, 1916.

Gilfond, Henry. "Workers' Dance League." *Dance Observer* 1, no. 8 (1934): 89–90.

Gold, Michael. *Jews without Money.* 1930. Reprint, New York: Carroll and Graf, 1958.

———. "John Reed and the Real Thing." In *The Mike Gold Reader.* New York: International Publishers, 1954.

———. "The Loves of Isadora." *New Masses* 4 (March 1929): 205–21.

———. "Strange Funeral in Braddock." In *Mike Gold: A Literary Anthology,* edited by Michael Folsom. New York: International Publishers, 1972.

———. "Toward Proletarian Art (1921)." In *Mike Gold: A Literary Anthology,* edited by Michael Folsom. New York: International Publishers, 1972.

Goldman, Harry Merton. "*Pins and Needles:* An Oral History." Ph.D. diss., New York University, 1977.

Gornick, Vivian. *The Romance of American Communism.* New York: Basic Books, 1977.

Graff, Ellen. *Stepping Left: Dance and Politics in New York City, 1928–1942.* Durham, N.C.: Duke University Press, 1997.

Graham, Martha. "Affirmations, 1926–1937." In *Martha Graham,* edited by Merle Armitage, 96–110. 1937. Reprint, Brooklyn: Dance Horizons, 1966.

———. *Blood Memory.* New York: Doubleday, 1991.

———. "Graham 1937." In *Martha Graham,* edited by Merle Armitage, 96–110. 1937. Reprint, Brooklyn: Dance Horizons, 1966.

———. "The Modern Dance. An Interview with Martha Graham." *Martha Graham and Dance Group.* Si-Lan Chen Collection, Tamiment Institute Library, New York University.

Gramsci, Antonio. "Americanism and Fordism." In *Selections from the Prison Notebooks of Antonio Gramsci.* New York: International Publishers, 1971.

Green. "Some Questions of the Work of the CPUSA." In *The Communist International in America: Documents, 1925–1933.* New York: Bolshevik League, n.d., 69–78. First published in *Communist International* 10, no. 17 (1 September 1933).

Hall, Carolyn, ed. *The Thirties in Vogue.* New York: Harmony Books, 1985.

Hardy, Camille. "Ballet Girls and Broilers: The Development of the American Chorus Girl, 1895–1910." *Ballet Review* 8, no. 1 (1980): 96–127.

Hawkins, Frances. "Economic Status of the Dancer." *Proceedings of the First National Dance Congress and Festival,* 77–80. New York: 66 Fifth Ave., 1936.

Heller, Agnes. "The Historical Dynamics of the Bourgeois World of Feeling." In *A Theory of Feelings.* Assen, The Netherlands: Van Gorcum, 1979.

Hellinger, Mark. "All in a Day." *Daily Mirror,* 25 July 1932.

Herndon, Angelo. *Let Me Live.* New York: Random House, 1937.

Hersey, Rexford B. *Workers' Emotions in Shop and Home: A Study of Individual Workers From the Psychological and Physiological Standpoint.* Philadelphia: University of Pennsylvania Press, 1932.

Heymann, Jeanne Lunin. "Dance in the Depression: The WPA Project." *Dance Scope* 9, no. 2 (1975): 28–40.

Horkheimer, Max, and Theodor W. Adorno. *Dialectic of Enlightenment.* Translated by John Cumming. New York: Continuum, 1999.

Horwitz, Dawn Lille. "Fokine and the American Musical." *Ballet Review* 13, no. 2 (summer 1985): 57–72.

Hove, Arthur, ed. *Gold Diggers of 1933.* Madison: University of Wisconsin Press, 1980.

Hutchinson, George. *The Harlem Renaissance in Black and White.* Cambridge, Mass.: Harvard University Press, 1995.

Hyman, Collette A. *Staging Strikes: Workers' Theatre and the American Labor Movement.* Philadelphia: Temple University Press, 1997.

Issacs, Edith J. R. "Setting Sail: Broadway in Prospect." *Theatre Arts Monthly* 20, no. 10 (October 1936): 759–768.

Jameson, Fredric. *Postmodernism, or the Cultural Logic of Late Capitalism.* Durham, N.C.: Duke University Press, 1991.

———. *The Political Unconscious: Narrative as Socially Symbolic Act.* Ithaca: Cornell University Press, 1981.

Jelavich, Peter. *Berlin Cabaret.* Cambridge, Mass.: Harvard University Press, 1993.

Kirstein, Lincoln. "Blast at Ballet (1937)." *Ballet: Bias and Belief. Three Pamphlets Collected and Other Dance Writings of Lincoln Kirstein.* New York: Dance Horizons, 1963.

———. "The Dance as Theatre." *New Theatre* (May 1935): 20–22.

———. "Revolutionary Ballet Forms." *New Theatre* (October 1934): 12–14.

Koritz, Amy. "Re/Moving Boundaries: From Dance History to Cultural Studies." In *Moving Words: Re-Writing Dance,* edited by Gay Morris, 92–98. London: Routledge, 1996.

Kracauer, Siegfried. "Girls and Crisis (1931)." In *The Weimar Republic Source Book,* edited by Anton Kaes, Martin Jay, and Edward Dimendberg, 565–566. Berkeley: University of California Press, 1994.

———. "The Mass Ornament." In *The Mass Ornament: Weimar Essays,* edited by Thomas Y. Levin, 75–88. Cambridge, Mass.: Harvard University Press, 1995.

Kruger, Loren. "A People's Theatre." In *The National Stage: Theatre and Cultural Legitimation in England, France, and America.* Chicago: University of Chicago Press, 1992.

Laban, Rudolf, and F. C. Lawrence. *Effort.* London: Macdonald and Evans, 1947.

"A Labor Union Goes into the Show Business with a Sparkling Musical Revue." *Life,* 27 December 1937, 53.

Larsen, Neil. *Modernism and Hegemony: A Materialist Critique of Aesthetic Agencies.* Minneapolis: University of Minnesota Press, 1990.

Latouche, John, and Earl Robinson. *Ballad for Americans.* Victrola America Historical Recordings, recorded 1 February 1940.

Laurentz, Robert. "Racial/Ethnic Conflict in the New York City Garment Industry, 1933–1980." Ph.D. diss., State University of New York at Binghamton, 1980.

Levine, Lawrence W. *Highbrow/Lowbrow: The Emergence of Cultural Hierarchy in America.* Cambridge, Mass.: Harvard University Press, 1988.

Leyda-Chen Papers, Tamiment Institute Library, New York University.

Lloyd, Margaret. "Interview." *Christian Science Monitor,* 26 May 1945.

Locke, Alain. "The Legacy of the Ancestral Arts." In *The New Negro.* 1925; reprint, New York: Atheneum, 1970, 254–267.

Lorentz, Pare. *FDR's Movie Maker: Memoirs and Scripts.* Reno: University of Nevada Press, 1992.

Lott, Eric. *Love and Theft: Blackface Minstrelsy and the American Working Class.* New York: Oxford University Press, 1993.

Love, Paul. "The Dance in America." *Theatre Guild Magazine* 7, no. 8 (1931).

Lutz, Catherine A. "Engendered Emotion: Gender, Power, and the Rhetoric of Emotional Control in American Discourse." In *Language and the Politics of Emotion,* edited by Lila Abu-Lughod and Catherine A. Lutz, 69–91. Cambridge: Cambridge University Press, 1991.

MacAloon, John J. "Olympic Games and the Theory of Spectacle in Modern Societies." In *Rite, Drama, Festival, Spectacle: Rehearsals toward a Theory of Cultural Performance,* edited by John J. MacAloon. Philadelphia: Institute for the Study of Human Issues, 1984.

Manning, Susan. "Black Voices, White Bodies: The Performance of Race and Gender in *How Long Brethren.*" *American Quarterly* 50, no. 1 (1998): 24–46.

———. *Ecstasy and the Demon: Feminism and Nationalism in the Dance of Mary Wigman.* Berkeley: University of California Press, 1993.

Martin, Carol. *Dance Marathons: Performing American Culture in the 1920s and 1930s.* Jackson: University of Mississippi Press, 1994.

Martin, John. "The Modern Dance 1: Its Place in the Field." *American Dancer* 10, no. 2 (1936): 15, 28.

———. "The Modern Dance 3: How It Functions." *American Dancer* 10, no. 4 (1937): 15, 24, 47.

———. "The Modern Dance 4: Its Technical Basis." *American Dancer* 10, no. 5 (1937): 15, 42.

Marx, Karl. *Economic and Philosophic Manuscripts of 1844.* Moscow: Foreign Languages Publishing House, 1961.

Mazis, Glen A. *Emotion and Embodiment: A Fragile Ontology.* New York: Peter Lang, 1993.

McCarren, Felicia. *Dancing Machines: Choreographies of the Age of Mechanical Reproduction.* Stanford: Stanford University Press, 2002.

McDermott, Douglas. "The Theatre Nobody Knows: Workers' Theatre in America, 1926–1942." *Theatre Survey* 6, no. 1 (1965): 65–82.

McDonough, Rosin. "Ideology as False Consciousness: Lukács." In *On Ideology*, 33–44. London: Hutchinson, 1977.

Mellencamp, Patricia. "The Sexual Economics of *Gold Diggers of 1933*." In *Close Viewings: An Anthology of New Film Criticism*, edited by Peter Lehman, 177–199. Tallahassee: Florida State University Press, 1990.

Melosh, Barbara. "Manly Work." In *Engendering Culture: Manhood and Womanhood in New Deal Public Art and Theater*. Washington, D.C.: Smithsonian Institution Press, 1991.

Meyerhold, Vsevolod. "Biomechanics." In *Meyerhold on Theater*, translated and edited by Edward Braun. New York: Hill and Wang, 1969.

Michaels, Walter Benn. *Our America: Nativism, Modernism, Pluralism*. Durham, N.C.: Duke University Press, 1995.

Misler, Nicoletta. "Designing Gestures in the Laboratory of Dance." In *Theatre in Revolution: Russian Avant-Garde Stage Design, 1913–1935*, edited by Nancy van Norman Baer, 156–175. San Francisco: Fine Arts Museum of San Francisco, 1991.

Mizejewski, Linda. *Ziegfeld Girl: Image and Icon in Culture and Cinema*. Durham, N.C.: Duke University Press, 1999.

Močnik, Rastko. "Ideology and Fantasy." In *The Althusserian Legacy*, edited by Ann E. Kaplan and Michael Sprinker, 139–156. London: Verso, 1993.

Morgan, Barbara. "Dialogue with Photographs," *Massachusetts Review* 24, no. 1 (spring 1983): 65–80.

———. *Martha Graham: Sixteen Dances in Photographs*. Dobbs Ferry, N.Y.: Morgan and Morgan, 1980.

Morris, Gay. "Post-War American Dance: A Sociological Study of the Avant-Garde." Ph.D. diss., Goldsmiths College, University of London, 2001.

Naison, Mark. *Communists in Harlem during the Depression*. New York: Grove Press, 1983.

Noble, David F. *America by Design: Science, Technology and the Rise of Corporate Capitalism*. New York: Alfred A. Knopf, 1977.

Ocko, Edna. "The Dance." *New Masses* 13, no. 10 (1934): 30.

———. "Dance in the Changing World: A New Trend." *Proceedings of the First National Dance Congress and Festival*, 25–28. New York: 66 Fifth Ave., 1936.

———. "Dance Reviews." *New Theatre* (April 1936): 37.

———. "The Modern Dance in America." *New Theatre and Film* (April 1937): 34–35.

———. "The Revolutionary Dance Movement." *New Theatre* (June 1934): 27–28.

———. "Reviewing on the Left: The Dance Criticism of Edna Ocko." Selected and introduced by Stacey Prickett. In *Of, by and for the People: Dancing on the Left in the 1930s*, edited by Lynn Garafola, 65–103. Studies in Dance History 5, no. 1. Madison, Wis.: Society of Dance History Scholars, 1994.

"The Old Left: An Exchange." *New York Review of Books*, 23 June 1994, 62–63.

Olsen, Tillie. *Yonnondio: From the Thirties*. New York: Delta/Seymour Lawrence, 1974.

Oral History of the American Left. Tamiment Institute Library, New York University.

Orvell, Miles. *The Real Thing: Imitation and Authenticity in American Culture, 1889–1940*. Chapel Hill: University of North Carolina Press, 1989.

Outhwaite, William, and Tom Bottomore. *Blackwell Dictionary of Twentieth-Century Social Thought.* Oxford: Blackwell, 1993.

Pfister, Joel. *Staging Depth: Eugene O'Neill and the Politics of Psychological Discourse.* Chapel Hill: University of North Carolina Press, 1995.

Philip, André. *Le problème ouvrier aux Etats-Unis.* Paris: Librairie Félix Alcan, 1927.

Pinch, Adela. *Strange Fits of Passion: Epistemologies of Emotion, Hume to Austen.* Stanford: Stanford University Press, 1996.

Prentis, Albert. "Basic Principles." *Worker's Theatre* (May 1931): 1–2.

Prickett, Stacey. "Dance and the Workers' Struggle." *Dance Research* 7, no. 1 (1990): 47–61.

———. "From Worker's Dance to New Dance." *Dance Research* 7, no. 1 (1989): 47–64.

———. "Marxism, Modernism, and Realism: Politics and Aesthetics in the Rise of the American Modern Dance." Ph.D. diss., Laban Centre for Movement and Dance, 1992.

———. "'The People': Issues of Identity within the Revolutionary Dance." In *Of, by and for the People: Dancing on the Left in the 1930s,* edited by Lynn Garafola. Studies in Dance History 5, no. 1. Madison, Wis.: Society of Dance History Scholars, 1994.

Program and Constitution of the Communist Party of America. Adopted at the Joint Unity Convention of the United Communist and Communist Parties. N.p.: Central Executive Committee of the Communist Party of America, May 1921.

Rabinowitz, Paula. *Labor and Desire: Women's Revolutionary Fiction in Depression America.* Chapel Hill: University of North Carolina Press, 1991.

Rancière, Jacques. *Le Partage du sensible: Esthétique et politique.* Paris: La Fabrique, 2000.

Ricoeur, Paul. *Lectures on Ideology and Utopia.* Edited by George H. Taylor. New York: Columbia University Press, 1986.

Rivière, Jacques. "Le Sacre du Printemps." In *What Is Dance?* edited by Marshall Cohen and Roger Copeland, 115–123. New York: Oxford University Press, 1983.

Robertson, Pamela. "What Trixie and God Know: Feminist Camp in *Gold Diggers of 1933.*" In *Guilty Pleasures: Feminist Camp from Mae West to Madonna,* 57–84. Durham, N.C.: Duke University Press, 1996.

Rogin, Michael. *Blackface, White Noise: Jewish Immigrants in the Hollywood Melting Pot.* Berkeley: University of California Press, 1998.

———. "'Democracy and Burnt Cork': The End of Blackface, the Beginning of Civil Rights." *Representations* 46 (spring 1994): 1–34.

Roosevelt, Franklin Delano. "Address at San Diego Exposition, October 2, 1935." In *The Public Papers and Addresses,* vol. 4. New York: Random House, 1938.

Rubenstein, Annette T. "The Cultural World of the Communist Party: An Historical Overview." In *New Studies in the Politics and Culture of U.S. Communism,* edited by Michael E. Brown, Randy Martin, Frank Rosengarten, and George Snedeker, 239–260. New York: Monthly Review Press, 1993.

Rubin, Martin. "The Crowd, the Collective, and the Chorus: Busby Berkeley and the New Deal." In *Movies and Mass Culture,* edited by John Belton, 59–92. New Brunswick: Rutgers University Press, 1996.

———. *Showstoppers: Busby Berkeley and the Tradition of Spectacle.* New York: Columbia University Press, 1993.

Rukeyser, Muriel. "The Dance Festival." *New Theatre* (June 1935): 33.

Schnapp, Jeffrey T. *Staging Fascism: 18BL and the Theater of Masses for Masses.* Stanford: Stanford University Press, 1996.

Schomburg Center for Research in Black Culture, New York Public Library.

Scott, Joan Wallach. *Gender and the Politics of History.* New York: Columbia University Press, 1988.

Segal, Edith. "Directing the New Dance." *New Theatre* (May 1935): 23.

Seldes, Gilbert. Review of performance of *Kykunkor, or Witch Woman.* Shologa Oloba, New York. *Esquire* (August 1934).

Sellars, Marion. "The Dance Project—WPA Stepchild." *New Theatre* (August 1936): 24.

Seltzer, Mark. *Bodies and Machines.* London: Routledge, 1992.

Shea-Murphy, Jacqueline. *The People Have Never Stopped Dancing: Contemporary Native American Stage Dance and Modern Dance History.* Forthcoming.

Shubert Archive, Shubert Foundation, New York.

Smith, H. Allen. "It's Scientific, It's Rhythmic, and It's Worth $23.86 per Week." *New York World-Telegram,* 20 August 1936.

Snyder, Robert L. *Pare Lorentz and the Documentary Film.* Reno: University of Nevada Press, 1994.

Soares, Janet Mansfield. *Louis Horst: Musician in a Dancer's World.* Durham, N.C.: Duke University Press, 1992.

Sohn-Rethel, Alfred. *Intellectual and Manual Labour: A Critique of Epistemology.* Translated by Martin Sohn-Rethel. London: Macmillan, 1978.

"The Solo Recital." *New Dance* (January 1935): 5.

Sternhell, Zeev. *The Birth of Fascist Ideology: From Cultural Rebellion to Political Revolution.* Translated by David Maisel. Princeton: Princeton University Press, 1994.

Storrs, Landon R. Y. *Civilizing Capitalism: The National Consumer's League, Women's Activism, and Labor Standards in the New Deal Era.* Chapel Hill: University of North Carolina Press, 2000.

Stratyner, Barbara. *Ned Wayburn and the Dance Routine: From Vaudeville to the Ziegfeld Follies.* Studies in Dance History no. 13. Madison, Wis.: Society of Dance History Scholars, 1996.

Tagg, John. "The Currency of the Photograph: New Deal Reformism and Documentary Rhetoric." In *The Burden of Representation: Essays on Photographs and Histories.* Minneapolis: University of Minnesota Press, 1988.

Taylor, Frederick Winslow. *Principles of Scientific Management.* 1911. Reprint, New York: Norton Library, 1967.

Thomas, Edward. *Industry, Emotion, and Unrest.* New York: Harcourt, Brace and Howe, 1920.

Tish, Pauline. "Helen Tamiris (1902–1966)." In *Jewish Women in America: An Historical Encyclopedia,* edited by Paula Hyman and Deborah Dash Moore. 2 vols. London: Routledge, 1997.

Tomko, Linda. *Dancing Class: Gender, Ethnicity and Social Divides in American Dance, 1890–1920*. Bloomington: Indiana University Press, 1999.

Turner, Victor. *The Ritual Process: Structure and Anti-Structure*. New York: Walter de Gruyter, 1995.

Vogel, Lise. *Marxism and the Oppression of Women: Toward a Unitary Theory*. New Brunswick, N.J.: Rutgers University Press, 1983.

Wald, Alan M. *Writing from the Left: New Essays on Radical Culture and Politics*. London: Verso, 1994.

Waring, James. "Five Essays on Dancing." *Ballet Review* 2, no. 1 (1967): 65–77.

Warren, Larry. *Anna Sokolow: The Rebellious Spirit*. Princeton: Princeton University Press, 1991.

Weales, Gerald. "Waiting for Lefty." In *Critical Essays on Clifford Odets*, edited by Gabriel Miller. Boston: Hall, 1991.

Williams, Jay. *Stage Left*. New York: Charles Scribner's Sons, 1974.

Williams, Raymond. *Drama from Ibsen to Brecht*. New York: Oxford University Press, 1969.

———. "Structure of Feeling." In *Marxism and Literature*. Oxford: Oxford University Press, 1977.

Wolff, Janet. *Aesthetics and the Sociology of Art*. Ann Arbor: University of Michigan Press, 1996.

"Workers Dance League." *New Theatre* (January 1934): 16.

Wright, Richard. *Black Boy (American Hunger)*. 1945. Reprint, New York: Harper Collins, 1993.

Žižek, Slavoj. "The Spectre of Ideology." In *Mapping Ideology*, edited by Slavoj Žižek. London: Routledge, 1994.

Index

About the Author

Mark Franko is a dancer, choreographer, and professor of Dance and Performance Studies at the University of California, Santa Cruz. He has presented his choreography in the United States and Europe since 1985. He has published *Dancing Modernism/Performing Politics* (1995), *Dance as Text: Ideologies of the Baroque Body* (1993), and *The Dancing Body in Renaissance Choreography* (1986). He has also coedited *Acting on the Past: Historical Performance Across the Disciplines* (2000). He has been a Getty Fellow and recipient of research grants from the American Philosophical Society, the American Council of Learned Societies, and the France/Berkeley Fund.